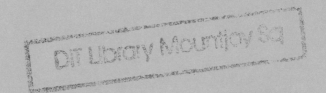

AUSTRALIAN STUDIO GLASS
THE MOVEMENT, ITS MAKERS AND THEIR ART

AUSTRALIAN STUDIO GLASS
THE MOVEMENT, ITS MAKERS AND THEIR ART

NORIS IOANNOU

CRAFTSMAN HOUSE

G+B ARTS INTERNATIONAL

to my family

Distributed in Australia by Craftsman House,
20 Barcoo Street, Roseville East, NSW 2069
in association with G+B Arts International:
Australia, Austria, Belgium, China, France, Germany,
Hong Kong, India, Japan, Malaysia, Netherlands,
Russia, Singapore, Switzerland, United Kingdom,
United States of America

ISBN 976 8097 60 4

Design   *Craig Peterson, Handpress Graphics*
Printer   *Kyodo, Singapore*

Plate 1 (frontispiece): Brian Hirst, *Object and Images series — Votive*, 1994,
blown-cast glass (bowl) with sheet-glass (panel), engraved, polishing-gold,
enamels, acid-etched; 30x 40 diam. (bowl), 97.4 x 66 cm (panel). Photo:
Hiroyuki Okamato

1. Studio Glass — Australia. 2. Social History — Australia. 3. Decorative Arts
— Australia. 4. Cultural Theory.

This project has been assisted by the Commonwealth Government through
the Australia Council, its art funding and advisory body.

Contents

FOREWORD 7

INTRODUCTION 11

CHAPTER 1   *STARTING OUT:* THE SEMINAL YEARS   19

CHAPTER 2   *THE GLASS COMMUNITY:* DEBATE AND EXCHANGE   41

CHAPTER 3   *ON THE PLINTH:* THE EXHIBITION STORY   61

CHAPTER 4   *KILNFORMED GLASS:* AN AUSTRALIAN TRAIT   81

CHAPTER 5   *BLOWN GLASS:* FLUID DIRECTIONS   115

CHAPTER 6   *ALTERNATE GLASS PRACTICES*   139

CHAPTER 7   *HEART OF GLASS:* POESIS AND PRAXIS   169

ENDNOTES 190

BIOGRAPHIES 193

SELECT BIBLIOGRAPHY 235

INDEX 236

Foreword

This book, Australian Studio Glass, captures our heart and soul. Its timely launch at the 9th biennial conference of the Australian Association of Glass Artists (Ausglass) titled 'Heart of Glass', and held in Adelaide, Australia, is a fitting celebration of our movement.

I have been involved with studio glass for the last fourteen years, and my Ausglass Presidency has allowed me to have a profile in, and make a contribution to, the glass community in Australia. My husband and friends are studio glass artists, and my acquaintances glass collectors, curators, and educators. I'm surrounded by glass objects at work and at home. My involvement in the studio glass movement began at art school in Gippsland, Victoria where I saw Stephen Skillitzi give a demonstration of hot glass using a make-shift furnace, and the 'industrial experience year' of my teaching diploma was spent working in Richard Marquis's studio in California.

I have always felt strongly the need to unravel the intricate story of the recent glass movement. I even began an attempt in the late seventies to collate information on glass practitioners world-wide: this effort was taken over by Stephen Skillitzi who has always shown that he cares about the story. He deserves our thanks for sowing the seed for this book with the publisher, and for recommending Ausglass as the resource for contacting glass practitioners in Australia.

As the author Dr Noris Ioannou himself points out, this book is not a definitive history of the movement so much as an attempt to capture a moment in time. It chronicles the diversity of form and technique used by glass artists in Australia; it gives a glimpse of the practitioners, their art, their independent invention and inheritance; and their means of exchange of technical information. Although a resume of the formative years is presented, this book is primarily the story of the last ten years of studio glass, how it unfolded and where it is now. The studio movement itself is imperfectly understood and this publication, in its attempts to tie these and other themes together, brings us closer to an understanding of how it ticks. The text also links all centres of studio glass activity in Australia and, together with the illustrations, gives an unparalleled expansion to previous writings.

The choice of style of this book is the province of the author in consultation with the publisher. The responsibility for illustrative material, and some of the content for possible inclusion was to the practitioners themselves. In a letter sent out in the form of an invitation, artists were asked to submit three transparences plus their curriculum vitae as well as an artist's statement. Four hundred and fifty invitations to submit material were sent to Ausglass members and to non members alike; word of mouth was also valuable in contacting people. On behalf of the Ausglass executive I would like to thank all practitioners who provided material: the response was gratifying.

In writing a book of this type it is usual, indeed indispensable, to draw on the knowledge and writings of other authors, relevant magazine articles and exhibition catalogues. Noris Ioannou's scholarly research

Plate 2 (opposite)
Pamela Stadus (b. 1953)
The Gleaming, 1993
sand cast with glass
and enamelled-copper inclusions;
40 x 25 x 7 cm

has encompassed all of these avenues of information, giving due credit where necessary. As well he has conducted numerous telephone and personal interviews: practitioners, educators, and curators were all valuable sources of information. I am grateful to Noris for his critical interpretation of the facts presented to him and for the tenacity of his research. This show-case of contemporary studio glass will surely be seen as a testimonial to this creative area of practice in Australasia in 1995.

Australian Studio Glass also represents to me tangible evidence of the power of a unified group. As Tony Hanning stated in his address 'The real value of Australian Glass', at the Glass Weekend held in Melbourne in September 1993: 'We are all too busy being independent to realise that the key to success lies in being interdependent'. Here is an example of the furtherance of Australian studio glass as a whole being within our own best interests.

To the publisher, Nevill Drury of Craftsman House, who has been supportive in allowing the scope and content of this publication to expand considerably beyond the original project, the Australian glass community is deeply appreciative. I feel especially privileged to be the President of Ausglass at the time of the research and publication of this book.

It is my opinion that this book will be enormously valuable to practitioners for the kudos a published work receives; as a reference for social historians, theorists, curators, and collectors, as well as for educators and their students. I commend this 'story of glass' to you, the reader.

Pauline Mount
Ausglass President

critical framework of current glass and craft theory generally. These include the dynamics of technique and creativity and their relationship to the peculiarities of the medium; the recent heightened concerns for originality; the alleged 'seduction' of the medium; the shifts in balance between crafterly and fine art values; the exploration of historical glass processes within a contemporary setting; and the international network of social links, and information, ideas and skills exchange. These and other emergent trends point the way for studio glass as it approaches the end of a millenium.

Especially salient to this narrative of glass culture are the personal accounts of the various participants who were involved in the founding and in the expansive years of the studio glass movement in Australia. Given that their oral evidence must be evaluated against existing material and documentary evidence, this source sounds out a variety of views, presents personal insight and, through the voices of these participants, restores the human side of the picture. In this manner, it may be possible to come closer towards a gestalt of glass.

Explanation and acknowledgements

Some explanation is necessary of the various major technical categories of studio glass, the processes and terms used to describe them. As this is a relatively new area still in transition, much of the language has yet to stabilise and achieve uniform usage. For example, the historic terminology, the American Hot Studio Glass Movement, has already given way to the lucid, 'studio glass movement'. The use of 'hot' specified the historic innovative use of a small furnace for glass manipulation within a studio or artistic scale. Later, the terms kilnworked and kilnformed emerged and became virtually interchangeable, despite the differences of meaning: this text uses the preferred term 'kilnformed' to refer to the broad diversity of techniques and processes where the kiln is central to the activity. Hence slumping, draping, fusing, laminating, mosaic work, *pâte de verre*, and kiln-casting are all encompassed by kilnforming or kilnformed. Furnace-working refers to glass blowing and solid-working, as well as furnace-casting (including sand-casting). Cold-working involves cutting and grinding, polishing, engraving, sand-blasting and acid-etching, assembling and cold-laminating (glueing) — these are processes which may be used on work first formed in the furnace or which result from kilnforming. Then there is flame-working, a less-frequently used process which is sometimes referred to as bench-working and which involves the extensive use of the blow-torch rather than kiln or furnace. Finally, leadlighting, the preferred term, is often substituted by stained or flat glass.

Some further comments are necessary regarding the inclusion, and seeming exclusion, of the various works illustrated in this book. There were a number of criteria on which selection was made: the work had to be essentially the outcome of practitioners who used glass as their primary medium; a proportional representation of all the distinctive areas of practice of glass has been attempted, although this has been based in part on their current levels of popularity; the works illustrated represent practitioners who have either made a significant contribution over the past decade or so, or they are newly-emergent and show promise. Over the past decade some glass practitioners have fallen by the wayside or moved into other areas of practice; others are long-stayers, while yet others are new to the scene. Aside from a handful of innovators, traditional stained glass is not covered as its practice falls outside of the parameters of this book. The location of the illustrations is generally based on the major topics or themes of each chapter, although some, such as those in the introduction and first three chapters, are used to introduce practitioners or images and ideas relevant to the text. All caption measurements first give the maximum height followed by the width and depth in centimetres.

In closing, I would like to thank those who assisted me in my research and writing of this book: they are as numerous as the practitioners and others mentioned in the text, and I thank them for the long talks we had and their open willingness to share their stories and insights. Some deserve special thanks: Tony Hanning, Klaus Moje, Maureen Cahill and Rob Knottenbelt. I could go on, but their names are to be found in the endnotes.

Pauline Mount has been an enduring presence, providing assistance and a sounding board whenever necessary. Both Pauline and I also thank Clare Belfrage for her assistance in the task of collating the illustrations and biographical details submitted by the glass practitioners; Roger Buddle has my sincere appreciation for performing the arduous task of compiling the initial biographies. I am especially grateful to both Pauline and Stephen Skillitzi for their valuable suggestions following their reading of an early draft — this book is all the more improved thanks to their efforts. Finally, this book could never have come to being without the original spark of encouragement from Stephen Skillitzi who realised its timeliness, and Nevill Drury, the publishing manager of Craftsman House, whose assurance and support has been crucial to its eventual realisation. I am also grateful for a grant from the Visual Arts/Craft Board of the Australia Council, which not only assisted me during my work on the final stages, but also underscored the Board's recognition of the value of this project.

In closing, I would like to mention how opportune it was that I had been asked by Klaus Moje and Elizabeth McClure to present a paper at the Ausglass conference in 1993; this led to my subsequent invitation by David Williams to participate as writer-in-residence in the glass workshop at the Canberra School of Art in late 1993: these two activities prepared me in advance for this present task, especially as the latter gave me valuable hands-on experience and insight into the manipulation of and fascination for studio glass.

Noris Ioannou
Adelaide

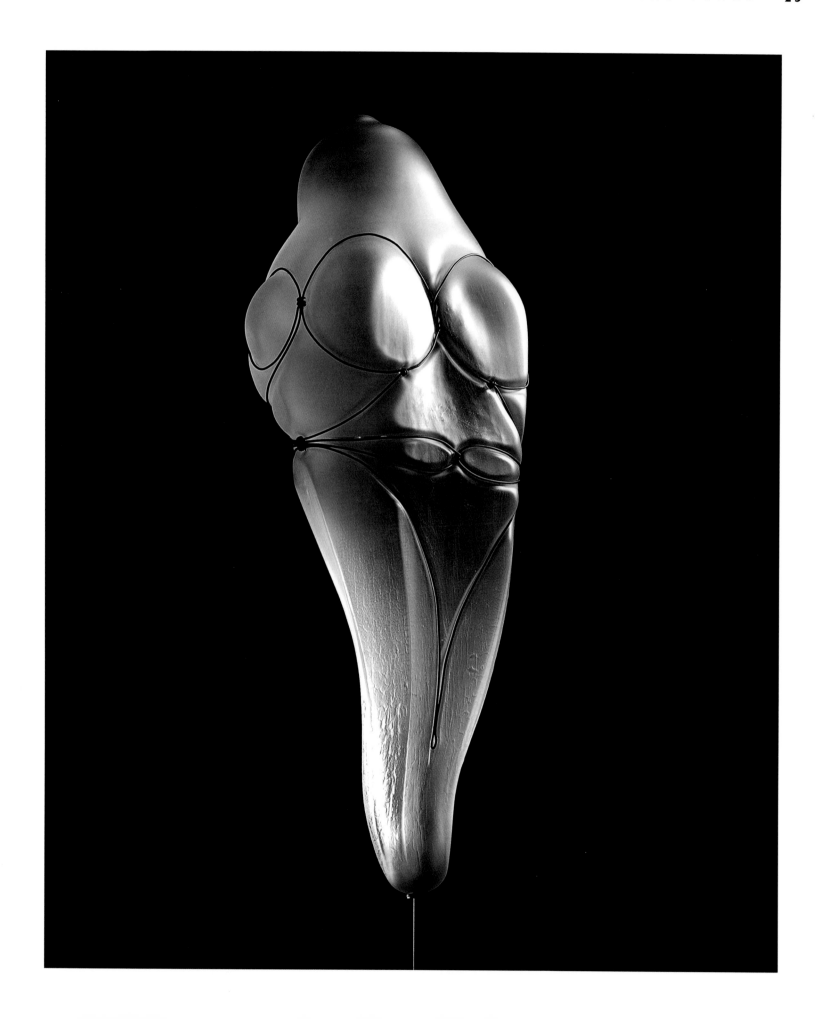

Plate 6
John Elsegood (b. 1940)
Bowl, 1988
kiln cast glass;
7 x 14.5 x 14.5 cm

evolution of the studio glass movement over the ensuing years. As graduates departed from these places to set up their own studios, or became teachers themselves, they seeded the country with their own centres of creativity and enterprise. In this manner, the chain reaction set up by the first handful of players, became a critical mass which has since been self-sustaining.

Over the late 1970s, a number of other glass courses were commenced about the country: in his role as degree co-ordinator of the School of Design in Adelaide (then of the South Australian School of Art and later the Underdale campus of the University of South Australia), Skillitzi instigated a glass studies course in 1976, in association with ceramics; until his retirement in 1987, he was a full-time lecturer. Gerry King (b. 1945) became co-ordinator of the glass studies from late 1985, later becoming the head of the School of Design in 1993. The Ceramic and Glass Course at the School of Design continues to offer a wide scope of study in furnace, kiln and cold-working glass techniques and processes to substantial levels of expertise. Significantly, students are also involved in design study in ceramics and cement, so that the school's emphasis is on the training of designers, rather than glass or ceramic practitioners: such a priority, of design over glass, has taken the course from a 'school of art' to a 'designer-maker' model. Its graduates include Vicki Torr, Rod Smith, Rosemary Prentice, Sally Hunter, Meg Keslake, Matthew Larwood, Kate Hayhurst, Bettina Viscetin, Judith Candy, Annie Lipschitz, Neville Smith.[7]

Dennis O'Connor established the hot glass facilities at Monash University (then Caufield Institute) together with one of the earliest formal hot glass programmes available in Australia in 1977, albeit as part of a long-established ceramics programme (see also Chapter 6). Also in Melbourne, the establishment of the Meat Market Craft Centre included a cold, and later, hot glass workshop in 1985 and 1988 respectively.

Plate 7
Keith Rowe (b. 1952)
Vase — Inferno Series, 1993
blown and sanblasted glass,
on kinfused glass;
vase 35 x 22 cm
photo: Rob Charters

John Elsegood (b. 1940) established a glass course at Charles Sturt University (formerly the Riverina College of Advanced Education) in Wagga Wagga, New South Wales. Elsegood was another of the handful of individuals who had been in contact with the American Hot Glass Movement of the early 1970s. His studies at the College of Ceramics at Alfred University in New York State during 1971, had brought him into contact with Andre Bellicci who was in charge of the glass course; this led Elsegood to reduced his clay studies to take up glass blowing. On his return to Australia, he was later successful in applying for a position at Charles Sturt University (formerly the Riverina College of Advanced Education) where, following Bill Boysen's glass-blowing demonstrations there in mid-1974, he established a glass facility as part of the ceramics study course in 1978. This hot glass furnace and workshop had some influence over the ensuing years of the decade with Sam Herman and Eva Almberg also demonstrating techniques there. Its presence also determined the eventual initiation of a national studio glass collection in the Wagga City Art Gallery. This resulted through Elsegood's inspiration of one of his students, Judy Le Lievre, the subsequent director of the gallery (see Chapter 3). Indeed, Elsegood and Le Lievre were among those who attended Stephen Skillitzi's glass workshop at the crafts summer school (run by the Crafts Council of South Australia) at Tatachilla south of Adelaide in 1978. This event, and subsequent overseas travel which gave Le Lievre a chance to view public collections, further inspired her interest and predilection in glass — eventually leading to the founding of the National Art Glass Collection at Wagga.

Other courses in other locations about the country were relatively late in coming: it was not until the late 1980s that Rod Smith introduced glass studies at the College of Art in Brisbane, and 1991 when Perth instigated glass in combination with ceramic courses at the Curtin and at Edith Cowan Universities. Compare Australia's ten glass courses in 1994 with the 100 or so courses in the United States in 1974, reduced to 70 in 1988, and down to between 30 to 40 in 1994. Of the latter, Richard Whiteley considers that only about ten of these are comparable to the four major glass programmes in Australia, namely those of the Canberra School of Art, the Sydney College of Arts, the School of Design (Adelaide), and Monash University (Melbourne). Whiteley also points out that in Australia, glass programmes provide an opportunity for students to major in the medium from the onset, whereas in the United States, it is generally not until later in the course that glass becomes the major focus of study.[8]

While Australia's aforementioned tertiary glass courses all contributed their various influences on the glass scene, that of the Sydney College of the Arts had a considerable impact over the 1980s. In 1978, Maureen Cahill set up Glass Studies as part of the visual arts programme, with the first glass workshop in the country which emphasised kilnforming techniques. Cahill had chosen to study this area of glass practice during her period of overseas study in Stourbridge, England on the basis that she felt that kilnforming 'was the best approach for developing and conveying ideas — there was a more lateral way of thinking through kilnforming ... glass blowing was not experimental enough ...'.[9] It was not so much that she anticipated an expansion of interest in this area in the 1980s, than it was her aim to set up a course which gave students a broad knowledge of a range of techniques or 'a working vocabulary on which to base ideas ...'. Cahill's bent towards the conceptual, as well as the practical, placed her in the lead when it came to articulating the interpretation of idea into glass and its historical links; this emerged in a paper she gave to the first glass makers' gathering in 1978, as well as in her later architectural installations which came to characterise her work (see Chapter 6).

The Sydney College of the Arts had an influence too, on the diversity of glass work that was produced, extending it beyond the typical exhibition object into that of the installation. Over the past decade or so it has earned a highly-successful vocational record with at least half of its graduates establishing their own studios. These include James Minson, Sergio Redegalli, Deborah Cocks, Keith Rowe, Giselle Courtney, Jennifer Farley, Jane Cowie, Anthony Hoffmann, Phillippa Playford, and Michelle Tilgen. The success of the glass course at the Sydney College of the Arts was such that works by not only Cahill, but also by three students — Giselle Courtney, Michael Anderson, and Reiko Saito — were selected for the 1981 Contemporary Glass exhibition held in Japan. The exhibition included Canadian, American and local Japanese work, as well as that from other Australians, namely Brian Hirst, Gerry King, Rob Knottenbelt, Warren Langley, Stanislav Melis, Nick Mount, Stephen Skillitzi, and David Wright.[10]

Another associated enterprise emerged from Maureen Cahill's realisation for the need to regularly hot-glass workshop in Australia in 1977. (Julio Santos' own hot-glass studio established in 1973, has operated for twenty-one years and is therefore probably the longest-established glass studio). Budgeree Glass was very successful, being retailed throughout Australia, and even in in California by 1984.

Unlike the prevailing trend of glass practitioners to develop — over a long period of some years — a distinctive series or genre which becomes their signature work, Mount has remained diverse in his exhibition work; he has therefore tended to be identified through his production work, which has itself been considerably prolific and distinctive due to the strong visual and historic associations of the work to the Venetian aesthetic. This is despite the fact that Mount's philosophy of glass blowing informs both areas — production and exhibition work (see Chapter 5).

Over the 1980s, Mount regularly visited the United States: he spent a further six months working with Dick Marquis in 1980, and he was a teaching assistant at the Pilchuck Glass School on four occasions from 1985 to the most recent in 1993. During these visits he had considerable contact with celebrated glass blowers such as Lino Tagliapeitri and Dante Marioni. Mount emphasises that working in a private studio is an isolating process and 'you have to make the effort to get out and make contact with others'.[18]

From 1977 to 1985, Mount's Gippsland studio emerged to make a significant contribution to the training of a generation of glass blowers: it offered a hot-glass blowing facility whereby graduates from a variety of tertiary institutions, as well as glass-blowers from the Jam Factory, became trainees (under funding from the Visual Arts and Crafts Board). Among these were Brian Hirst, Robert Wynne, Keith Rowe, Michael Hook, Anne Hand, and Michael D'Aquino; all of these subsequently established their own hot-glass careers. Today, they and other glass blowers, adhere to a hot-glass philosophy whereby production work underpins their use of glass as a medium for artistic expression. Yet, because of their strong links to production work, the tendency has been to highlight this activity rather than their exhibition work — a tendency which is less likely with practitioners involved chiefly in kilnforming.

The latter is a crucial point which cannot be over-emphasised. In the ensuing text, it will become apparent, for reasons which will be disclosed, that the kilnformed area of practice has a considerable profile compared to that of glass blowing within studio glass as a whole in Australia. And whereas the glass workshops in the Canberra School of Art became a catalyst and nexus of a national and international network of glass practitioners involved in kilnforming especially, the Jam Factory has not maintained an equivalent profile or role as a centre of glass blowing over the past decade. The active network which was constructed and fostered by Klaus Moje, during his term as head of the glass workshop in Canberra, one which linked curators, writers, educators and practitioners, has simply not been as well defined in the area of glass blowing. As a result, Pauline Mount considers that, over the past ten years, 'blown glass has been out in the wilderness since the rise of kilnforming in Australia'. Nick Mount surmises that another reason for this condition is due to the fundamental infrastructure required for glass blowing: notably the expense of a furnace, and its demands on production for its support. Whereas the latter condition is not necessary with kilnformed work which simply requires a small kiln. This means that the work practices of the former are more within the sphere of craftwork, whereas the latter permits the model of the artist-craftsman, as in ceramics, to be the prime activity.

Plate 9
Peter Tysoe (b. 1935)
Gunyah, Flinders Ranges series, 1991
glass cast over steel moulds, with added
colour inclusions,
jarrah wood and steel-bolt base;
51 x 67 x 20 cm
photo: Eric Algra

How then may glass blowing be given equal recognition? Mount points to seasoned glass blowers such as Richard Royal at Pilchuck Glass School in the United States, whose work is considered on the same level as that of kilnformed or other areas; the reasons for this are to be found in the 'cooperative spirit and teamwork approach and support he receives'. The networking achieved by glass blowers in the United States is based on this united approach which is deemed essential if this area is to receive its due recognition. In a limited extent, this cooperative approach to glass blowing may be seen in Victoria where a group of glass studios which specialise in the area are clustered in a wide area about Melbourne. These studios include Rob Knottenbelt's, Michael Hook's and Richard Morrell's, and have forged strong links between themselves and the glass studios located in Monash University and at the Meat Market Craft Centre. Hence they are able to provide support to emerging new generations of glass blowers. Consider one of these practitioners, Clare Belfrage, for example: she graduated from the glass course at Monash, then worked in the hot glass access workshop in the Meat Market, then worked in Knottenbelt's and later, Hook's glass studios. She followed this with a two-year traineeship at the Jam Factory, then a spell in Nick Mount's studio in Adelaide. In 1994, Belfrage took up a teaching position in the new glass and ceramic course coordinated by Kerry Williams at Curtin University in Perth (see Chapter 6). It was a long sequence of studio-hopping which gave Belfrage a solid grounding in glass blowing and other hot-glass studio practices. But it was the network linkages of this scattering of studios which permitted her, and other graduates, to take advantage of the sites where glass-blowing experiences was available (another group of glass-blowing studios is active in the south-west corner of Western Australia).

By 1988, Mount, together with an increasing number of craftspeople, had become disillusioned with the small-scale business philosophy of studio craft, to the extent that he made the decision to move into a designer-maker role. He established a factory workshop with a considerable infrastructure where he designed prototypes and made large-scale production runs with a team of fifteen. After three years the business was closed due to financial and other problems and Mount, after taking a year off to re-think his ideas and aims, re-established a studio glass workshop in Adelaide (see Chapter 5). His considerable experience and profile in small and large-scale production glass blowing, eventually led to his successful move to become the present head of the Jam Factory Glass Workshop from early 1994.[19]

In this capacity, Mount intends to enlarge the glass workshop's role as a facility for glass education across a broad range. This will include the education of trainees based on production work, design and marketing, and generally to impart a philosophy of glass making: 'I want glass practitioners to realise that the team approach is a strength which can underpin individual work'. He also sees the need for the glass workshop to attract seasoned glass practitioners to use its considerable facilities, as well as educate a broader public in the aesthetics, design demands and skill requirements of studio glass. He especially wishes to 'reinstate the glass workshop in the Jam Factory as a focus for glass blowing in Australia'. This will be instigated through a programme of visiting overseas and local practitioners: the most recent in 1994 were Dick Marquis and Dante Marioni, who were invited to Australia by Ausglass through Nick and Pauline Mount. Mark Douglas, Richard Clements, Ben Edols, Scott Chaseling and Tony Hanning were among the successive visiting practitioners who undertook workshops at the Jam Factory in that year.

The Canberra School of Art Glass Workshop

Whereas the Jam Factory had its greatest influence on the glass movement during its early formative years, the Glass Workshop in Canberra School of Art has been the foremost authority over the past decade. And while the former fostered glass blowing, the glass workshop at the Canberra School of Art was exemplary in the area of kilnforming glass techniques and processes. The arrival of Klaus Moje (b. 1936) in Australia in late 1982, to instigate and head the Canberra School of Art's Glass Workshop, from the beginning of the following year, marked a pivotal point in time in the growth of the glass movement. Over his ten-year appointment kilnforming techniques and processes infiltrated the glass community to arouse the same sense of excitement and level of activity as glass blowing initially had induced almost a decade earlier.

Henceforth, the kilnformed genre of studio glass was to become increasingly attractive, eventually emerging by the late 1980s as a characteristic feature of the glass scene in Australia.

Not long after arriving in Australia, Klaus Moje travelled to Adelaide where the third Ausglass Conference was held in early 1983. Sampling the local work as exhibited in the second Ausglass show in the Jam Factory, he recalls his impressions that 'in general, Australian glass was fifteen years behind the work in Europe and America': the former excelled in technical development, whereas for the latter it was aesthetics. Also, 'Australia did not have the backing of industry nor the history of glass'. Moje's judgement seemed somewhat drastic in the context of the then small handful of experienced Australian glass artists. However, these comments were not surprising given that he had arrived at the time when studio glass was yet to grown out of its formative years to enter a succeeding phase of development. This would see it shift from a level characterised by a relatively narrow technical base and a limited aesthetic expressiveness, to one of wider expertise and greater expressive sophistication.

Moje's crucial influence in this specialty area of studio glass in Australia, stems from his particular background training and experience in Germany. This began with his trade or guild style of education in 1952, when he was apprenticed as a glass-cutter in the family workshop becoming a certified journeyman, and three years later at the Glass Schools Rheinbach and Hadamar, where he studied and obtained his Master's Certificate. However, aside from this European educational grounding, Moje was also subsequently influenced through his contact with two ex-Bauhaus teachers. The first was in 1958 with Lothar Schreyer (1886–1966), one of the nine original Masters of Form at the Bauhaus, as they were termed; he started the theatre workshop which operated on an avant-garde theory which aimed to create 'a single organism'. Schreyer also designed painted abstract figures he described as 'non-objective, sculptural, coloured works of art', words which are coincidentally applicable to Moje's later glass work.[20] Working for Schreyer on a project of thirteen meditation windows for a chapel which also incorporated kilnformed glass, Moje had 'long on-going discussions with the ex-master', absorbing some of his unique design ideas. A few years later, in 1966, Moje met the ex-Bauhaus silversmith Wolfgang Tuempel (1903–1978), who was instrumental in bringing him in contact with the contemporary craft scene in Germany. According to Moje, 'Bauhaus tradition infused the movement'.[21]

The Bauhaus system of craft education had a strong influence on Moje's ideas and his subsequent teaching: Walter Gropius, the founder of the Bauhaus, which was established in 1919, aimed to train creatively-skilled craftsworkers through a philosophy based on a type of utopian-Medievalism. He asserted and emphasised that 'There is no essential difference between the artist and the craftsman: the artist is a craftsman raised to a higher power … *but a foundation of craft-discipline is essential to every artist'.*[22] Manual skills were imparted through the workshop system, and students were termed apprentices and journeymen; there was also an emphasis on one-to-one training and on the freedom of expression and creativity of each student.

Klaus Moje's brief at the Canberra School of Art was to establish a workshop which covered all aspects of glass making. As his kilns and other equipment had accompanied him from Germany, and because his expertise lay in that area of practice, he decided to first set up a kilnforming workshop. His

Trailblazing in glass was initially due to the efforts of just a handful of individuals including Peter Minson, Richard Clements, Denis O'Connor, Stephen Skillitzi, Julio Santos, Rob Knottenbelt, Maureen Cahill, Warren Langley and Nick Mount: they were the individuals who took the courageous steps of embarking on a career in what was then a novel medium in the crafts movement in Australia. In the following years many other individuals became similarly infected with an ardour to work in the medium, themselves becoming pioneers of various glass techniques and approaches — a pattern which continues to this day. It was within this relatively short period too, that some of the issues and themes which are still a feature of contemporary studio glass, had begun to emerge: the stress on international networking; the differentiation of specific generations of glass practitioners; and the broadening of approaches which led to the current diverse field of practices.

CHAPTER TWO

The Glass Community: Debate & Exchange

'… a reasonably small and elite group of practitioners … linked together by a sort of Masonic bonding anchored in a shared knowledge of the alchemical properties of that most seductive of all materials: silicon dioxide'.[1]

Studio glass practitioners as a group are especially participatory within their tribe: involved in one aspect of a set of social practices which characterise the cultural make-up of contemporary life, they display a discernible esprit de corps, and hence, have strong sense of peer group identity.

There is little doubt that the formation of various medium-specific institutions within the sphere of craft, including one for glass, have been largely instrumental in facilitating the transfer of technical information, setting incentives, and establishing conceptual or ideological directions in glass activity. In this manner, various institutions have determined the current make-up of the glass movement, and to a considerable degree, the nature of its output. The discussion on the glass workshops at the Jam Factory and the Canberra School of Art, for example, revealed how the background of particular masters and the guiding educational policies of the two centres determined the manner in which studio glass was approached in terms of favoured techniques and the particular genres of formal expression: they also revealed the considerable influence such institutions can have on the glass movement as a whole.

Guilds of specialist makers have always exerted a powerful effect on the standards, output, the profile, prosperity and activity of their members. Since its formation in 1978, Ausglass, the Australian Association of Glass Artists, although not the longest extant medium-specific forum in Australia (the Potter's Society of Australia precedes it by some seventeen years), its impact on the glass movement has been substantial. And as David McNeil, head of Art Theory Workshop at the Canberra School of Art, has pointed out, Ausglass is 'something of a barometer to the current concerns of art glass in this country'.[2]

Bronwyn Hughes, practitioner and editor of Ausglass' journal, has commented 'Attending an Ausglass (or any other) conference is almost like entering a time loop. It offers participants the opportunity to examine and reflect on 'real' world activities, and to absorb and distil new and old ideas'. From another perspective, Nola Anderson has outlined a succession in which 'Ausglass and its related exhibition program, seem to develop a life of their own'. In this latter view, rather than being indicators of artistic and other developments in glass, the institution is seen as actually determining and imposing specific ideologies, narratives and debates onto the field.[3]

Plate 12 (opposite)
Deborah Cocks (b. 1958)
Animal Pleasures — The Hen, 1994
slumped and enamelled glass;
Diam 58 cm
photo: Peter Schardin

Plate 14
Richard Whiteley (b. 1963)
Madonna and Child, 1993
Industrial-blown glass, enamel-painted,
rubber and latex;
20 x 14 x 6.25 cm
photo: R. Whiteley

were given by Ausglass members, or makers invited from overseas. Although considered 'lightweight' by some when it was later compared to the following 1991 conference, the programme nevertheless reflected a number of emergent trends and issues pervading the crafts community at the time.

Over the 1980s, the drift of craft practice and its organisational infrastructure shifted to embrace the new marketing pragmatism, heightened professionalism, and a re-unification of craft, design and industry. Accompanying these developments was a broadening and acceptance of the multiplicity of approaches, processes, and representations. Plurality instilled an underlying sense of confusion and much debate, the latter focussing on the contemporary role of the craftsperson, the relevance and meaning of craftwork and its relationship to the visual arts, design, industry and the broader spectrum of cultural practices generally.[9] By the end of the decade, the blurring of boundaries and the increasing alliance of craft with the fine arts, was being increasingly questioned by a number of writers, historians and makers, who saw this direction as antithetical to craft's integrity and ongoing vitality.[10] Although this predicament was typical of most areas of professional studio craft activity at the time, including glass, for some practices such as ceramics, the crisis was perhaps more immediate.

There was no sense of urgency for the 1989 conference, which only included a single participating academic, Jenny Zimmer. She presented a paper which focussed on the re-evaluation of craftsmanship over the pervasiveness of conceptual directions in glass. In an historical overview she emphasised that 'Glass is uniquely appropriate and immensely suited to the functional and ornamental and much more rarely suited to art'. She concluded, 'We should praise the life-enhancing qualities of good design and craftsmanship and the pleasure inducement of the ornamental'.[11] Notwithstanding this endorsement to be decorative and functional, some participants nevertheless saw such statements as 'anti-intellectual', while others interpreted this as meaning that too much studio glass was being made which was not suitable to the medium. This was a similar opinion to that voiced by Peter Emmett some three years earlier during the Art Works Glass exhibition.

This perennial theme now formed a central focus for Nola Anderson who scrutinised Ausglass in one of her 1991 glass narrative essay series. She argued that the organisation predetermined the 'critical approach applied to glass', as indicated by the manner in which certain categories of glass works were rejected in preference to others; specifically, production work was denied access to survey exhibitions, that certain values of glass, such as beauty had been 'outlawed', and that the 'exclusivity' imposed on the medium had led some areas of glass practice, namely glass jewellery and contemporary sculpture, to be discouraged from 'participating in other relevant narratives'.[12] Anderson also pointed the finger to Ausglass, as the culprit in determining the exclusive 'narrative of glass' as it emerged over the 1980s.

The underlying assumption of this narrative, according to Anderson, was that, as Auglass grew in size and in its level of operational sophistication, so too has studio glass become progressively refined. The past decade has, however, arguably shown this to be the case: glass practice has certainly progressed in terms of its expressive sophistication, in tandem with the continuous maturity of its association, but more significantly, because the technical expertise of its members has become increasingly refined.[13]

A turning point: 'know thyself'

By the beginning of the 1990s, these and other allied issues had reached a crescendo in the craft scene, including glass. As a result, a mood of reflection and re-assessment formed the central theme for the 1991 Ausglass Conference held at the University of Sydney. Titled Contemporary Making — Current Thinking, it was considered by many as a turning point for the institution, motivated as it was by a groundswell of feeling which encouraged critical viewpoints to be aired and debated. Whereas the very first conference of Ausglass had looked at 'how' members made glass, and while subsequent conferences had raised philosophical issues to a limited degree, the first conference of the 1990s was incisively focussed on 'what we are making as practitioners and how are we being evaluated by theoreticians'. The conference theme especially sought to encourage dialogue on a perennial and now contentious issue, articulated as 'whether it is possible to meld together a medium-based aesthetic which explores the intrinsic properties of glass, its light transparency, opacity, and reflection with the fine art principles of painting, sculpture and architecture which have a questionable relationship to these unique qualities'.[14]

As well as attempting to specifically discuss these queries, the programme also aimed 'to extend the practice of glass making' through day-long focuses on three areas: the presentation by art historians, theorists, curators and critics, of theoretical and historical frameworks as a setting for contemporary practice; elaborations of personal and medium-based philosophy; and an investigation of the 'environment' within which glass practice was developing in Australia and overseas. It was the most sophisticated programme Ausglass had convened, particularly because of its balance of theory and practice and its apparent success in melding the two. Significantly, its chief approach for stimulating the debate was through an effective mix between practitioners and non-practitioners in the make-up of panels and in the presentation of talks.

Art historian Sylvia Kleinert presented an opening paper which located glass practice within the historical context of visual arts, and tracing its emergence in Australia through the broader issues raised by modernism, post modernism and regionalism. This included a resume of how divisions and hierarchies between the fine and decorative arts had been created since the Renaissance, and the resultant privileging of the theoretical over the practical and material by current Western intellectual traditions.

Although logical, it has been rare for commentators to compare glass developments with those of the other craft media despite the obvious links to be found. Kleinert, for one, elaborated how the emergence of studio crafts in the post world-war two period were based on the modernist premise of functionalism and 'truth to materials'. Ceramic practice especially promulgated this view, primarily through Bernard Leach's teachings: his Anglo-Oriental aesthetic and approach to making swept through the Western craft revival movement in the 1950s and 1960s until the abstract-expressionist motions of American ceramist Peter Voulkos initiated an alternative approach, one which linked with the 'anything goes' attitude of pop and funk art in the late 1960s. It was this disposition favouring a highly-explorative and expressive set of craft practices which also enervated studio glass in its first five years in Australia.[15]

This modernist model and its prescriptive dogma of 'communing through the medium' was, Kleinert pointed out, constraining and unrealistic for it suggested that the artist was somehow isolated from the set-

Plate 15
Gerry King (b. 1945)
Such is Life, 1994
kiln and flame-formed,
laminated, mosaic, cold-worked,
etched and frosted, glass;
40 x 60 x 45 cm
photo: M. Kluvanek

ting of daily life 'with all its multitude of political, social economic and cultural issues and influences'. She posited the prevailing post-modernist perspective which did away with existing value systems to replace it with the semiotic notion that 'all aspects of our culture operate as signs which communicate the ideas and values of society'. She proposed 'a new, broader definition of glass, one which does not try to define parameters for practice which may in the end prove restrictive to both the practice and reception of contemporary glass'. It was an ideology of glass which eschewed time-worn hierarchical categories to embrace 'a practice and a range of semantic meanings which flow along a continuum from the fine arts of painting and sculpture through architecture and industry'.[16] In this democratic approach, Kleinert was essentially promoting an interdisciplinary or even, material culture, point of view which saw cultural productions

quest for originality can too easily be diverted into a defence against the charge of derivativeness and mimicry'; the location of Australian glass, at the centre or on the periphery, determined the power to value or devalue work, whereas alternative perspectives, including post-modernism, valued regionalism and difference.

Rowley's paper finished by drawing on literature, modern art and scientific rationalism to make a number of observations on the 'culturally-formed meanings of glass'. These included danger, ritual, purity, fragility and glass as a metaphor for the imagination; she especially emphasised the medium's 'cool contemplation' through 'science's privileged mode of vision'. Glass practitioners were urged to be sensitive to these symbolic, cultural and historical associations as 'they compliment the formal and technical interest that the media holds'. She concluded: 'And given the centrality of objects in our lives, making these symbolic investments in materials the subject of critical investigation through the work may offer us the chance to reflect on the condition of our lives and our world, which I believe is the responsibility and challenge of art'.[28]

Another paper: Private Visions, New Models, given by the author of this book, presented an 'antipodean perspective' which shifted the focus from external factors, such as geographical location and national origins, to scrutinise introspective processes and attitudes as they are affecting Australian studio glass development. The argument, that critical re-evaluation may effectively begin by first taking a look at the location of glass in respect to other areas of craft practice, was generally in accord with other speakers' views. In particular, the paper raised the clay and glass cross-over, specifically examining the parallel development between the two allied media as a means of comparing and predicting ongoing trends. Originality was then tackled through an examination of what 'the language of glass' meant, how this could be extended and how the creative act translated inner vision and experience into artistic reality: these comprise some of the themes examined at length in Chapter 7.[29]

It was not all talk or theory: an International Summer School followed the 1993 conference. Over a period of two weeks there were courses or demonstrations across a range of hot and cold-kilnforming techniques and processes; aside from local instructors, this period of skill exchange involved a large group of overseas practitioners. Among these was American glass blower Richard Royal who has worked as a gaffer on Dale Chihuly's team: the latter himself made a rushed excursion from the United States to make an appearance at the conference and play a video documentary on his museum installations.

Other international practitioners included Elizabeth Tapper an experienced platemaker who perfected the process of intaglio printing plate glass, and is the master printmaker at Pilchuck Glass School; Franz Xaver Holler, a German glass artist and lecturer in glass design at the School for Glass making in Zwiesel, Bavaria and is renowned for his glass casting and sculptural wheel cutting; Catherine Thompson, an American glass artist known for her innovative use of stained-glass painting techniques on blown forms; Maud Cotter an Irish stained glass artist whose sculptural background has led to an innovative approach to this area; William Carlson, professor of Sculpture and Glass at the University of Illinois, whose glass programme is considered pre-eminent in the United States; the British glass artist David Reekie known for his figurative sculptures in cast glass; Hiroshi Yamano, the celebrated Japanese glass artist and the first to be invited to teach at Pilchuck; Katsuya Ogita, winner of the grand prix 1991 World Glass Now exhibition; Richard Whiteley, an Australian, but then teaching in the University of Illinois Glass Programme; and John Croucher, a New Zealander specialising in production glass.

This strong overseas representation maintained the interchange of goodwill, ideas and techniques between the glass scene in Australia and the international movement. It also highlights the concern detailed earlier regarding the power relations of the centre-periphery system: networking is clearly essential, but inevitably it also tends to reinforce the dominance of overseas values and stylistic or other trends — especially within the circumstances whereby Australian practitioners dote excessively on international glass.

During the writing of this book, the 1995 Ausglass conference was well into its advanced planning stages: entitled 'Heart of Glass', its focus was planned on the motivation of practitioners working in the Asia Pacific region, as well as 'an examination of the the spiritual and emotional development of our movement'. In part, it was a theme which arose from comments by a number of speakers at the previous conference, concerning the glass discipline's highly defined and essentially closed boundaries, and their concerted encouragement that adherents venture beyond the practice to find inspiration elsewhere. In this instance, the alternative source was the medium of film, and director Werner Herzog's 1974 film *Heart of Glass*, became the title of the conference. It is a cogent and ambitious theme, brought to the awareness of the Ausglass committee through a critical essay by United States art historian and critic Donald Kuspit, who discusses the film as the basis of an elaboration of stylistic issues in contemporary glass-making.[30] Kuspit's thesis, which pivoted about the perceived tension between 'the very character of glass and conventional social meaning ...', especially dwelling on its metaphorical potential, has considerable ramifications and relevance to contemporary studio glass and is discussed in Chapter 7.

The 1995 conference also included a week of workshops, each structured to include two heads from differing fields of practice, hence anticipating cross-disciplinary formulation. Workshops included: Installation — Cork Marcheschi and Neil Roberts; Glass painting and metalwork — Linda Lichtman and Greg Healey; Glass Engraving and glass painting — Alasdair Gordon and Deb Cocks; *Pâte de verre* and textiles — Judy Bohm-Parr and Bernadette Will; and Lampworking and beadmaking — Richard Clements and Bernie Stonor.

Summary

In reviewing the social operations of Ausglass, especially the participants, themes and tone of its conferences, it becomes apparent that the association is not secure from the political processes and pressures which are seen to occur within most craft or, for that matter, other social organisations. All such fraternities or guilds have their complex of relationships, peer group alliances, rivalries and competitiveness. It sufficient to recognise these dynamics as having a bearing on the values and motivations of the movement, as well as the make-up of its conferences, exhibitions, the perceptions of observers and, to a degree, the direction of member's work.

In her delivery during the 1993 Ausglass Conference, Sue Rowley noted that the glass community is 'likely to place a strong value on "disciplinary" integrity'. Reinforcement of disciplinary values and the

boundaries of the glass community can become the means whereby existing power structures within the group are reinforced, hence impeding change. The consequences of this conservative outlook, Rowley warns, includes the 'narrow band of criteria' used to determine the works for exhibitions, and a reliance on international trends in glass, especially American and European, for setting the directions of Australian glass. It also highlights the potential for conflict with the inevitable progression of the movement as new pacesetters, values and standards replace the previous generation.[31]

Over its fifteen years of growth, Ausglass has developed from its inception as a loosley-formed social group to become an organisation of political, promotional and cultural influence. Members have recently observed that there was also a stronger element of camaraderie in the early conferences, together with an emerging sense of belonging to a world-wide group; today the former is perceived by some as having become diminished, in part due to the inevitable factions and politicising that developed over the past decade — although this viewpoint is not necessarily unanimous. Warren Langley has commented: 'I share more with the international community than fellow glass makers in Australia; we're all on our own paths these days ...'. Concurrently, the collaborative nature which once infused the movement diminished in the competitive setting of the late 1980s, although by 1994, awareness of this tendency saw collaboration emerging as a catch-cry of the movement.[32]

The trend in the contemporary crafts over the past decade has seen practitioners strive for independence to the point that commentators have remarked on this, together with a perceived devaluation of the vital, interdependent, links between people and groups. The issue was recently elaborated by Bronwyn Hughes, who made the salient plea that the organisation should 'expand its thinking beyond the mere self-promotion of individual members ... Ausglass has an opportunity to provide leadership for a diverse number of interested glass groups ... to aim for less is to deny the potential and influence of a growing, effective organisation ...'.[33]

Plate 17 (opposite)
Denis O'Connor (b. 1953)
Fragment of Venus, 1993
kiln cast glass, patinated copper, sandstone;
58 x 28 x 12 cm

CHAPTER THREE

On the Plinth:
The Exhibition Storey

'This is too important a matter to leave to the art historians or curators to deal with. We, the artists are the most competent and only we know what is good or bad ...'[1]

As a site of display and social activity, the exhibition provides a portal into the unfolding story of Australian studio glass: it permits a sampling of technical and stylistic trends, it highlights the achievements of chief practitioners, and it reveals critical and audience responses to the medium.

Even so, it is necessary to recognise that the potential of the exhibition to accurately represent developments in studio glass is limited for a number of reasons. These include the method of selection which is often based on the jurors' or curator's particular aesthetic, political and psychological leaning towards certain categories of work and artists. Objectivity may also be also compromised by the undeniable fact that exhibitions generally are 'the principal medium for institutional promotion and show-casing of the works of selected artists and craftspeople; in this manner the institution sets and indicates standards of artistic or craftsmanly qualities'.[2]

All exhibitions are temporary, they can never be duplicated at a later date; even if the actual works were preserved and brought out at the same site, the audience and setting have irrevocably changed over time, as are the perspectives from which works are viewed. In addition, over a period of time, some exhibitions gain in stature while others fade into insignificance. This is demonstrated by prior documentation of studio glass, and whether catalogues or reviews recorded the event and its impact.

Given the aforementioned, rather than a comprehensive chronology of glass exhibitions, this chapter surveys a selection of the more salient shows, those which occurred at critical points in the unfolding of the studio glass movement, primarily over the past decade.[3]

Neo-dadaist beginnings

From the time of its founding, Ausglass, the Australian Association of Glass Artists, has held major exhibitions concurrently with its biennial conferences. The first national exhibition of Australian studio glass was the Ausglass 'With Care' show, held in April 1979 at the Jam Factory. Although now far removed from the present, a glimpse at its exhibits and the predictably mixed response which it elicited throws some insight into the foundations of the glass movement, as well as providing a point of comparison for more recent exhibitions. Thirty-two 'studio glass makers' as they were called at the time, exhibited work which was

Plate 18 (opposite)
Stephen Procter (b. 1946)
The Gatherer, 1990
blown glass with prismatically-cut edge, wood base;
105 x 42 cm
photo: Johannes Kuhnen

Plate 19
Katsuko Eguchi (b. 1946)
Scene 100, 1994
painted and fused glass sheets (3)
wood frame;
60 x 120 x 7.5 cm

either blown or flat glass. *The Australian* critic Peter Ward then commented that 'the standard of design and technical achievement … [was] uneven'. Warren Langley, the foundation president of Ausglass was quoted as having noted 'that Australia has on its hands an important "nascent revival of glass as an artistic medium" '.[4] There were works by Sam Herman as well as those by trainee glass makers influenced by his approach: these works mostly consisted of small-scale, irregularly-shaped organic forms with swirling murky colours; other blown glass included Stephen Skillitzi's attenuated wavey-necked bottles, an extra-ordinary 'moon' form by Julio Santos, sea-form vessels by Stanislav Melis, and swirling glass platters by Nick Mount. In a departure from the predominantly blown glass work there was a small offering of dis-crete kilnformed, cast and cut glass mosaic cubic forms by Maureen Cahill; and of course there was a good representation from the flat glass makers with a number of autonomous panels by Cedar Prest, Klaus Zimmer, David Saunders and David Wright.[5]

One participant in particular stood out: Rob Knottenbelt, one of the first batch of Jam Factory trainees, displayed a work entitled 'The Suitcase of Mac Fiorucci Milli Fiori'. It consisted of an old leather suitcase filled with the 'obscene pedimenta … of the travelling artist-salesman', and which included a dildo, and was intended to be a subversive comment on the question of artistic quality in glass, as well as the market-conscious attitude already apparent in the area. It had the effect of upsetting viewers, especially his colleagues, a response which Knottenbelt felt vindicated his perception of the highly-conservative attitude towards artistic expression which was typical of glass makers at the time. Although his intention was clear to at least one critic, another dismissed Knottenbelt's work as a 'publicity gesture', while describing conventional blown glass works as 'tasteful, craftsmanly and inoffensive'. Some twelve years later, yet another critic commented that the suitcase 'effectively took the micky out of the then glass "establishment" '.[6]

vessel forms; the commentarial or interrogative object; and the two-dimensional work or autonomous panel. The former category was exemplified by Stephen Skillitzi through the narrative complexity of his figurative sculptural work 'The Fall of Man' (lost wax casting); by Gillian Mann's provocative stylized female genitallia 'Icons' (*pâte de verre*); Brian Hirst's painterly panels of his 'Cycladic Series' (laminated sheet glass, carved and engraved with gold lustre); and Warren Langley's symbolic 'Druid Site' (fused glass and patinated bronze). Falling into the second category were Patrick De Sumo's (b. 1958), 'Simple Vessel Series' which directly appealed through their celebration of functionalist, formal and material qualities (hand-blown and cast base); Helen Aitken Kuhnen's intelligently-designed glass lamp 'Light' (kiln-cast); Janice Blum's bricolage chalice 'Dick-Nose Bear' (blown, fused, lampwork, paint, *pâte de verre*); and Richard Morell's monumental satirical 'Bowl of No Meanings' (blown, kilnformed, cut and polished). The complexity of technique and variety of conceptual approaches saw their blending in sculptural, functional, figurative or commentarial classes. Hence, in addition to the preceding, one may point to Anne Hand's (b. 1960), 'Fire Cone', an organic-shaped lamp (blown and fused); Patrice McKeown's (b. 1965), 'Castle of Sighs', a multimedia assemblage (painted, glass, collage, found objects); and Paul Sanders 'Archaisian Forms' of a coloured vessel placed on a granite slab (blown and kiln-fired).

Especially evident in the exhibition, and apparent in the aforementioned, was the wide-ranging eclecticism of the glass-forming processes and techniques used, some pure, others mixed, and included blown glass, engraved lead-crystal, complex assemblages, and leaded stained glass panels; kilnforming processes such as casting, lost-wax methods and *pâte de verre* were also prevalent (see Chapter 4). Yet, whatever the wide-ranging and imaginative use of these numerous techniques, and whatever the sculptural, vessel or symbolic class of exploration undertaken, most of the works indicated that the earlier tendency of privileging the idea over the qualities of the material had diminished considerably. As this exhibition demonstrated, the late 1980s had seen many practitioners clearly exploiting, indeed revelling, in the qualities of the medium — concurrently with the expression of idea. This was evident in the use and celebration of colour, the heightening of texture, and of other light-affecting qualities unique to glass.

Plate 22
Marc Grunseit (b. 1952)
Capricornia, 1993
kiln-formed, fused and slumped glass'
Diam. 50 cm

Compared to its predecessor, the 5th Wagga National Studio Glass Exhibition in 1991, which concurrently celebrated the tenth anniversary of Wagga's survey shows, was widely perceived as 'a let down'. It was especially revealing of the processes leading to its make-up within the setting of the glass scene. Its jurors, John McPhee and Glenn Cooke, curators of the National Gallery of Victoria and the Queensland Art Gallery respectively, were forceful in expressing their concern at the quality of the work submitted by eighty-four artists. McPhee was especially critical in his catalogue comments: 'The amateur nature of these submissions shocked and disappointed me'. After numerous submissions were rejected, compared to the fourth triennial of 68 works by 45 artists, the fifth show was reduced to 36 works by 13 artists — a diminished representation for such a major survey exhibition. Of these, nine of the selected artists were women, apparently a proportion only slightly higher than the total number of entries. It was difficult to disagree with the jurors' sentiments: whereas the previous exhibition demonstrated a considerable degree of technical virtuosity and a mature attitude towards conceptual risks these qualities were not as discernible in the fifth triennial, perhaps because of the reduced number of entrants. The lack of support by significant hot and flat glass artists was considered to be part of the reason why sculptural (and architectural) elements — then prevalent in both Australian and international studio glass and which had increased in scale — were under-represented.[13]

The exhibited works, without exception, were characteristic of the personal style distilled by each glass maker over their mostly, short careers. There were assembled shard vessels by Jan Blum; unassuming *pâte de verre* vessels by Judith Bohm-Parr; baroque vessels by Barbara Jane Cowie; form and pure-colour goblets by Benjamin Edols; abstract colour-field platters by Judi Elliott; illusionist cityscape cameo jars by Tony Hanning; sculptural-vessel combinations by Irena Kaluza; decorative champagne glasses by Elizabeth Kelly; multi-worked and painterly perfume bottles by Elizabeth McClure; deconstructed archaic sculptural forms by Paul Sanders; finely-etched and layered glass panels of the Fossil Record series by Graham Stone; vigorous fused-colour bowls by Vicki Torr; and boldly-coloured modernist blown glass bottles by Maureen Williams. If the exhibition was to be taken as representative of the glass movement as a whole — which it arguably was not — it suggested that there had been a swing back to the vessel, for at least two thirds of the works were either bowls, bottles, dishes or platters of a modest scale.

Among the critical comments raised by the exhibition, Tony Hanning was the most trenchant first criticising the Jurors' statements, especially McPhee's comments that 'goblets … this most useful area of production has always seemed to me to have been neglected by Australian artists'. Hanning pointed out the large number of glass practitioners making such items since the early 1980s and who have suffered 'the effects of the "curatorial stigma" that was associated with tableware and the high ideals of galleries who would only exhibit work which "challenged the traditional notion of glass"'.[14] Maureen Cahill's focus was pragmatic: 'Glass must be packed carefully and if a work is too spiky or too big or too delicate, these became criteria for selection and they become restrictive. The vessel therefore becomes a preference and artists generally tailor-make pieces for a travelling show which therefore may not be an accurate representation of current work and ideas'.[15] More than anything, exhibitions reflect the predilections of its jurors, positioning the fifth triennial as a salient reminder of how assiduously survey shows needed to be planned by curators — and how cautiously they should be approached and interpreted by the viewer.

Despite its limitations, there were some exceptional works in the fifth triennial: Paul Sanders' *Archaisian Form*, was a sequel to his earlier work whereby he had moved from representation through the manipulation of the timeless vessel to a brutal image of technological allusion, and reinforcing this shift by combining glass with metal instead of natural stone; his masterful use of kiln-formed processes to achieve subtle patination effects further heightened the sense of complexity and symbolism. Jan Blum's lamp-worked fragmented and painted vessel form similarly caught the eye: this work, exemplary of the post-modernist deconstructivist imagery so prevalent in contemporary ceramics and jewellery, demonstrated that this influence had been infiltrating studio glass since the mid-1980s; Deconstruction, as an approach which informed the works of Warren Langley, Gillian Mann, Meza Rijsdijk, Peter Tysoe, Stephen Skillitzi, Velta Vilmanis, and Richard Whiteley, to name a few, are examined in detail in Chapter 7.

The sixth Wagga National Studio Glass Exhibition, *The Cutting Edge*, was organised and selected at the time of writing of this text in mid-1994. Divided into two sections: the invitational and the general, the former was reserved for eight invited major artists and included a considerable ($20,000) fund for purchases. The response was disappointing, forcing the showing of 33 works by invited practitioners only; of these, the majority were pioneers — newcomers were scarce. However, as this exhibition was not to be toured, the works would have limited exposure; instead, planning was under way to tour, during 1996, for some fifty works by major artists selected from the now historic National Art Glass Collection, together with a sub-stantial catalogue as a means of showcasing and promoting the presence of the permanent collection — a logical stratagem given the relative isolation of Wagga from the main population centres of Australia.

A more recent initiative of this gallery has been to support glass artists through a series of specialist exhibitions called Studio Glass Design: Limited Edition Series, the first held in 1991 and the second in 1993. The idea of promoting limited edition work through exhibitions was one outcome of the recession of the late 1980s and early 1990s which saw income from exhibition work fall considerably for many glass practitioners, most of whom are disadvantaged by Australia's distance from the lucrative collectors market in the United States. The recession saw a return to the balance between production and exhibition work as a means of economic survival; this, in turn, has seen a growth of giftware and tourist pieces as well as functional tablewares.

For the Limited Edition Series exhibitions, eight glass practitioners were selected and asked to design and make an art work which could be suitable adapted to production as a limited edition. The idea was to entice potential collectors with works from established artists at prices below those of one-off pieces. Le Lievre was generally disappointed with the response she received from the practitioners: 'Not all artists produced work which was suitable for reproducing as a limited series run. Blown work is not so suitable as it can resemble production work, whereas cast glass is better for this kind of exercise. The exhibition itself was was poorly supported ... we'll persevere and put it on again in 1995'.[16]

The concept of limited series runs has certainly been successful in the professional crafts in the past six years, perhaps more notably in jewellery and less so in furniture and glass. Clearly, success depends in part on the nature of the medium, as well as on the design skills of the maker in prototyping forms suitable for series production. The essential point about this area of craft, design and making is that, aside from

Plate 23
Alison McMillan (b. 1947)
Just Desserts, 1992
slumped, painted and sandblasted glass
on sand-cast glass 'rock' feet;
enamelled, painted and lustre;
40 x 40 x 10 cm

considerations of efficiency and economy, the requirement that the reproduced item retains signs of its sourcing in craft and handwork. In glass, casting in moulds is less likely to diminish the individual and appealing, craftsmanly qualities of one-off works; it is a challenge which may provide a growth niche for the enterprising glass maker in the late 1990s.[17]

Given its bush location and the size of Wagga Wagga as a regional urban centre — features which paradoxically magnify the significance of its glass collection — Judy Le Lievre has endeavoured to maintain the impetus of the Wagga City Art Gallery. Its permanent collection of glass and the exposure the programme of exhibitions has given to glass practitioners over the past thirteen years have arguably had their greatest impact throughout the 1980s. The 1990s require new strategies, and the impending national tour over 1996, of a sizeable number of works from the permanent National Art Glass Collection, will spearhead this new initiative.

International exposure

Besides its regular survey shows, Wagga City Art Gallery also organised exhibitions which have toured overseas, hence expanding the collector's market and contributing towards the international profile of Australian work. Art Glass From Australia, for example, travelled to Germany and Holland in late 1990 and early 1991: it featured four vessel-based works and three sculptural pieces by seven, then well-established, glass artists: Brian Hirst, Robert Knottenbelt, Warren Langley, Peter Tysoe, Richard Whiteley, Denis O'Connor and Janice Blum.

Exhibitions exposing Australian work to overseas audiences had been initiated in the early 1980s beginning with the first major show Glass From Australia And New Zealand. Comprising sixty-three works by forty-five Australian glass makers, and accompanied with eleven works by ten New Zealanders, the exhibition toured Europe from October 1984. Although care was taken to ensure that the selection process

Plate 24
Sallie Portnoy (b. 1954)
Contemplate,
Made Platter Series, 1993
fused and slumped, gold lustre;
38 x 46 x 50 cm

was non-discriminatory, one of the organisers, Jenny Zimmer, pointed out 'many of our prominent artists were missing'.[18] Nevertheless, a number of significant artists were represented.

Over a quarter of the work in Glass From Australia And New Zealand was flat glass — a very high representation which reflected Zimmer's specialty and which coincided with the release of her book on stained glass.[19] The exhibition included works by Cedar Prest, Klaus Zimmer, Terry Beaston (b. 1951), David Clegg (b. 1943), John Greig (b. 1950), Wayne Rayson (b. 1963), Gerhard Emmerichs, Berin Behn (b. 1951), Alison McMillan (b. 1947), Philippa Roberts (b. 1962), Anne Atkins (b. 1942), Daniel de Chalain (b. 1960), Gisela Hunter (b. 1939), Dylan Thornton (b. 1960), Lorraine Bodger (b. 1962), and Christopher Bingley (b. 1959). The majority of these artists had graduated from the innovative flat glass course at Chisholm University (then Institute of Technology), whose senior lecturer was Klaus Zimmer. Not unexpectedly, many of the flat glass exhibits — which were presented as autonomous panels — demonstrated the incorporation of the, then novel, hot-glass kilnforming processes, in combination with traditional painting and leaded techniques (see Chapter 6).

Glass artists who worked in kilnforming techniques included Warren Langley whose kilnformed work was suggestive of his later and current textured and sculptural forms; Brian Hirst who had then already distilled the essence of his on-going imagery in his Cycladic series; Stephen Skillitzi whose Ground Zero Nuclear Game exhibit demonstrated his complex assemblage and multi-skilled approach which incorporated performance; Maureen Cahill whose Kite Series of slumped and sand-blasted glass exemplified her evolving architectural forms; Gerry King whose satirical, modestly-scaled mould-blown work indicated to his later social-commentary sculptural forms; Rob Knottenbelt, whose cynical, fused-glass and gold-leaf Postcard series, maintained his position as a rebel in the glass scene; and Pauline Delaney's blown glass vessel: a progenitor of present-day works.

Of course, the year in which the exhibition was held precluded the distinctive kilnformed work which was to shortly emerge from the Glass Workshop at the Canberra School of Art established a year earlier (see Chapters 1 & 4). Instead, many of the artists represented in Glass From Australia And New Zealand were graduates of the Chisholm Institute, a handful had trained at Jam Factory Glass Workshop, others had trained in various institutions in Europe before migrating to live in Australia, and a few were self-trained. It was also notable that, while the majority of the artists had had five years or less experience in the medium, indications of the participants' future directions were already evident. Political and social issues, or personal concerns and interests expressed in the works also reflected the current concerns of the times: from nuclear proliferation to modern-day social anxiety, from the abstract representation of the Australian environment to human emotion. Aesthetic and formal approaches were also diverse and ranged from an unrestrained expression of decorative potential of the medium, through to painterly and sculptural explorations. The exhibition reflected the state of Australian studio glass as it had developed in the short period of twelve or so years.

International Directions in Glass which toured Australia in 1982, was the earliest significant showing of multinational work which received considerable exposure; it was a pivotal exhibition of its type in the early history of the glass movement in Australia, exposing a range of international studio glass works to the fledgling movement.[20] An eclectic collection representing 54 glass artists, it emphasised American work which ranged from the vessel and small object to sculptural, installation and two-dimensional works: especially evident was the versatility of technique and freedom of expression in glass. Eleven years on, Marc Grunseit recollected: 'the technical and conceptual inspiration that the collection created passed like an earthquake through the glass art scene, particularly as no Australian works were, at the time, considered worthy of inclusion'.[21]

The exhibition drew much criticism at the time, from a number of Australian glass practitioners whose work had been denied representation. There had been calls to include an Australian component but the need to expose overseas artists' works for the benefit of the Australians had been considered to be a greater priority. Without doubt, Michael Esson the selector found it extremely difficult to make aesthetic and political decisions about his own local peer group — hence the avoidance of the whole issue. This was despite the presence of a handful of Australian glass artists who were then producing world-standard work, including Stephen Skillitzi, Gerry King, Warren Langley, Julio Santos, Nick Mount, Maureen Cahill, Cedar Prest, Klaus Zimmer, David Wright, and Anne Dybka.

More significantly, the exhibition demonstrated to Australian glass practitioners that there was, not only a strong tendency towards the sculptural treatment of glass, but also the primacy of concept over technique was the aim of most, if not all, of the represented overseas artists.[22] Given the enthusiasm with which the work was received, it suggested the taste for things to come on the local scene. As it eventuated, sculptural work did not flood the scene in the following years, perhaps because of market limitations: it has always remained an option.

It was the lack of Australian work in the first International Directions in Glass Art which toured in 1982, and which became one of the incentive for mounting its successor — albeit a decade later — with Australian work. International Directions in Glass Art was organised by the Art Gallery of Western Australia as one component of three shows comprising Design Visions, the Australian International Crafts Triennial, held in Perth in October 1993. It was also timely from the perspective of the Ausglass conference held a few months later in early 1993 and which had origins and originality as its theme. International Directions in Glass included the work of eight Australians and the New Zealander Ann Robinson. This was out of a total of forty-six participants comprising thirteen from the USA, one from Canada, sixteen from Europe, and seven from Japan: Australian representation was therefore generous. This was even more so if one considered the additional five glass works displayed among the miscellaneous craft exhibits of the complementary Australia — New Design Visions component of the Triennial.

Who were the glass artists chosen to represent the condition of the Australian scene, and how did they compare with their international counterparts? First, a selection of works by thirteen out of the five hundred or so glass practitioners in this country could not by any means be considered representative. Moreover, flat or stained glass was entirely bypassed in favour of strictly hot-glass approaches; however, what was eventually included did portray an idea of the achievements of Australian studio glass in terms of its technical, expressive and cultural traits some three years into the 1990s.

Among the various observations to be made it was notable that, whereas International Directions in Glass had one woman among seven male glass artists, the five whose work was exhibited in the Australia

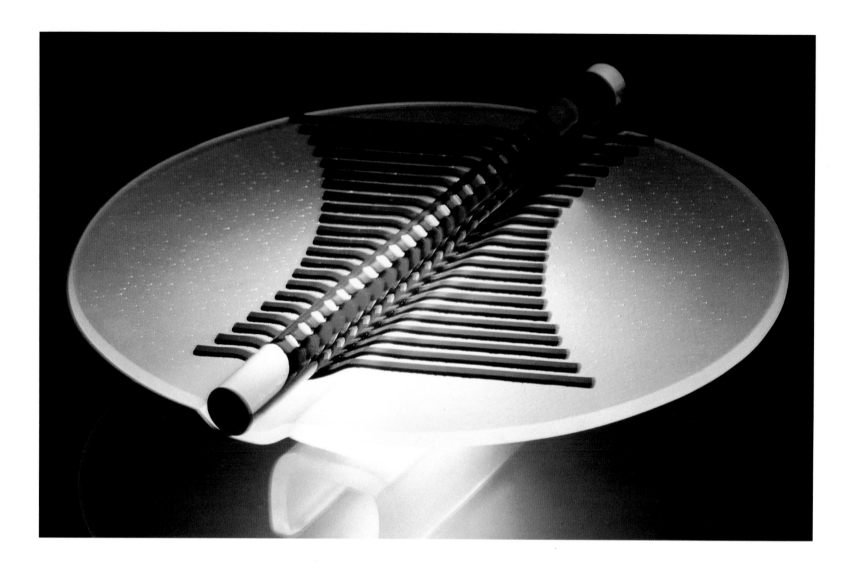

Plate 25
Velta Vilmanis (b. 1949)
Table Light, 1993
fused, slumped glass with crystal rod;
Diam. 45 cm

— New Design Visions component, were all women. And, with the exception of Vicki Torr, all of the participating women of both exhibitions — Judith Bohm-Parr, Helen Aitken Kuhnen, Judi Elliott, Kirstie Rea, and Meza Rijsdijk — were graduates of the Glass Workshops of the Canberra School of Art. The influence of this institution on glass in Australia is further underscored when we note that their teacher, Klaus Moje, also participated in International Directions in Glass. In part because of this strong representation from Canberra, and in part because of the international trend to favour kilnformed glass, especially casting, fusing, moulding and *pâte de verre*, the combined Australian work of the two exhibitions especially emphasised this genre of work. Out of the thirteen Australians, the nine who displayed pieces of this genre were Judith Bohm-Parr, Helen Aitken Kuhnen, Judi Elliott, Kirstie Rea, Brian Hirst, Klaus Moje, Gerry King, Warren Langley, and Vicki Torr.

Each of these glass makers had utilised a particular blend of kilnformed techniques and process, some combining cold-working techniques for finishing effects as well. Naturally, each also had their own aesthetic and conceptual approaches: Bohm-Parr explored the relationship between material, form and historical technique through her deceptively modest *pâte de verre* vessels, pursuing the sensualist qualities of this genre, especially its tactile, visual and decorative virtues; Aitken Kuhnen used kiln-cast lead and Bullseye

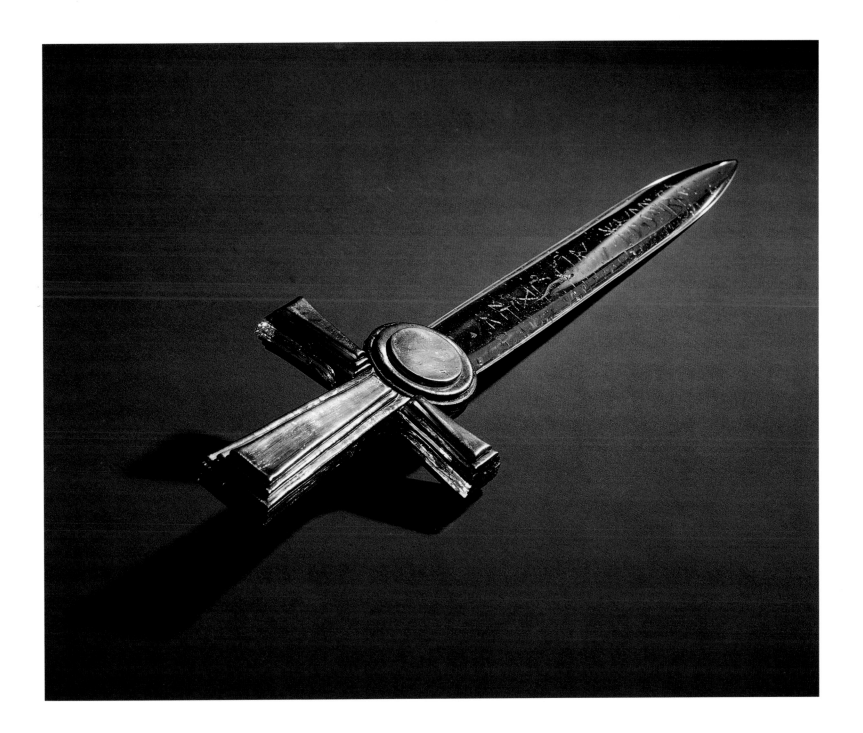

Plate 29
Sergio Redegalli (b. 1962)
Ritual Blade,
Martian Warrior Series, 1994
laminated, gold-fused and polished glass;
38 x 10 x 2 cm
photo: Roger Dekker

this does not prevent the subsequent re-working or deformation of the basic form to extend the possible outcomes as the following chapters elaborate.

A critical point in the development of the genre was achieved in 1988 when a two week symposium, the International Masterworkshop in Kilnformed Glass, was held in Canberra in April through to May: it was an event which especially underscored the national and international profile of innovative kilnforming activity in Australia. Incredibly, this was the first time such a workshop, which brought master glass practitioners of this specialty together, had been held world-wide. Convened by Klaus Moje, half the glass artists were invited from overseas while the other half were local. The Masterworkshop in Kilnformed Glass was a milestone in the international glass movement's history: it set standards for kilnformed work; demon-

Plate 30
Helen Aitken Kuhnen (b. 1952)
Sculptural Light, 1993
Kiln cast glass and anodised aluminium;
36 x 29 x 29 cm

strated the potential diversity of methodology, application and expressions; and exposed practitioners within the glass community who worked in this specialty.[2]

The theme of the glass masterworkshop centred about fusing and kilnforming techniques, the master glass practitioners sharing techniques and ideas with locals and students in practical workshop and discussion sessions. The former included Colin Reid and Diana Hobson from England; the New Zealander Ann Robinson; Stephen Weinberg from the United States; Antoine Leperlier (b. 1953), from France (grandson of Francois Decorchemont, 1888–1971); and Willi Pistor from Germany. The other participants were Stephen Skillitzi, Warren Langley, Rob Knottenbelt, Meza Rijsdijk, Richard Whiteley, and Elizabeth McClure — a group of Australian glass artists who were specialists in kilnforming processes, although McClure had only recently arrived from the UK to lecture at the school.

These visiting and local artists explored a variety of fusing and kilnforming processes including *pâte de verre*, the lost wax method of casting, sand-casting, mosaic glass making, fusing and slumping, making glass jewellery, vessels, and figurative or abstract sculptural work. As well as consolidating this area of practice in Australia, the symposium also promoted a shift in the prevailing focus on conceptual, fine arts issues, to the making process itself, and an examination of the relationship between hands, material and creativity, a theme explored at depth in Chapter 7. As an observer at the time, the latter was investigated through a series of articles by Nola Anderson.[3]

Not unexpectedly, the masterworkshops also revealed the degree of rivalry which existed between glass blowing and kilnforming at the time: during a slide lecture Warren Langley provocatively stated that 'the future of glass lay with the kilnformed, and that blown glass was at least comatose if not dead'. Another observation was the dichotomy of approach between the conservatism of the European practitioners on the one hand, and the freer expressions of the United States and Australian practitioners on the other, a fact generally sublimated by the camaraderie of the occasion.[4] In addition, Skillitzi later surmised that the workshop was not so important in terms of teaching any new techniques, than providing 'a kind of small Pilchuck,' with its attendant stimulating atmosphere and peer-group network of overseas and local glass practitioners.

In association with the symposium was Kilnformed Glass: An International Exhibition. This featured the work of twenty-four glass artists, including the twelve aforementioned together with Helen Aitken Kuhnen, Maureen Cahill, Allan Crynes, Judi Elliott, Gwendoline Ford, Gerry King, Gillian Mann, Ian Mowbray, Sallie Portnoy, Kirstie Rea, Vicki Torr, Richard Whiteley and David Wright. The handful of participating non-Australians also included those overseas artists who were involved in the workshop, with the addition of visiting French practitioner, Antoine Leperlier.[5] In 1990, Judi Elliott, Warren Langley, Klaus Moje, Kirstie Rea, Meza Rijsdijk, Richard Whiteley, Vicki Torr, Ann Robinson, and Gillian Mann — all then specialists in kilnforming — were selected by Klaus Moje for the exhibition Australian Kilnformed Glass, which toured four cities in the United States: New York, Los Angeles, Fort Lauderdale and Detroit. The two exhibitions, especially the latter, underscored the comparatively high level of activity and the vitality of kilnformed glass in Australia from the late 1980s, as well as raising its profile in the United States.

In 1994, another exhibition of kilnformed work, once more selected by Moje from 13 former gradu-

ates of the Canberra glass workshop, was shown at the Jam Factory in Adelaide. Clearly, Moje's promotion of his past students has been a critical factor in their on-going high profile. His colleague, Dale Chihuly in the United States, has similarly been strongly supportive of his students in this manner.

A close analysis of the Wagga City Art Gallery's 4th National Studio Glass Exhibition held in 1988, manifests the degree of popularity which kilnforming had reached by the late 1980s in Australia. Of the 68 works by 45 artists which comprised the show, at least 18 were exclusively created through kilnformed techniques and processes with an additional 7 works which were combined with other techniques (mostly blowing). This exhibition, with its large number of exhibits chosen from a very large pool of works (240 by 70 artists), more so than any other held between the mid to late 1980s (and possibly the largest submission of the movement's history), was indicative of the direction studio glass had taken. With 37 per cent of works kilnformed, compared to 24 per cent furnace blown — the remainder were either mixed assemblages (12 per cent), flat-stained (9 per cent), lamp-worked, engraved lead-crystal and other (18 per cent). A comparison of these figures with their counterparts in the United States and Europe, suggests that about 50 per cent are furnace blown and about 20 per cent kilnformed: this would appear to reinforce the observation that kilnformed work characterised studio glass in Australia.[6]

Who were among the represented and chief glass practitioners utilising kilnforming techniques and processes as revealed by the Wagga show? There were the first generation or masters: Stephen Skillitzi, Warren Langley, Gerry King; and subsequent generations of glass artists: Vicki Torr, Richard Morrell, Velta Vilmanis, Gillian Mann, Richard Whiteley, Peter Minson, Kirstie Rea, Helen Aitken Kuhnen, Karl Brugel (b. 1931), Judi Elliott, John Elsegood, Etsuko Nishi (b. 1955), Anthony Rake (b. 1954), Peter Crisp, and Meza Rijsdijk. Other artists utilised kilnforming processes as a critical part of their work and included Paul Sanders, Janice Blum, Patrick De Sumo, Don Wreford, and Bronwyn Hughes.

In later years, the prevalence of kilnforming was underscored by two subsequent exhibitions in particular: International Directions in Glass, and the Australia — New Design Visions; both were components of the International Crafts Triennial held in Perth in late 1992, and both emphasised kilnformed glass. Taken together, the exhibitions also highlighted the dominance which the Glass Workshop at the Canberra School of Art had achieved in the area: with the exception of one exhibitor, Vicki Torr, the rest were all graduates of the Glass Workshop and included Judith Bohm-Parr, Helen Aitken Kuhnen, Judi Elliott, Kirstie Rea, and Meza Rijsdijk. Klaus Moje, who also participated in International Directions in Glass added his own imprint so that, out of the 13 Australian exhibitors in total, 9 displayed work of this genre, while an additional 2 had utilised selected kiln-procedures as part of their work.

Each of these glass practitioners, like many others, honed their own particular blend of kilnformed techniques and processes which they apply to various aesthetic and conceptual approaches. For example, the historical links between ancient or more recent cultures, in regard to kilnforming, broaden the expressive language of the medium adding a further dimension which enhances and re-interprets this genre's prismatic and other qualities; this approach is effectively exploited by an increasing number of glass practitioners including Paul Sanders, Warren Langley, Peter Tysoe, Ann Robinson, John Elsegood, Judith Bohm-Parr, Gillian Mann, Richard Morrell, Allan Crynes and Judith Candy.

Plate 31 (opposite)
Richard Morrell (b. 1953)
Bowl for a Lost Heart, 1994
kiln cast glass, metal oxides
and coloured-glass shard
inclusions, acid etched
and cold worked;
25 x 27 cm

Plate 32 (opposite)
Gillian Mann (b. 1938)
Icon, 1988
cast glass;
21.5 x 17.5 x 6 cm

On the other hand, the exploration of kilnforming approaches in combination with the vessel form — its aesthetic, sculptural or metaphorical allusions — sometimes in association with the preceding historical angle, forms yet another area of strong interest for a number of practitioners, including Ann Robinson, Peter Tysoe, Richard Morrell, Klaus Moje, Paul Sanders, Meza Rijsdijk, Velta Vilmanis, Judith Bohm-Parr, and Allan Crynes.

More recent practitioners who are concentrating on this genre seem to be especially interested in exploring its potential to represent psychological or humanistic states, including Stephen Skillitzi, Judi Elliott, Robyn Campbell, Itzell Tazzyman, Mies Grybaitis, Marc Kalifa, Luna Ryan, and Roger Buddle.

Inevitably, there are cross-overs of conceptual intent and of technical exploration in the preceding, as well as in the work of the following whose work ranges from social or political commentary, personal narrative, symbolic, figurative or sculptural as found in the work of Gerry King, Warren Langley, Ian Mowbray, Denis O'Connor, Sergio Redegalli, Kirstie Rea, and Paul Sanders.

Considering the diversity of combinations and possibilities which expands the range of explorative areas of the aforementioned, what are the particular reasons these and other practitioners choose to work in kilnforming, what are their individual approaches and current concerns, and what have they achieved?

Lost wax and casting

Kilnformed glass processes had a gradual start, first being used as early as 1972 in Australia by Stephen Skillitzi, although he acknowledges that his predominant activity at the time and for the following few years was in blowing glass. Skillitzi established his glass studio, Glass Earth and Fire, in Adelaide in 1987: his art practice has always included ceramics, mixed media, and sculptural glass, but never market-driven production ware. To Skillitzi, such a commercial focus would be contrary to Harvey Littleton's 1959 maxim: 'Glass can be a sculptural medium'.[7]

Since 1981 Skillitzi has centred preoccupations around three genres: First, 'glass as a material', whereby kiln and furnace cast works, up to 150 kilograms, as units for wall sculptures, screens or fountains for corporate or domestic settings, and temporary site-specific commercial glass installations for concept development purposes; 'glass with a message', his second category, consists of his more widely-known and modestly-scaled, lost wax, kiln-cast glass, usually embellished with with electroformed metals of copper, nickel or gold. These have conceptual or allegorical human figurative themes, and have been primarily marketed to United State museums and collectors. His third category of work 'glass with spirit', consists of 'playable games' of mixed media and glass with satirical, and as he puts it, 'attitude-challenging, contemporary-issue themes'. Sometimes these games — which began in 1978 and reached their apotheosis in the late 1980s — are integrated with 'street theatre', or presented by Skillitzi as Master of Ceremonies. These non-commercial works in space and time serve to extend 'his frustration at the static nature' of his more conventional sculpture, his figurative moulded glass, into the arena of mimed allegories.

In 1994, Skillitzi returned to creating sculptural interpretations of his game series: Snakes and Ladders, Anyone? combines large-scale child figures with actual snakes and ladders in playful reposes. Here the innocence of youth is juxtaposed with the danger of the venomous reptile, hence evoking the insecurity of life.

Plate 33
Judith Bohm-Parr (b. 1953)
Ripples, 1992
pâte de verre, cast legs;
Diam. 17 x 8 cm

Through his idiosyncratic approach, Skillitzi has embraced the metaphysical substances of glass, earth and fire, which he translates respectively as: 'the material, technical body: the rational, narrative mind; and the unfettered spirit essence'. This practitioner also sees a biographical perspective as essential to understanding his seminal 1987 work, Tomb of the Unknown Glass Artist, which he considers his 'most darkly reflective work to date'. Seemingly a gravestone, this 150 kilo clear-glass cast with human face images and installed at the Adelaide Cemetery, was a neo-dadaist work 'miming the artist's career cycle'.

His current preoccupation with lost-wax casting began in 1979, albeit in a multi-media manner. Three years later, following an extended European study tour, Skillitzi set up his present-day studio in suburban Adelaide when he 'put away his glass-blowing pipes' and built a kiln to accommodate various casting techniques. Skillitzi had come to the realisation that a number of other artists were to come to over the ensuing years, that glass blowing was limited in its sculptural potential; and in particular, he had always been

Plate 34
Vicki Torr (1949–1992)
Double Cone, 1991
pâte de verre;
20 x 47 cm

committed to representing the human image. Skillitzi has since specialised in kilnforming techniques and processes, specifically with the ancient *cire perdue*, or lost wax method, and allied kiln-casting approaches. With a self-confessed omnivorous appetite in his thematic choice, Skillitzi's work has free-ranged from exploring issues as diverse as the Persian Gulf War to current environmental concerns, from sexual politics to timeless questions of human existence and aspirations.

Ambiguity, illusionism, and allegory are Skillitzi's preferred conceptual tools: these direct an impressive technical virtuosity in the manipulation of glass to result in figurative imagery. His medium-scaled works often depict interlocking faces, figures and symbolic architectural or other fragments, the whole engaged in a complexity of expression. It is this intricacy that communicates his ideas and outlook of a world of brutal reality, of contradicting emotions and behaviours. The human image as half-face, half-mask is his preferred idiom, one which projects the duality of the psyche: autonomy versus societal control, creative freedom versus ego-destructive restraint, and optimism versus pessimism.

The lost wax method for casting gives Skillitzi textural, colour and other qualities which extend his formal imagery; he develops these even further through the innovative use of copper or nickel metallic depositions which are applied through an electroforming process. Because this process depends on electrical power manipulated by him during the application stages, Skillitzi argues that it adds a metaphorical 'aura-derived life-field of the Russian Kirlian type'. Hence the crafting process, evident in the cast glass and its organic-like metallic encrustations, interplay with and contribute to artistic intent (see also Chapter 5).

The lost wax method has also been the New Zealander, Ann Robinson's (b. 1944), central technique since her entry into glass in 1980. Coincidentally, Robinson's discovery of this method was not unlike that of Skillitzi's: during her art school course she took up glass as an option, and although the focus was on on glass blowing, she experimented and succeeded in adapting bronze-casting procedures into glass casting; it was a necessary pathway as manuals or teachers of this method simply did not exist or were unavailable. For a decade, Robinson worked in a production studio blowing glass, concentrating on glass casting solely on her days off. Casting permitted the making of basic mould forms which could then be carved to develop pattern; it also gave her a freedom of expression unavailable in blowing: 'glass blowing is faster, extroverted, whereas casting allows you to attend to details and to work on your own, its introverted'.[8]

Robinson developed her command of technique and material, a high-lead crystal glass made locally, to explore the qualities of glass through the timeless form of the vessel and its decorative potential. Although the work of the early twentieth-century glass French designer, René Lalique, was a major inspiration — especially in his deft use of clear, frosted and opalescent glass; Robinson has similarly developed her own technical and expressive skills. She especially works on a considerably expanded scale, often using up to 40 to 50 kilograms of glass for a vessel. A fondness of natural forms as observed in the native foliage of New Zealand flora such as palm leaves, has led to an intense investigation of repeat patterns and motifs centred about angularity; the dramatically-eroded volcanic coastline near her home at Karekare (Maori for agitated or excited), has also inspired her decorative work. Her affinity for the vessel is especially strong, and a Polynesian influence is evident in the forms and their size, and emerge from the ubiquitous large wooden ceremonial bowls of Maori and other Pacific Island cultures found in New Zealand.

Robinson has conducted a number of workshops in her casting techniques and processes in Australia and overseas. These occurred after her participation at the master glass workshops in Canberra in 1988. In 1986, she won the New Zealand Phillips Glass Award with one of her cast glass works, the judge being Maureen Cahill who recognised its quality of artistic expression and craftsmanship. In 1992, Robinson taught lost-wax casting at Pilchuck in the USA where she was 'amazed at the lack of knowledge of casting there'. She was especially critical of the Americans' approach to the annealing stage which was simply executed through 'intuition', whereas she had derived and used precise mathematical calculations. Robinson observed at the time that, 'kilnforming has taken off more strongly in Australia than in the USA'. This is not to suggest that kilnforming does not constitute a sizeable portion of studio glass practice in that country, but rather that the interest has, proportionally, been much less notable than in Australia (see Chapter 7).

The intrigue of lost-wax working continues to progressively attract practitioners to its time-consuming, but satisfying, process. Bridget Hancock (b. 1959), is one practitioner who has been casting in this method over the past three years. Her large encrusted vessels have an ice-like appearance which exemplifies clearglass, wax-casting and emphasise the play of pure light. Hancock also exercises a wide rage of other casting techniques including slumping, and the forming of deeply-textured glass surfaces through the use of sand moulds. Lately, she has moved into the area of photo silk-screening to produce surface imagery on glass in order to create the illusion of textures, such as sand-ripples of the shoreline.[9]

Peter Tysoe (b. 1935) is another glass artist who has concentrated on kilnforming as a specialty in his career. He was educated at Oxford Technical School, Oxford School of Art and Goldsmiths School of Art and London University, graduating in 1957. His studies of Oceanic and Australian Aboriginal cultures and travels in Italy and Greece, gave him considerable exposure to their art and architecture; form has subsequently been an essential element in his work, usually allied to controlled texture and colour. He first exhibited works in slab glasses combined with metal structures with Bernard Leach, Barbara Hepworth and others. The influence of these major British artists was reflected in his later work, with flat areas of coloured glass being suspended in spatial constructions with thin steel bars.[10]

In 1966 Tysoe set up a studio producing architectural commissions in glass and multi-media for major clients in the UK and the Middle East. Hot glass elements for architectural works were made under his direction at the newly formed Dartington Glass factory in North Devon. In 1970 he was awarded a Churchill Fellowship to study glass production and design in Scandinavia and Finland. His meeting with Bertil Vallien who was then working in cast glass at the Kosta Boda glass factory reinforced his desire to explore casting further. Sand-casting was very much in fashion in England during the 1970s. In 1976, Tysoe had sand-cast large dish forms which were exhibited in the British Craft Council's Exhibition Centre in London.

During the 1970s, Tysoe also made two tours in the USA, visiting the Corning Museum and factory and working in hot glass in Vermont. This first exposure to the actual manipulation of hot glass led him to undertake courses at the recently formed Glasshouse in Covent Garden, London and other places. In the 1980s, sculptural pieces were developed, casting hot glass into sand moulds. Unique glass box forms were made utilising graphite moulds: two cast boxes from this period are in the permanent collection of European glass at the Kunstsammlungen der Veste Coburg, Germany. In 1980 Tysoe met Klaus Moje in Hamburg, and who was then already creating his familiar mosaic work; Tysoe realised that 'there was a notable degree of kilnforming and cast work about in Europe then, a lot of developing ideas, especially rediscovering the techniques of glass designers and makers such as René Lalique and Francois Decorchemont'.

In 1985, when he was appointed as head of the Glass Workshop at the Jam Factory in Adelaide (Chapter 1). Although mostly instructing trainees in glass blowing, Tysoe maintained his affinity for kilnforming which he mostly utilised for his own exhibition work. He combined this approach with a keen sense of observation of his newly-adopted country. The experience of travelling to the coastal and outback areas of South Australia and the Northern Territory first became reflected in his Willunga series of blown vessels in black-cased glass, which have been acid etched, and in the more recent developments in *cire perdue*, lost wax castings in glass, where the original model is beset in a refractory mould, into which the glass is cast. Lost-wax procedures were developed by Tysoe from his 1970s metal casting which had then moved into lost-material casting using industrial foams; conventional wax replaced this material in 1988.

Three sculptures in cast glass and steel, with themes based on the relationship of the land with the indigenous people, were included in the Art Glass from Australia exhibition. In his more recent works, the

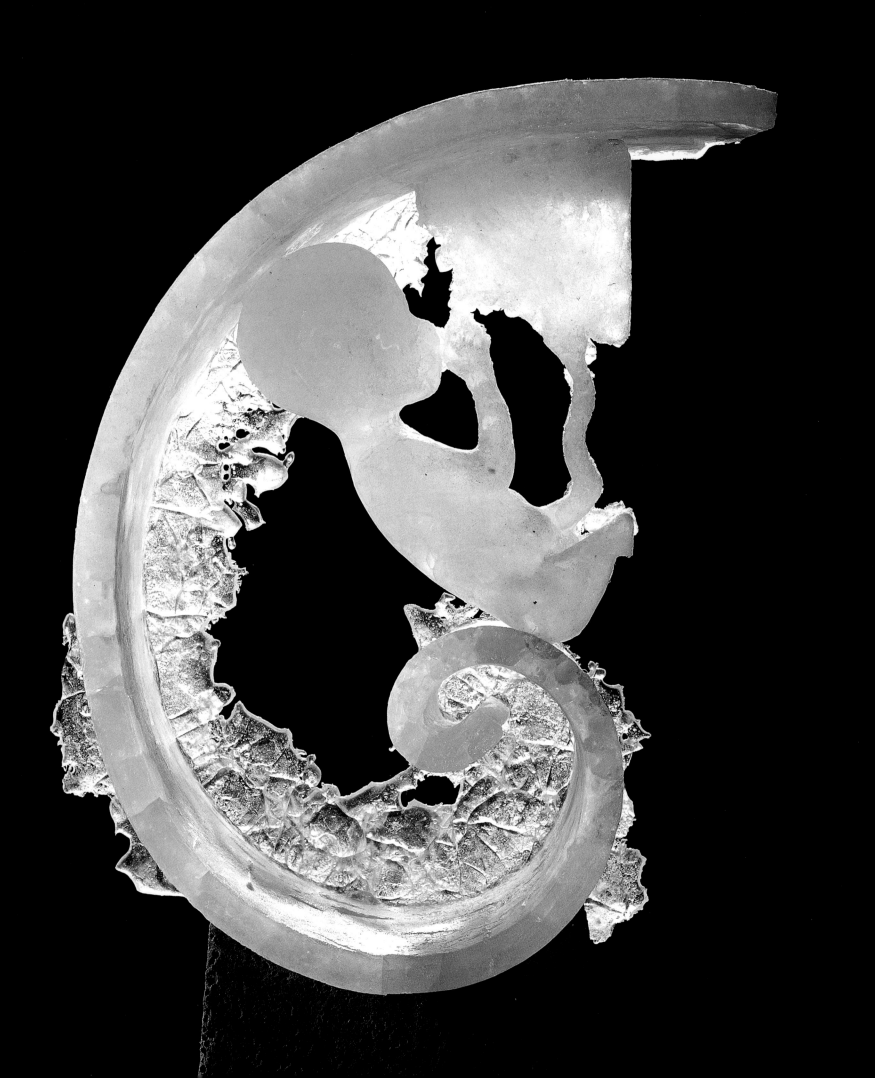

increasingly begun to work in casting techniques, an influence he attributes to recent travels in Europe where he noted this area was becoming prominent in artistic expression in glass.

The intrigue of pâte de verre

In the traditional sense, *pâte de verre* — literally, glass paste — is finely crushed glass of varying colours which is mixed with a liquid binding agent to produce a malleable paste. This is modelled into the desired form, or placed into a mould produced from plaster and wax which produces the final shape. Long firing cycles with a lengthy annealing period, often risky and prone to fracture, are necessary to fuse the ground glass; its a long, exacting and highly-controlled process, yet it often yields unpredictable results in a manner not far removed from the 'gifts of the gods' effects sought for during certain ceramic processes: such as wood-firing or salt-glazing. The resultant *pâte de verre* object may resemble ceramic, alabaster, marble or translucent crystal.

Originating in ancient Egypt some 3,500 years ago, the technique of *pâte de verre* was revived throughout the past centuries on at least two occasions: in the 1760s, James Tassie (1735–1799) a Scottish artist who experimented and perfected the casting and imitation of precious gemstones and cameos from a vitreous paste; the formula which was kept secret was lost with his death, although subsequent analysis showed it to be a lead potash glass.[15] *Pâte de verre* was revived once more and considerably extended in 1884, first by the French artist Henri Cros, and subsequently from about 1900, by a handful of designers, ceramists and sculptors including Argy-Rousseau, Francois Decorchemont, Georges Despret, and especially, by Emile Gallé. A variation of this work which the famed French glass artist Gabriel Argy-Rousseau, especially elevated, is *pâte de crystal*. By the 1920s, alongside the making of one-off studio pieces, limited-edition production by larger workshops had ensued, but the scale was usually relatively modest.

It was not until after an interim between the 1930s and mid-1960s, that *pâte de verre* became revived for the second time this century; its intriguing and exceptionally challenging process, together with its rich cultural associations, are among the reasons it continues to attract practitioners in Australia. Although it may not have the highest profile, *pâte de verre* has attracted considerable attention to become one of the vigorous offshoots which constitute the contemporary stream of glass activity.

Glass practitioners are intent on exploring the singular relationship between material, form and historical technique which *pâte de verre* embodies. Out of the set of characteristics which distinguishes *pâte de verre* from any of the other popular kilnforming techniques in Australian studio glass, its most outstanding feature is its sensuous surface: exceptionally tactile, *pâte de verre* delights both the hand as well as the eye. Soapy-soft to the touch, *pâte de verre* objects may range from a dense, opaque polychrome appearance, through to a paper-thin delicacy of rich, translucent colouring streaked with bubbles, veins and other light-enhancing effects.

Among the dozen or so glass artists around Australia who choose to work in what is a difficult, and often, unpredictable technique, Judy Bohm-Parr most closely follows the revived and labour-intensive French interpretation of *pâte de verre*. Through her deceptively modest *pâte de verre* vessels she pursues the especially sensualist qualities of this genre — its tactile and visual virtues. Eschewing the cold, hard and

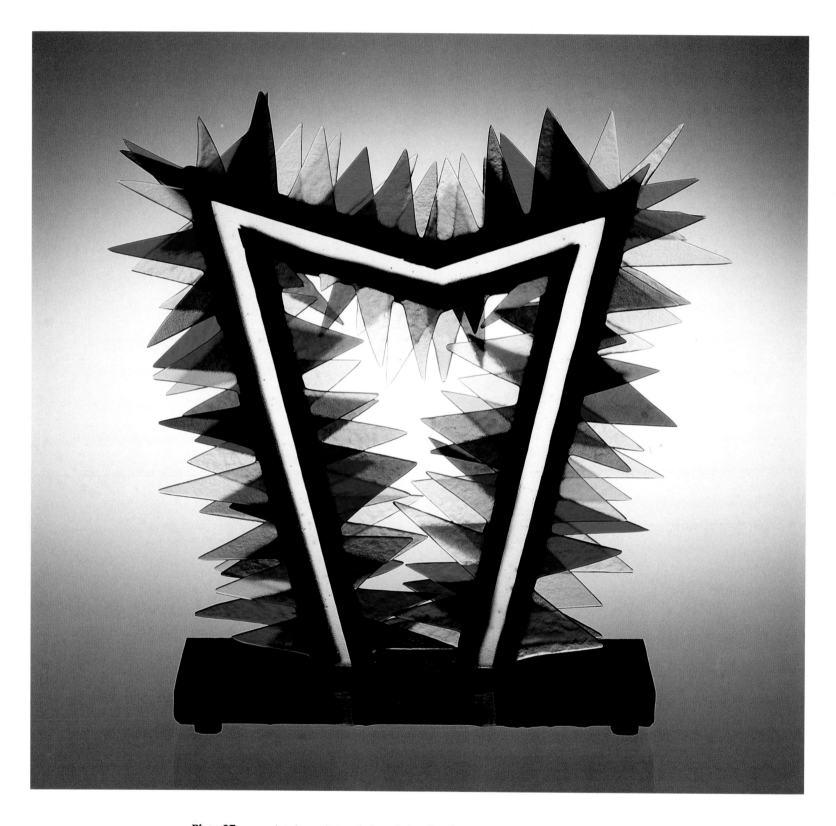

Plate 37
Ian Mowbray (b. 1955)
Panacea for the Addled Mind, 1989
pâte de verre, assembled;
37 x 30 x 1 cm
photo: Grant Hancock

brittle qualities of glass, Bohm-Parr first experimented with casting techniques in trying to achieve an alternative, warmer 'look'; she soon realised that this approach was not going to be the means of achieving her aim. It was in 1988, during the glass master workshop symposium in Canberra, when the *pâte de verre* masters Ann Robinson of New Zealand and Diana Hobson from England revealed its potential to 'humanize' our concepts of glass. 'If you want to do *pâte de verre* for its own sake, you're a maniac! The process is only worthwhile pursuing in the results it yields,' she has stated.[16]

So began Bohm-Parr's interaction with this genre. Emulating the earlier French revival of the technique, she has since concentrated her *pâte de verre* aesthetic explorations about the tradition of the vessel; 'simple vessel forms are best for probing and bringing out various qualities'. Bowls, platters and even sake cups also permit intimate interaction: they allow the user to handle and touch the work, hence experiencing the sensuous, tactile surfaces, as well as taking delight in the sensual play of light and colour so characteristic of *pâte de verre*. The haptic response is always a fundamental consideration — she speaks of a 'feeling appearance', the hand exploring the rim of a bowl, as the eye enjoys the form rising to the surface, its curves and symmetry.

There is an intense sensitivity in Bohm-Parr's approach: she is particularly involved with the decorative aesthetics of her material exploring technique and form as it affects the interplay of colour, texture, and function. The intricate grainy texture of her vessels draws the eye along the seams of colour which integrate form and structure both physically and visually. Proportions and their relationship to the mass of the object are also key qualities this and other practitioners who work in the genre seek to control and perfect.

Bohm-Parr has articulated a philosophy of 'visual communication' which borrows from Oriental, as well as Western, concepts of beauty. Her use of colour is strongly influenced by Oriental beliefs in the power of various colours: 'blue points to the realm of the transcendent; it signifies faith and beckons our spirits, whereas green is contentment and hope …'. The softly glowing depths from which colour and light emerge in her pieces is another of the peculiarities of this genre, and is due to the refraction of light by the facets of myriad particles of glass within the fabric of each work. The translucent colours and ripples of water are a favourite source of inspiration. The French Impressionists have also influenced her use of colouration: 'I have endeavoured to capture those rare "in between moments" in our lives where we are most vulnerable'. Bohm-Parr's perseverance of glass practice within the French tradition of *pâte de verre* has led to her characteristic style, one which embodies a particular philosophical outlook: 'I like to think of my work as something that beautifies and enriches our lives and it worries me to see that some people have forgotten the need for beauty'.

Judy Bohm-Parr has established her present studio in Cairns where, as well as on-going work for exhibitions, she is developing a range of production *pâte de verre* including jewellery. This is aimed at providing high-quality crafted glass souvenirs for the tourist market in Cairns. Lately, having been inspired by the tour-de-force decorative works of the early twentieth century French glass makers, the Daum brothers of Nancy, she has begun to explore the combination of blown glass with *pâte de verre*. In this manner, the potential expression of decorative traditions in studio glass within this specialty are thus becoming further extended.

The lost-wax and *pâte de verre* processes first captured the attention of Allan Crynes (b. 1948), in the early 1980s. Similarly to Ann Robinson's experience, he was forced to investigate and develop the necessary technique from basics. This led, in 1986, to his experience as Klaus Moje's technical assistance in a *pâte de verre* workshop conducted at Pilchuck. Two years later Crynes visited Pilchuck again to attend a sand-casting workshop, this time led by Bertil Vallien. Crynes supports his exhibition work through lines of

slumped and iridised, as well as *pâte de verre* and decorative tablewares. His work reveals an affinity with history typical to this specialty: he recollects a small Egyptian *pâte de verre* pendant seen at the Corning Museum in 1986, which dates from 1450 BC, the earliest known example; cone-formed glass amphoreskos (small flasks which date from 1400–1360 BC). Crynes has managed to increase the scale of his *pâte de verre* to considerable proportions: his Grecian Vase contains 30 kilograms of glass, the pressure of which originally created considerable problems with the moulds which he eventually solved. Pieces such as this, which combine classical form, sea-shell encrustations and dense, semi-transluscent glass effects, evoke a strong mood of antiquity.[17]

Roger Buddle (b. 1940), a recent graduate of the ceramics and glass design course at the School of Design (University of South Australia), has been investigating the richly-expressive field of lost-wax casting and *pâte de verre* since 1992. He has produced some innovative work which combines blown components with the former technique; his series of Mushroom Lights effectively combine blown stems and *pâte de verre* caps which have a luminescent and organic imagery reminiscent of the art nouveau style; Debut, a clear mould-fused glass sculptural work depicting a vulnerable human embryo and fern-leaf curled, membranous, placenta, especially demonstrates how sculptural forms created through this process can evoke an extraordinary degree of delicacy rarely achievable through other means.[18]

Judith Candy (b. 1953) is another practitioner fascinated with *pâte de verre* and other historic kilnforming processes; her studies, also in the School of Design, led her to investigate early techniques, from the Egyptian era through to the turn-of-the-century French glass masters — even to the extent of translating portions of Argy-Rousseau's diaries. A study tour of India and Nepal furthered her knowledge of glass techniques a well as bronze casting. Her main approach utilises the ancient Egyptian technique of casting with mosaics. In this process, millifiore, or decorative fine canes, are pulled in the furnace from pre-fused glass or blocks of coloured glass, then re-arranged, re-fused and stretched in the furnace. These components are further cut into finer pieces depending on the intended finished thickness of the vessel. The mosaics components are then layered and fused into the mould where they become cast into the desired form. Moulds vary from simple open forms to more complex ones for the lost-wax method. Various finishing techniques are then employed to produce waxy, stone-like, velvety or glossy surfaces: its a very lengthy process. Candy is particularly skilled at combining this cast glass, usually in the form of a vessel, with cast-bronze bases of figurative, and sometimes, Egyptian, form. These works effectively evoke an archaic imagery with strong ritual overtures.[19]

The investigation and development of historical cast-glass techniques, similarly underpinned Ian Mowbray's and Vicki Torr's involvement in studio glass. These two practitioners worked as a partnership until the latter's premature death. Mowbray (b. 1955) came from a self-taught background in flat glass which he had begun in 1979; whereas Vicki Torr (1949–1992), had a training in glass and ceramics run by Stephen Skillitzi at the School of Design, later majoring in glass kiln processes for her degree. In 1981, Mowbray and Torr attended a lecture given in Adelaide by Boyce Lundstrom and Dan Schwoerer, directors of the American company Bullseye, the world's largest producer of kiln-compatible glass as used by studio practitioners: this event enticed them into glass. They set about enthusiastically investigating kilnforming, and by 1987 had established their studio MoTo Glass, a studio which represented the fusion of Torr's kiln work and Mowbray's flat glass. Torr concentrated on perfecting a double-cone casting technique, using an internal and external mould to achieve her familiar cone-shaped vessels. In this process the mould is packed with numerous crushed pieces of coloured glass then kiln-fired. Torr's architectonic, double-cone vessels had a strength of colour and integration with form rarely seen.[20]

Mowbray, on the other hand, concentrated on developing his personal idiom through the *pâte de verre* process. It has been the work he developed from 1989 which has especially been foremost: this consisted of miniature *pâte de verre* representations of human figures and domestic objects which were assembled within glass domes filled with water and glass 'snow'. Based on the souvenir, and often vugarised, place domes, Mowbray's encapsulated tableaus were familiar, homely scenes — living rooms, bathrooms and kitchens complete with tables set for a meal. From 1990, he began to present his figures in open tableaus or sand-pits. These consisted of rectangular, shallow, glass trays filled with sand in which colourful *pâte de verre* figures could be artfully arranged by their owners: beach and aquarium scenes were typical. For his most recent work, developed from 1994, Mowbray created small coloured cast images of everyday objects — cars, boots, strawberries or faces — and then re-cast these into clear blocks of cut and polished glass; the three-dimensional forms appear 'frozen' within bubbly swirls, an effect Mowbray especially strives to achieve.

Further innovative approaches to kilnformed glass have been originated, or developed from existing techniques, on a number of occasions by a handful of practitioners in Australia — as noted in the preceding instances. Among these, intriguing cross-overs between ceramics and glass often occur, as has been the case with Paul Sanders' work. His Archaisian series especially, emerged during his post-graduate studies when he developed a process for creating aged patina effects on glass. His teacher at Charles Sturt University in New South Wales, Denis O'Connor, encouraged the exploration of ideas, and Sanders, who had studied ceramics as part of his earlier education, hit on the idea of simulating the unique raku process in glass. His technique of packing sand-blasted glass vessels in vermiculite layered with reducing and metallic salts, and then firing this combination, led to the post-fired patination outcome now recognised as his signature work.[21]

The progression of Sanders' work first saw a shift from his exploration of the blown vessel, in combination with stone bases, to an architectural combination of glass tubes with metal and concrete. The late 1980s pre-occupation with the art-versus-craft debate then led him to the decision to move away from the vessel with its historical craft and material connotations, to sculptural treatments of glass. The avoidance of functional forms suggested to him the use of fragments of glass which similarly seemed devoid of historical connotations. Pieces of window glass are put through the same post-fired patination process, then balanced on concrete bases which have been treated to appear as a dark stone. These shards, with their aged colouring and sharp-edged wedge shapes, articulate sculptural concerns without any allusions as fragments of a known form. As a further phases in Sanders' Archaisian series, these fragments are intriguing in that they signal the unique qualities of the medium concurrently with their representation of glass as sculpture.

John Elsegood is yet another glass practitioner who made the decision to shift from glass blowing to

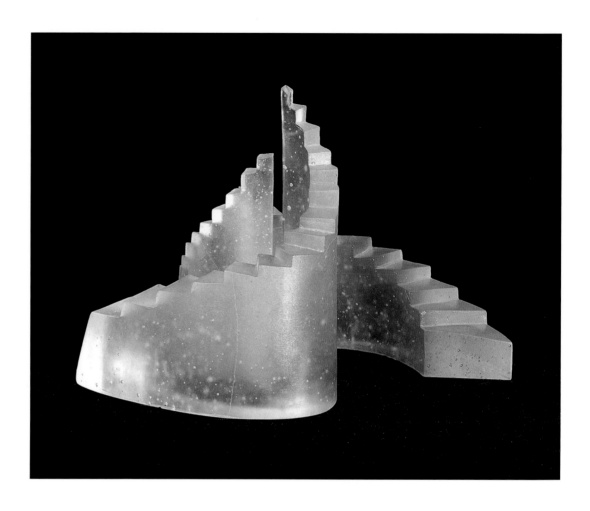

kilnforming. His present studio on the north coast of New South Wales at Coff's Harbour was established in 1983; essentially a one-man glass-blowing workshop, he finally decided by the late 1980s that 'glass-blowing was producing much work around the country which looked alike'. By 1987, he had shifted into the exploration of kilnforming processes, especially glass casting to create thick-walled, crystalline-like vessels; these are often placed on similar cast-glass stands, hence simulating an Oriental aesthetic in glass. More recently, Elsegood has begun to explore combinations of glass with copper and other metals.[22]

Design, painterly and other approaches

Highly conceptual, symbolic, design and fine art approaches to kilnforming have also characterised this area in Australia, as the following group of practitioners indicates.

Gerry King has had an especially long involvement with glass; besides his influence on the glass scene through his role as an educator and through Ausglass, he has made an additional contribution through his is personal glass work. King brings a highly-controlled methodology to his making of miniature glass sculptures which are infused with his interpretation of broad cultural and political issues.[23]

He became involved with glass working in the United States at the New York College of Ceramics (Alfred University) from 1973 to 1974. He subsequently undertook glass studies in Canada, Australia, New

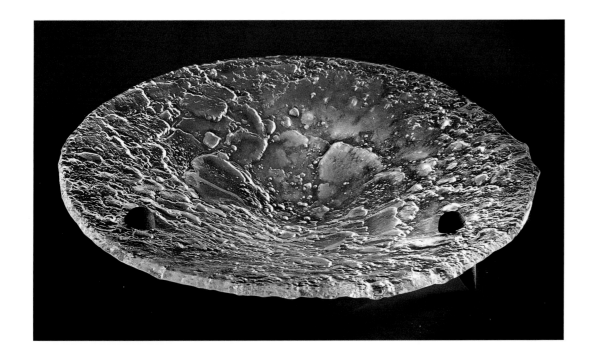

Plate 39
Bridget Hancock (b. 1959)
Vessel, 1994
sand-textured, slumped glass with
cast-iron feet;
Diam. 68 cm
photo: John Norton

Zealand and at the Pilchuck Glass Centre; he has also extensively lectured and presented workshops in these countries. He is currently Head of the School of Design at the University of South Australia. Originally trained in glass blowing, he has studied and now teaches aspects of kilnforming, cold working, and furnace and kiln casting.

King's present work shows only tenuous links to his early 1980's free-blown forms which punctured and rejoined glass to create the Yukat series — works evocative of garments and of the human torso. Succeeding series developed a more complex origin, presenting hints of his myriad intentions, rather than providing explicit statements with single interpretations; a background of ceramics and especially fine art and design, is evident in ongoing series. Although he began kilnforming from the late 1970s, it was not until a decade later that King whole-heartedly shifted into this genre to express selected socio-political concerns: in the View With A Room series, the work, Room For A Nuclear Family, used the dual meanings of the term 'nuclear' to combine speculations of the social debilitating of the nuclear family, with manifest evidence of the nuclear devastation of architectural form: ruination overlays the structure and order of both family and architecture, intensified by the combination of eroded imagery and fused glass.

The Cicatrix series are the most recent group of works beginning this decade: as with earlier works a socio-political focus permeates the references and allusions of the imagery. These works address the topic of cultural colonization in Australia as a layering of image and symbol — once more imposed upon an eroding structure — and variously depicted as geographic, architectural or artefacts. And whereas there are clear references to Australian Aboriginal images, this series is not about the Aboriginal people or their art. Instead, the intention is to communicate the idea of colonization as an act of the dominant rather than that of the dominated party — hence these works are more closely associated with the cultural practice of transplanted Europeans. The series may be subdivided into several groups. The Cicatrix Shields are elongated bowl forms suggestive of the Wirra (an Australian Aboriginal wooden elliptical bowl). The opaque patterned glass forms stand upon isolating frosted translucent plinths imitating the manner in which museum displays alter the context of the exhibit. The Cicatrix Shadows employ the shadow cast from a solitary remaining wall of an eroded building to depict the layering of one cultural practice upon another. The decaying and abandoned farm houses found in the arid and desert regions of Australia inspired the use of architectural fragments in this series.

Other recent works are lifesize glass renditions of furniture and fragments of buildings seemingly real yet translucent and contradictory in their apparent fragility. The work, Please Don't Sit, beckons the viewer to ignore the request of the title: the form is that of a chair, yet it signals caution as the texture is that of corrugated iron. Hence King uses the chair in its symbolic portrayal of demarcation between societies and status groups.

These examples amply demonstrate how narrative and other expressive aspects are conveyed through a precise formal imagery and symbolism. This combines kiln and flame-formed, laminated and mosaic techniques with cold-worked, etched and frosted, glass processes: erosion, decay and the detailed over-layering of cultural references are thus directly evoked or intensified through the manner Gerry King treats glass.

Contrast this tightly-controlled vocabulary with that of Judi Elliott (b. 1943), who sees herself as a colourist, drawn to glass because of its brilliance, colour and opacity. In the late 1980s, the bold, precise lines and shapes of her early work gave way to massed colour and a design freedom which led to a more expressive style. Architectural images, inspired by an appreciation of old buildings and the memories of their former occupants, now dominate her work. At first, the corrugations and colour patterns of her kiln-slumped containers were sufficient to evoke the vernacular elements of rural Australian architecture.[24]

More recently, these images have become overlaid with the further complexity of Jungian symbolism as it relates to the nature of the domicile. The metaphorical 'shadow' of Carl Jung's writings — the side of ourselves kept hidden from others — prompted her to explore this facet of human personality through the inclusion of shadows in her House series: hence the backs of houses on the reverse side of some tablets permit the exposure of both sides, or else the shadowed side may be kept 'private'. Another approach has been to incorporate small mirrored windows into the panels which act reflect the viewer, to permit them to share the 'house'.

Overcoming the physical limitations of kiln size, Elliott's tablets later shifted into a new phase with changes to scale, shape, texture and intent. This is evident in the Orchard Street Collection, now installed in a restored Georgian building in Bristol, England. These works were commissioned by a psychologist who had been investigating theories relating to colour preference and various personality types; the collection therefore explores specific themes, as revealed by their titles including Inspiration; Right Brain, Left Brain; and Id, Ego and Superego. Elliott's use of the house as a metaphor of human life has currently developed into the Black Box series; as these works take their name from the electronic flight recorder in aeroplanes, they represent life voyages. The geometric perfection of her earlier series has also lately been heat distorted in her attempt to achieve 'a more painterly human quality'.

Judi Elliott also makes large-scaled commissioned architectural installations for restaurants and offices;

and surface patterns. Portnoy's clay background is also evident in her expression at the delight of 'surprises the fire of the kiln brings'.[30]

Denis O'Connor's pioneering work as an educator has already been recounted (Chapter 1); since 1987, his lecturing in drawing, sculpture and glass studies, in the School of Visual and Performing Arts (Charles Sturt University, Wagga Wagga), has regenerated his focus on the human figure in his glass work. Not surprisingly, this has become closely associated with his drawings and prints of the human figure. In 1993, he departed from the earlier influence of the glass blowing process which resulted in his characteristic eroded spherical forms, into kilnforming to represent the human face. O'Connor is yet another practitioner who models extensively with clay to derive his cast-glass works; these have an ethereal appearance, with faces seemingly emerging from a translucent diaphanous fabric.[31]

Although Deborah Cocks (b. 1958), works mostly in enamelling, she also produces a small output of appreciable cast glass figurative works (see Chapter 6). These are generally presented as sculptural tableaus, the idea usually being developed from a found object — a rusted tin, an old wooden plane — which is then used as a container or setting for Cocks' peculiar glass characters as they 'journey through a bemused sort of life'. The glass components of these works are made from crystal glass, with 'a ridiculous amount of hand polishing and a final acid polish'. Sometimes engraved and oil painted, Cocks imbues her figures with a provocative psychological intensity which effectively draws the viewer into her inner vision.[32]

Aside from the teaching of glass blowing by the American Ron Street in Perth in 1973 and 1974, and Stephen Skillitzi's blowing workshop at the Fremantle Art Centre in 1974, Western Australia has been slow to accept hot glass as a medium of artistic expression over the intervening years. It was not until 1992 that courses in glass had again become available in Perth. Edward Arrowsmith (b. 1952), a ceramist and educator, was among the earliest to shift from ceramics into glass from about this time. His kilnformed pieces are still evolving, and generally consist of bowls or platters decorated with repetitive stippled patterning in gold and enamels, and often supported on glass feet which simulate a molten state. Kerry Williams is another Western Australian practitioner whose work in cast glass is discussed in Chapter 6.

Not surprisingly, since Klaus Moje's retirement, recent graduates of the glass course at the Canberra School of Art have continued to demonstrate a strong affinity with kilnforming: Robyn Campbell's interest is the investigation of 'structure of mind', particularly memory and its interaction with time, especially using spiral steps and architectural forms among her minimalist symbols: 'casting gives a delicacy of surface, a satin feel which expresses my idea clearly'; Mies Grybaitis is focussing on the social aspects and effects of shock and drug treatment on extreme psychiatric patients with an evocative and powerful figurative imagery; Itzell Tazzyman is exploring personal and social narrative and the geography of land and mind, setting out her work as a tableau reminiscent of stage or theatre design. Others have attended the course from overseas and have returned to take the influences of this workshop and its stress on kilnforming back to their home country: Francoise Bolli, from Switzerland, is casting a series of glass cubes to be later assembled into an architectonic structure; and New Zealander Marea Timoko is developing *pâte de verre* approaches to make delicate vessels or ship hulls infused with a personal symbolism.[33]

Plate 41 (opposite)
Marc Kalifa (b. 1951)
Guardian
Dreamers Series, 1993
kiln cast glass, patinated bronze,
textured wood base;
40 x 35 cm

Summary

All of the earliest masters in the area of kilnforming particularly, Stephen Skillitzi, Warren Langley, Klaus Moje, Gerry King, Maureen Cahill, Peter Tysoe, Allan Crynes, Richard Morrell and Ann Robinson, have remained ensconced within this specialty for a decade or more, their adroitness in kilnforming having become especially developed and evident. Because half of them were, and some still are, educators in tertiary institutions, they have passed on their attitudes and skills to successive waves of glass practitioners, many who have similarly chosen to work predominantly in kilnforming. Distinguished among these are the first and subsequent sets of graduates notably from the Glass Workshop in Canberra, the Sydney College of the Arts, the School of Design in the University of South Australia, and the Chisholm Campus of Monash University. They include Meza Rijsdijk, Helen Aitken Kuhnen, Richard Whiteley, Velta Vilmanis, Kirstie Rea, Judi Elliott and Judith Bohm-Parr, Kathy Elliott, Cindy Hill, Paul Sanders, Jan Blum, Sergio Redegalli and Bridget Hancock. Others who have entered the area are essentially self-taught, and include Allan Crynes, Mark Kalifa, Warren Langley, and Ian Mowbray.

In the past year or two, of the latest generation of glass practitioners who have just begun careers, a notable proportion are gravitating towards kilnformed glass. As noted earlier, graduates from Canberra are especially drawn to the area and include Luna Ryan, Itzell Tazzyman, Robyn Campbell and Mies Grybaitis; yet others have come from various glass courses about the country and include Roger Buddle, Janette Trenchard-Smith, and Judith Candy. Then there are those practitioners who, although specialising in another area, nevertheless utilise kilnforming as a significant part of their forte: among these are David Wright, Graham Stone, Cedar Prest, Klaus Zimmer, Marc Grunseit, Kazuko Eguchi and Alison McMillan: these and other practitioners have been dealt with in Chapter 6 as the essential flavour of their work emerges from a combination of disparate processes, especially blowing and cold-working with kilnforming, to comprise a set of alternative practices.

In reviewing this chapter, we have noted how adherents are drawn to kilnforming because of its flexibility and potential expressive range. From the early 1980s, kilnforming approaches tended to concentrate on fusing and slumping, but by the end of the decade the numerous practitioners working in the area had extended its parameters and were exploring a wider spectrum, especially casting, mosaic, and *pâte de verre*. Practitioners follow an approach of honing a particular facet of kilnforming to exploit its metaphorical qualities and explore his or her personal concerns — be they sculptural, aesthetic, figurative, painterly or commentarial. The diversity of representational imagery which has accumulated over the past few years is a testimony to the considerable energy expended in the exploration of this genre of studio glass. And despite a peculiar stance which surfaces from time to time which seeks to deny the outright appreciation of glass, its so-called seductive qualities on the basis of privileging 'artistic' or 'conceptual' content', the evidence is clear that most, if not all, practitioners working in this genre, manipulate these qualities as a matter of course: in part to investigate sculptural, decorative or conceptual aspects, or because of their willing surrender to the seductiveness of the medium.

Given the rush into kilnforming, this area of glass practice may appear to be reaching its zenith, and it may be that, like other areas which become widespread or fashionable for a time, this present run of interest may possibly diminish until its next cycle. Predictions, however, can only be accurate to a point, and in examining another area of distinctive activity — glass blowing — in the following chapter, it will become apparent that there will always be devotees who remain steadfast to their chosen specialty, and ultimately pass their enthusiasm on to others. Through its extended textural abilities, its rich dense translucency, opalescence, and jewel-like virtues, kilnforming will surely continue to perpetuate the language of aesthetics, the historical and cultural associations of glass, and its sculptural potential. Most certainly, it will continue to celebrate the unrivalled qualities of glass for many years to come.

Blown Glass: Fluid Directions

'... my pieces breathe in and out several times before they come to rest'.[1]

Glass blowing, as first revived by the 1960s American Hot Glass Movement, has had the longest development of all the forms of studio glass activity in Australia: twenty-four years have passed since the concept and techniques of glass blowing in the studio mode were introduced to this country by Stephen Skillitzi, to be reinforced by the wave of American glass blowers who followed in 1974 (see Chapter 1). The fascination for glass blowing peaked by the mid-1980s, to shift from its position as being the prime enterprise of the movement in Australia, to become simply one of a group of specialty activities within current studio glass practice. The salient point which emerges from this is that glass blowing underpinned the movement; lately, a groundswell of practitioners has begun to reinvigorate the area.

Towards the later 1980s, glass blowing had given up the spotlight to other areas, especially kilnforming, which seemingly displays a sense of vitality and allure that the former once commanded. Certainly, the crystalline, spectral and sculptural qualities of kilnformed work set it apart from the mercurial and organic nature of blown glass forms. It is true that many of the practitioners who began their careers in glass blowing in the first decade, have since shifted into kilnforming and other areas of activity; some have simply dabbled in the latter while others have taken to working in both areas, combining aspects of the two fundamentally-differing approaches to studio glass. Especially intriguing is the fact that a trickle of those who specialise in kilnforming, have more recently made forays into glass blowing, similarly combining a variety of techniques. As will be revealed in the following, glass blowing in its relatively pure form continues to contribute a vitality to the studio glass movement.

In contrast to the almost plodding pace with which kilnforming generally assumes, glass blowing is a volatile practice: when blowing glass long pauses are generally not possible and instead, the practitioner must be intuitive in a moment by moment process of appraisal of how form is emerging. The embryonic bubble form which always first results from glass blowing, also places some restriction on the possible range of expressive shapes that may eventuate, and hence, the ideas that may be expressed; unless of course, this cardinal technique is combined with others. The furnace, its life-span and prohibitive fuel costs, has similarly been an obstacle in attracting devotees, whereas kilnforming, as discussed in the preceding chapter, is more accessible to the independent practitioner. Even so, some find this approach with its crafting of moulds, steaming and other stages, tedious; these are practitioners who have an affinity for

Plate 42 (opposite)
Don Wreford (b. 1942)
Phase Transitions, 1987
blown, sandblasted
and carved glass,
with pre-blown glass
components;
33 x Diam. 22 cm
photo: G. Sommerfeld

handling the material in its molten state, who enjoy a collaborative approach to glass making, and who revel in blowing life into its glowing essence.

Innovative combinations

That glass blowing has not lost its potency on the world glass scene, was demonstrated by Brian Hirst's win of the 1994 Hokkaido Museum of Modern Art Prize. As the current trailblazer, Hirst (b. 1956), describes himself as a glass blower, hence stressing the principal process to the creation of his works.

It was the 1983 Ausglass conference, where Hirst met the glass blower Richard Meitner, and which he considers was the point from which his work began to coalesce into the current directions of his Cycladic, and later, Object and Image series. As the titles suggest, his works emerge from his affinity and explorations of ancient Cycladic art (c.2500 BC). Initially, Hirst created Cycladic figures (based on an original he viewed in the Art Gallery of New South Wales), which were laminated and etched then assembled with neon outlines; other medium and technique investigations led to etchings of these figures on glass plates, together with sketches of votive three-legged bowls and mould-blown bowls heavily dimpled, etched and engraved. Later, the dimpled bowl gave way for a period to a smooth-surfaced compressed form. Over this period of a decade, these various approaches began to be presented as a dialogue through his combinations of a glass panel, with etched imagery of free-standing vessels, with the mould-blown vessel.[2]

His peculiar innovative combination of blowing with kiln and cold-working techniques, result in additional rich, gold lustre and surface-cut patterns; this approach produces a surface texture which intensifies the decorative patterning and overall symbolism of the presented imagery. Acid-etching and sandblasting especially produce eroded, seemingly time-worn, vessel forms which allude to an ancient cultural heritage. Beyond the sensual ambience generated through such manipulation of form and texture, is the more overt symbolic communication: Hirst achieves this through his overlay of patterned motifs; the two approaches set up a dialogue, in tandem with that inspired by the juxtapositions of the three-dimensional vessel and its imagery on an accompanying two-dimensional panel.

Hirst's work exemplifies the manner in which glass blowing may be extended into greater potential expressiveness from its seemingly straightforward procedures. His present work, developed over the past decade from a distillation of notions from archaeological, cultural and fine art sources, relies on the interplay of medium, vessel and motif, together with the presentation of three-dimensional object and two-dimensional imagery. The totality of these achievement derive from his mastery of glass blowing and other techniques. Hirst has stated that 'to make a contemporary statement you have to know your field, otherwise you end up re-hashing … what I'm trying to do is absorb the history of my material and make a contribution to its future'. Hirst's work exemplifies too, how intensely-focussed conceptual possesses can become in association with actual handskills, and how the work may emerge as a personal narrative over a lengthy period of time.

Nick Mount is one of Australia's pioneer glass blowers, having begun as early as the watershed year of 1974 (see Chapter 1). Currently head of the glass workshop in the Jam Factory, his earlier teachers

included the master glass-blowers Dick Marquis and Paul Marioni; he has also had contact with the latter's son, Dante. Mount's blowing skills have mostly focussed on developing his line of lyrical vessels: goblets, vases, bowls and other forms, whose unifying characteristic is the consummate combination of refined profile and colour. His major exhibition series have include walking canes, funnels and fishing floats — all represented in the Wagga City Art Gallery National Art Glass Collection. These exhibition works relate directly to Mount's romantic notion of the historic link between glass makers and their

Plate 43
Pauline Delaney (b. 1959)
L'Amour Flame, 1993
free blown glass;
Diam. 31.5 x 18 cm

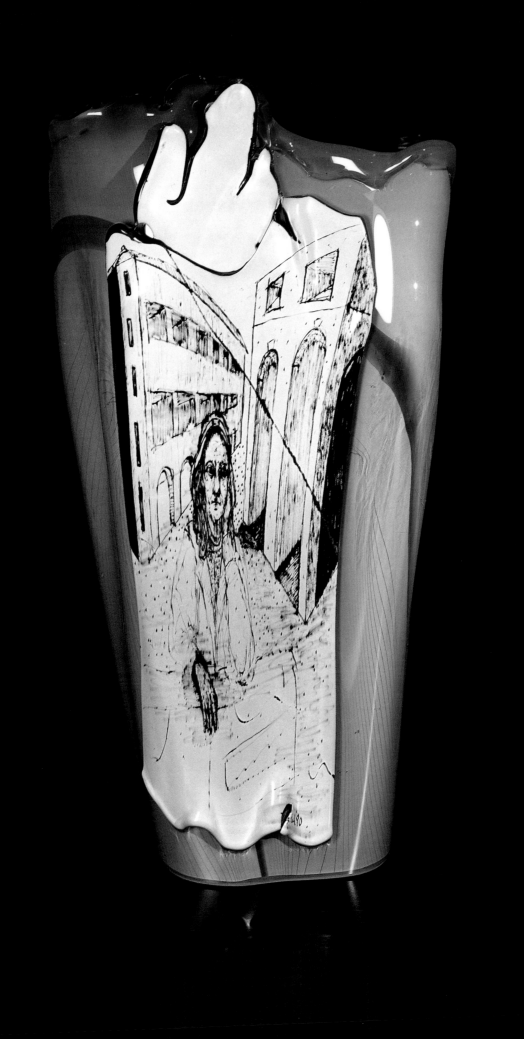

medium, a notion which emerged from a visit to Murano, Venice, in 1975. To Mount, Murano is an extra-ordinary sociological phenomenon which has 'created itself with its furnaces as the hub of activity … the pride that the makers had in their ability to produce still affects the way I feel about glass'. Mount's funnels, floats and walking sticks are a means of expressing his links to this history: 'walking canes had a mystical connection for these people, they kept evil spirits at bay … and they were made as 'friggers' (per-sonal folk works) during the glass maker's spare moments'. Similarly, the floats and funnels have their aesthetic or symbolic uses, in addition to their ostensible utilitarian functions.[3]

Plate 44 (opposite)
Garry Nash (b. 1955)
Standing Alone, 1990
free blown glass, engraved;
26 x 24 x Diam. 65 cm

Since 1991, following a break with glass manufacture in an industrialised mode, Mount has used his blowing skills to branch into a sculptural exploration of the human figure. He began with a year away from the furnace, practising life drawing before returning to express his visualised female torsos in glass. These are created by first making copper wire frames which manifest the line drawings into three-dimensions. Mount then blows glass into these wire outlines, filling them with 'one-shot blowing to develop the form … you can't labour over it'. Although the combination of metal and glass has been frequently explored, Mount's particular use of these two materials in the form of the human figure is novel in Australia.

The action is almost gestural, reminiscent of the pencil rapidly tracing across the paper — but this is glass. The earth-goddess icons of early humankind are invoked by Mount's glass torsos: by exaggerating various parts of the form, the copper matrix seemingly restrains the bulges while emphasising the con-juncture of breasts, buttocks and stomach: the resulting curvaceous, thrusting torsos have a palpable, sen-sual appeal. The forms vary and some have an elongated presentation which suggest classical references; all have an enticingly-frosted surface created through sand-blasting.

Mount points out how glass blowing 'stands apart from the traditional craft practices in that it relates to industry so intimately: after all, its primary focus is the making of functional items, such as vessels'. This association does not prevent the glass master from extending the basic process into expres-sive figurative form as Mount has achieved in this instance. These torsos were so potent that some found them 'offensive, sexist and chauvinistic', and even to the extent of projecting personal feelings, including notions of bondage, into the images. The description of these works by critic Jenny Zimmer as 'conceptu-ally dated … [they] belong to that unfortunate 1980s moulded "body-fragment" tradition', ignored the creative spontaneity with which they had been conceived through the act of blowing, as well as the erotic qualities glass as a medium may manipulated impart to the representation of the human form.[4]

The team approach and the Venetian model

The rise of popularity of the team approach to glass blowing in the United States over the late 1980s, has had its influences in Australia more recently over the past four years. Bronwyn Hughes has described this development and its benefits as a 'shift back to the more traditional organisation of glass blowing by some artists … to the employment of teams to achieve imaginative concepts and colossal forms. Although as disciplined and precise in its organised chaos as the old factory style of operation, the new team of the 1990s brings individual minds and skills into collaboration, with spectacular results'.[5]

The New Zealand glass practitioner Garry Nash (b. 1955) relies on the assistance of four to five experienced glass blowers when making these and other major works; he considers blowing has severe limitations, but sees the team approach as a method which permits a broadening of the potential range of expression in glass. Fusing images onto blown forms is another technique which also serves to extend this genre, to break away from the purely-blown form. Nash enjoys the link he has with the 'old school of glass blowers which is almost gone … their knowledge is kept alive by those in the studio system. You can't teach glass blowing with a book, its got to be through direct experience … I teach it as a method, a way of thinking about glass blowing'.[6]

Nash counts as particular influences the United States glass artists Dick Marquis and Bill Morris, as well as the Venetian master glass blower Lino Tagliapietra, although the latter's influence is mostly evident in his vessel-making. He also utilises a wide range of hot and cold processes to create large sculptures which combine free-blown glass with fused and engraved work. He has become especially proficient in a technique known as 'opalino-shard', whereby a fragment of glass is flashed with a covering of a contrasting colour, etched with an image, then attached to a larger glass piece which is blown out to expand the original image. Because the etched image was originally compressed, the blowing process expands it into a full picture. It is this particular combination of techniques and their visual expression which has given Nash's work a high international profile.

In reviewing the technical aspects of glass history, Nash comments that there has been 'little innovation in glass blowing other than in furnace technology and chemistry'. In his view, 'every glass blower should be able to blow a Roman goblet and be able to replicate other historical pieces … it is through going back to some of these ancient processes and experimenting with them that new techniques may develop'.[7]

Colin Heaney (b. 1948) arrived in Australia from California in 1966. A self-taught glass practitioner, he set up his own studio in 1982 to expand to the point whereby he now employs a team of 10 people working in the production of various forms, mostly for an expanding tourist trade. Through considerable research and experimentation he has developed and extended the iridising process to the point that its colour range and intensity typifies his work which mostly consists of goblets, platters and sculptural forms.[8]

Chris Pantano (b. 1948) has expanded his studio operations so that two blowers assist him in the making of his considerable range of successful glass works. These utilise a singular combination of glass techniques to create representations of Australian imagery. Pantano was first introduced to blown glass in 1980 by Peter Goss, Queensland's only glass blower at the time; some six years later he began the operations of his present studio in Queensland.[9]

Much of Pantano's inspiration comes from the Australian environment with its desert, rainforest and reef habitats, as well as from the nature of glass itself. His Outback series used warm colours to evoke the Australian desert and sunset sky: combining blown glass with kilnforming, he uses cane glass to 'draw images of trees, grass trees and aboriginal figures'. His Dreamtime themes evolved out of these series; for these, he utilises a combination of techniques to create a richly-textured, stone-like surface with images inspired by the cave and desert art of the Australian Aborigine. 'Drawn' symbols and images are applied

Plate 45 (opposite)
Chris Pantano (b. 1948)
Rainforest, 1994
blown glass with cased internal colouring;
36 cm
photo: Errol Larkan

Plate 46 (opposite)
Ben Edols (b. 1967) and
Kathy Elliott (b. 1964)
Blown Vessels, 1994
blown, ground and wheel-cut glass;
largest: 32 x 8 cm
photo: D. James Dee

using a fine cane and hand-held torch; symbols represent kangaroo tracks, water holes and meeting places. The Rainforest series are bold vessel forms with internal colouring, produced with techniques developed over a number of years, and applied in layers to create an effective three-dimensional impression of the entanglement of palms, liana vines and other flora. The Reef series is approached in the same way to create a fracas of blues, turquoise and aquamarines, grading into bright coral colours, and with pre-made sea forms attached to the lower half of the vessel. Other works include his sculptural Wandjinas, totem-like figures inspired by the Aboriginal cave art of the Kimberly region. Pantano creates these with a variety of techniques including sand-blasting and hot-drawn cane-work imagery. Sections of pieces have internally created imagery; they effectively capture the power of the Aboriginal mythological beings within the medium of glass.

In addition to the team approach, the stylistic influence of Italian glass making, specifically of Venice (or Murano) has left its mark on a number of Australian glass blowers. Its 'mastery of glass' philosophy has been spread by a number of Italian master glass blowers in the United States, through Dick Marquis and Dale Chihuly's visits to the Italy and their subsequent work, as well as the former's visits to Australia — the most recent being in 1994 when he came with his colleague Dante Marioni. Both of these practitioners readily acknowledge the strong impact of the Venetian glass virtuoso Ligno Tagliapetra on the American glass-blowing arena who started visiting in 1979 and then every year over the 1980s and 1990s. It seems that Italian glass maestros can still teach the Americans, and Australians, technique. Marioni executes work with the assistance of a team of two to four or more glass artists, a necessity for his larger-scaled pieces. This recent enthusiasm for large-scale work, one result of the revival of the team approach, was beginning to come to its human limits by the mid-1990s.[10] In addition to the influence of visiting American practitioners, Australian glass blowers have themselves travelled overseas to Pilchuck and other American institutions where Venetian methodology has been revived in terms of team workshop approaches, style and technique.

Among those Australians whose work emerges from or reveals aspects of the Italian tradition, we may name Nick Mount, Keith Rowe, Nick Wirdnam, Jane Cowie, Benjamin Edols, and Clare Belfrage. These glass blowers have each developed their own approaches and styles through the acquisition of a repertoire of techniques and processes.

Nick Wirdnam (b. 1956), has had a long experience in glass, including eight years blowing glass on the Isle of Wight (United Kingdom), and a workshop in Pilchuck, where he had access to glass practitioners only previously familiar through magazines and exhibitions: 'in reality the work was unbelievable, the technical ability — the achievement of scale and the finish was incredible'. The opportunity to observe and work with some of these artists and to be involved in their creative process, including Marioni, was 'an exhilarating one'. His present series entitled Excalibur Cups, consists of combined and segmented blown-vessel forms which demonstrate a sculptural intent, as well as demonstrating an affinity with Venetian glass; in effect, Wirdnam has translated the mythological sword and stone imagery into glass.[11]

Keith Rowe's (b. 1952), pure forms and swirling colours, have their roots in the traditions of the Italian masters. His aspiration, 'whether making the simplest of goblets or the most novel of art works, is

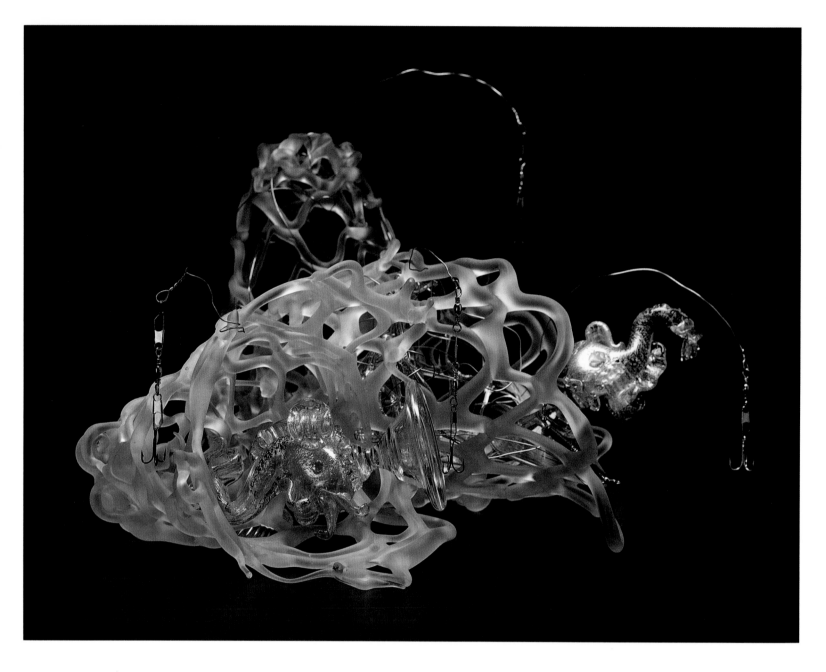

Plate 47
Jane Cowie (b. 1962)
Dolphins and Driftnets, 1992
hot-formed and sculptured glass,
and gold and silver leaf;
30 x 40 x 46 cm

to create objects that transcend the conventional … this is the beginning and ending of my search for each new design'. Although Rowe's forte, until recently, was in blowing, he has returned to exploring kiln-formed processes to extend his work. He has lately explored combinations of his blown and sandblasted vessels with landscape bases of highly-textured kiln-cast glass; this coexistence of processes is achieving exuberant images and generates dialogues between decoration and surfaces.[12]

Benjamin Edols (b. 1967) is producing some particularly exciting work in his relentless investigations of the Venetian model. Following the completion of his glass studies at the Glass Workshop of the Canberra School of Art, Edols had extensive experience in Pilchuck Glass School and other allied United States institutions between 1990 and 1993. He has considerable experience working as an assistant with Dante Marioni, Robert Levin, Dick Marquis and Lino Tagliapietra in particular and whose 'strength and fluidness … was inspiring'; indeed, Edols assisted Marioni and Marquis on their 1994 visit. Elizabeth

McClure has described Edols as possessing 'physical intelligence and a natural aptitude for hand skills'.[13]

Edols is also highly skilled in achieving striking balances of form and colour through a geometric design approach to vessel form. One series of works which involved such a formal design approach, consisted of unstoppered bottles combining spherical bodies and large cone-shaped mouths, the former made by the Italian style of fine cane work; the contrasting luminous colours and glossy versus satin surfaces form a striking functional imagery. Other sources of inspiration include the forms of the ceramic artist Hans Coper, his spheres, cylinders and combinations have been an inspiration, and is yet another example of the close links between the contemporary practices of ceramics and glass. Edols has also embraced the post-modernist philosophy of Memphis, especially its approaches to colour and function, its rejection of modernist theory and its own renouncement of ornament. The latter has especially resulted in explorations which have led to an alluring series of glass vessels. Made in collaboration with colleague Kathy Elliott (b. 1964), these consist of minimalist bottle forms imbued with delicate colour hues and energetic wheel-cut surfaces.

Elizabeth Kelly (b. 1960), has similarly had a strong grounding in vessel and colour combinations, the result of her training at the Glass Workshop at the Jam Factory, the North Adelaide School of Art (South Australia), and the glass course at the Canberra School of Art. Her blown glass vessels are allied to Edol's work insofar as they focus on the design elements of colour and form. The latter is often derived from classical proportions which are integrated with transparent, almost watery, secondary and tertiary colours. Although functional pieces, they are not created as production runs, but in limited editions.[14]

Mikaela Brown (b. 1966) is yet another glass blower who has been influenced by the Venetian tradition. This first occurred through her contact with Lino Tagliapietra, Richard Marquis and Dante Marioni in the Italian Glass Workshop in Auckland, New Zealand in 1990. Rather than their more formal language, however, Brown uses a more casual approach with humour as a vital element in her work, in order to 'entertain and evoke memories of enjoyment'. Popular culture and its constant onslaught of images through the media is a strong influence on Brown. Her unlikely figurative goblets provide a sense of release from the seriousness of every day life, concurrently striving to provide social commentary or satire; the use of text on the glass work reinforces narrative content and often adds a gibe or reinforces the visual joke.

Another of this younger generation of glass blowers emerging in Australia is David McLeod (b. 1966). A Canberra School of Art graduate and recent Jam Factory trainee, he uses blown vessel forms in a conceptual and sculptural manner to examine 'the inexorable progression of contemporary technology and its clash with classical philosophy'. He conveys this imagery by blowing classically-derived vessel forms of clear strong colours which he mounts onto spindly wire-metal frames set on small wheels, hence evoking a image of western civilisation precariously balanced on the 'wheels of progress'.[15]

Jane Cowie (b. 1962), exemplifies the path a number of Australians have taken to became a professional glass practitioners. Following her initial art school grounding, in this case the Sydney College of the Arts, she took an extended overseas tour, and later served a traineeship at the Jam Factory before finally establishing her own hot-glass studio in 1990.

Plate 48 (opposite)
Colin Heaney (b. 1948)
Ceremonial Bowl,
Quicksilver Series, 1994
blown, silvered and hot-joined glass,
wrought-iron support;
58 cm
photo: Suzanna Clarke

Cowie's overseas travel provided invaluable experiences for her; these included an invitation by German glass-artist Ursula Huth to assist in the production of sculptural glass, and to helping Iestyn Davis establish a hot-glass studio in England. Her American experience emphasised the potential of un-inhibited flamboyant and sculptural use of colour and glass. This rich background is evident in her prolific output which successfully combines production and sculptural processes. The latter is directed to the making of goblets which address a personal concern regarding the fragility of life: a recent series Dolphins and Driftnets, emerged from an investigation into Venetian glass-making and a photograph of trapped and dying dolphins. In this work, goblets created from delicate glass work graphically display dolphins seemingly caught in spun glass. Her current sculptural series of bound solid-glass human figures further develops this idea and sense of entrapment and enticement in the manner that it rebounds on humanity. Ultimately, the resolution she aims for is personal, but an invitation is also extended for the viewer's own reflective process. [16]

Not uncommonly as we have seen, Clare Belfrage (b. 1966) is another who came to glass from a ceramic background. She gained experience in glass blowing at the Hot Glass Access Workshop at the Meat Market Craft Centre in Melbourne, at Resolution Glassworks, then in 1991, as a trainee at the Jam Factory. Her liking of strong simple images is effectively translated in her tablewares, especially the coffee cups Cafe series which have a strong feel of exuberance achieved through her combinations of bright opaque colours, and the social associations which emerge from their intended practical use (see also Chapter 1).

Scott Chaseling (b. 1962) studied and worked in mixed media sculpture for four years, prior to becoming a trainee glassblower at the Jam Factory. This was followed by ten years of working in glass, including a spell at Pilchuck Glass School in hot glass sculpture with Pino Signoretto. He has also taught alongside Klaus Moje at the Canberra School of Art's glass workshop for eighteen months. He was also a teaching assistant to Richard Royal and Hiroshi Yamano, and in 1989, he was technical assistant to Dante Marioni, Dale Chihuly and Lino Tagliapietra. And more recently, Chaseling has worked collaboratively with colleague Ruth Allen. Chaseling has therefore had considerable experience, especially as a glass blower and in a number of modes of working, in Australia, the United States and Japan. [17]

This eclectic background is now informing his current series of works. These combine blown, kilnformed and fired-enamel techniques, especially reflecting various influences which emerge from his contact with the aforementioned glass masters. Chaseling's works embrace a number of concerns, and are especially explorative of the vessel: they range from small fragile works such as the Nest series, to that of larger, mixed-media, installations which sometimes have a Venetian imagery. All are permeated with an elegance and spontaneity that reflects the glass forming process. His grandiose Wreath series is a departure from the vessel format in that he utilises a combination of various hot-glass working methods to form a large circular and solid glass ring or wreath. This is then embellished with floral and foliate motifs to create an object of neo-baroque design. In this manner, his mastery of glass processes is especially imaginative and is an area in which Chaseling is successfully developing a unique personal idiom.

Plate 49
Elizabeth McClure (b. 1957)
Incalmo Bowls,
Basket Series, 1994
blown glass:
three-part incalmo, hot-joined,
high-temperature enamels,
painted inside and out,
sanblasted and etched;
26 x Diam. 26 and 31 x Diam. 26.5 cm
photo: Glenys NG

A diversity of approaches

The vessel form may be manipulated through the combination of any number of techniques and processes to produce a diversity of sculptural or decorative effects. Robert Wynne (b. 1959) was completing the final year of a ceramic course at the Monash University (formerly Gippsland Institute) when he met Nick Mount in 1976. Wynne was immediately 'captivated by the dynamic process of glass blowing … any form could be quickly and cleanly made when compared to the ceramic process which was muddy and time consuming'. Accordingly he spent time as a trainee in blowing glass in Mount's Gippsland studio, later travelling overseas to study glass in the United States. His personal vernacular includes work in both vessels and sculptural forms. The influences of art nouveau, especially Louis Tiffany and the contemporaneous French glass makers is evident in his iridised vessels with their refinement of form, surface patterning and colouring.[18]

Pauline Delaney's career as a glass blower demonstrates how a natural evolution of style and form may be generated through the honing of this technique, within its practically unadulterated form; her earlier works, the Tiara series, were simple bowls with a wrap of crimped hot glass forming a tiara around

Plate 50
Mikaela Brown (b. 1966)
Guru Surfin' Dude, Dream Dude,
Cocktail Kidney Dude, 1991
Blown and hot worked glass.
34 cm

the bowl; these were followed by the Two-Tone series, a result of two or three complimentary primary colours with a clear base and a white trail. Her experimentation with silver nitrate led to a series of black vessels marked by the traces of surface iridescence. Later, her bold use of colour shifted to a more calming emphasis on form using mainly clear and neutral tones on her Triton series of shell-shaped bottles. Over this period she also produced her Ice Flower series through an investigation and refinement of a technique of manipulating the glass on a punty to create floral forms. These are then applied to the vessel using hot trails, the assembly finally being treated to produce a frosted finish.[19]

Delaney was born in England in 1959, migrating to Australia in 1970. She studied ceramic design at Monash University, subsequently ending up in the glass course; a traineeship with the Jam Factory followed and extended her expertise, especially in the manipulation of combinations of colour, as well as a grounding in mould-blowing techniques and team approaches to glass-blowing. From 1988, as supervisor of the Hot Glass Access Workshop at the Meat Market Craft Centre in Melbourne, Delaney has combined the management of its operations with her personal blown work.

Her most recent bowls of the L'Amour Flame series, especially acclaim the free blown approach, embodying movement within the form. They achieve this effect through the rhythm of two colours, a ruby pink and a lucid blue, which 'have freedom in the clearness of the bowl but are then captured by the black rim'. These vigorous swirls of intense colour generate a movement suggestive of dance. The series

evolved from L'Amour Rouge, a similar style but with differing colours which evoked a bolder emotion, whereas the present work has shifted to a more sensual style which evokes a somewhat sombre mood.

Don Wreford's background and skills-development in glass blowing illuminate the directions of his current work. He first studied fine art painting and sculpture at the Hornsey College of Art, London; it was through his work as a self-taught glass artist, making stained glass windows that he was introduced to hot glass. In 1977 he arrived in Australia, working for a spell with glass blower Peter Docherty in his Gosford studio, before becoming a trainee under Stanislav Melis at the Jam Factory. He further studied glass blowing with Julio Santos at Monash University, eventually establishing his present studio in Daylesford, Victoria.[20]

Since 1984, the direction of Wreford's work has, according to him, 'followed a classical tradition based on training and experience and the conditioning of the patriarchal-dominated role model of blown glass'. In his interest to explore blowing techniques he has focussed on actually decreasing control over the hot glass, thereby 'allowing it to create its own forms and colours'. By first fusing coloured panels together then blowing these out, then sometimes re-fusing them again, he strives for a combination of random but ordered effects. He sees his philosophy as emerging from 'chaos theory', and unlike Dale Chihuly's work which is spun out with centrifugal force, 'my pieces breathe in and out several times before they come to rest'. Wreford (b. 1942), developed his technique in the mid-1980s during a period of isolation: it is intriguing to note that glass blowers in the United States have only recently begun to show curiosity in the process.

Wreford achieves his singular approach through the squeezing and indentation of the hot vessel until 'it collapses into itself, then blowing the form out'. Hence, instead of the usual progression towards greater control, this practitioner permits some randomness to 'allow the medium its own dynamics'. Its an unorthodox approach which necessitates an overcoming of the resistance to the habitual blowing out, 'rather like Jackson Pollock', Wreford says, 'you have to psych yourself to overcome barriers'. Wreford finishes his works with sand-blasting to remove 'the seductiveness' of the shine. The whole process requires more understanding and technique than this glass blower cares to admit: 'Is there ordered chaos?' he questions.

British glass practitioner and educator Stephen Procter (b. 1946), is currently head of the Glass Workshop at the Canberra School of Art. His interest in the integration of light and form led his to move from glass engraving to his present work in blown forms. He focuses on clear glass vessels as spheres or 'embracing forms' as he aptly calls them; some are designed to rock gently, whilst others are 'poised on the point of movement'. Equilibrium in form is a vital concern, and his perspective of 'finely tuning each piece like a musical instrument', achieves a delicate balance of form which he surmises is 'fundamental to all aspects of life, since every element is related, influencing every other, and so it is with the making of any vessel'.[21]

Procter's vessel-like forms, often made on a very large scale, are effectively 'gatherers of light, encompassing space and light within'. Through this glass and light manipulation, the open bowl is celebrated as a symbol for giving and receiving: 'I often think of my pieces as volumes of light, like still clouds filled to the

Plate 51 (opposite)
Elizabeth Kelly (b. 1960)
The Three Kings, 1992
blown glass bottles
with blown stopper tops;
39.5 cm
Photo: Steve Keough

brim with reflected light'. His concept of the 'sound' of a work is intriguing and throws some insight into his choice and use of technique: 'I am always conscious while working on a vessel form, of it's sense of sound, the resonance within. I think of the cutting and shaping of a form like tuning a musical instrument, searching for that particular rhythm and harmony'. To this end, Procter's vessel forms are frequently cut prismatically at their edges in order 'to reveal the elements of colour within pure light'.

Procter's inspiration comes from the landscape, not so much the visual elements than 'that intangible essence … an experience. I like to work with the qualities of this experience. It has something to do with an awareness of space, feeling stillness and movement, looking at opposites such as the heaviness of rocks contrasted with the lightness of clouds, the qualities of light and sound'. These qualities are exercised by Procter as themes for his work.[22]

Elizabeth McClure's brilliantly-coloured bowls and bottles are in complete contrast to the large, cool and clear-glass works of Stephen Procter. McClure's first encounter with glass was in 1975, during her first year of art school in Edinburgh, Scotland. Since completion of her studies in 1980, she has continuously worked with glass, as a maker, designer, and teacher. In 1985 she was working in Japan when she was invited to participate in an exhibition entitled BIN (Japanese for bottles). It was the first time she had considered the bottle as a vehicle for the expression of her ideas. Since then, she has become increasingly intrigued by the notion of bottles and their function as containers of liquids, especially of perfume; she sees scent bottles as a means of 'transporting the essences and fragrances of time, place, season and memory'. McClure's imaginative integration of unusual forms and exuberant colour combinations with this class of container, has been especially successful: 'As well as playing with the form of the bottle itself, I am exploring the intimacy of precious objects, materials and substances'. The flat, almost two-dimensional shape of her bottles is reminiscent of many styles of ancient flasks, as well as womens' powder compact cases and other cosmetic containers; they investigate detail, simplicity, colour, pattern and texture 'as an expression of the essence of perfume'.

In complete contrast to these small bottles, in scale as well as function, McClure also makes large, rounded and open vessels which have a strong affinity to woven baskets in the boldness of their shape and in the surface textural play of painterly strokes. Through these vessels she explores tradition: '… the notion of identification of vessels, particularly as associated with indigenous societies where women as gatherers, collectors and providers are the ones who also make, use and mark their vessels to decorate them, as well as to identify them as their own'. For McClure these bowls are about sharing, offering, giving, softness and containment: they also provide a canvas for painterly expression.

Although McClure's early work played down colour, her present painterly use of clear colours, conveys an elated disposition. She has linked this lively use of colour to the transition from living in the Northern Hemisphere and Japan, to Australia and New Zealand. Here, the light and colours 'are incredibly strong and rich'. For the last five years, she has restricted her palette to red, yellow, green, blue and black: essentially pure colours. These are applied in a masterful brush-enhanced patterning to explore what she refers to as 'mark making'. The distinctiveness of McClure's vocabulary: bold, simple forms and strong, splashy colours, has resulted in work of unwavering design sense which has most surely made its mark.[23]

Plate 52
Setsuko Ogishi (b. 1954)
Leaves and Stars, 1993
blown and sand-blasted glass;
65 x 12 cm

Plate 53 (opposite)
Scott Chaseling (b. 1962)
Wreath, 1993
solid-worked hot glass,
metal and granite stand;
72 x 60 x 28 cm

The diversity of approaches within blown glass are continuously expanding, as the work of the following three practitioners exemplify. Setsuko Ogishi (b. 1954) started her artistic career as a painter, later discovering a greater affinity with glass: 'it is a more flexible, purer and more honest medium'. While traditional Japanese art is an important influence in her work, Australia's 'futuristic mood and freedom', is especially conducive to her explorations of the potential flexibility of glass. Born in Japan, Setsuko arrived in Australia in 1981 and trained in the glass workshop at the Jam Factory in Adelaide, establishing her present glass studio in 1987 in Wollombi, New South Wales. As one of an increasing number of women glassblowers in Australia, Ogishi, whose physical stature is among the smallest as she has pointed out. She considers that 'an important advantage are her "woman's eyes"' which confer 'delicacy, softness and simplicity in her work'. Ogishi's vessels are highly-decorative and sometimes also sculptural treatments which often demonstrate a rare sensuality through her sensitivity of colour, form and textural effects.[24]

Jan Blum (b. 1948) has now been working within her own distinctive idiom for a decade. Her collages, composed of blown vessels covered in lamp-worked shards and fragments, suggest a punk vision of glass. More recently, her solid-colour vessels have sprouted twisted tendrils and spikes: they seemingly appear, through some mysterious attractive force, to have drawn flotsam and jetsam from their surroundings, covering themselves in a protective layer of jagged forms. Through this overt bricolage approach, Blum creates sculptural vessels with a humorous, though pungent edge: Trollop is a piece which makes reference to a friend who 'fitted the image … I did her in glass'. It is pertinent to reveal that Blum made a deliberate decision early in her career not to learn 'too many' glass methods, because she 'didn't want to fall into the trap so many glassworkers fall into — namely "death by technique"'.[25]

Collaborations: Santos and Skillitzi

The collaborative approach to the making of studio glass, has surfaced from time to time over the past fifteen years, but lately appears to be emerging as a more attractive model for many practitioners in the maturing movement of the 1990s, both in Australia and overseas. The 1960s and 1970s attitude which encouraged an almost aggressive independence on the part of the maker, has lately shifted to embrace a number of models. In the United States, the Dale Chihuly team approach where a single designer orchestrates the blowing and signs the finished work as his or her own, has total acceptance and suggests a return to the earlier, pre-studio or industrial mode of making as elaborated in the preceding section. Another alternative to this team approach or that of the customary studio artist-blower, is the collaborative activity of two practitioners who combine their design and making skills. The collaboration between Benjamin Edols and Kathy Elliott, and between Scott Chaseling and Ruth Allen have already been mentioned.

While glass blowers have nearly always employed assistants or trained apprentices, less common have been co-signed glass works produced by two or more independent practitioners, geographically distant and aesthetically divergent. Nostalgia for old times and a desire to reflect current teamwork attitudes prompted an instance of this collaborative activity between Julio Santos and Stephen Skillitzi in 1993. Following detailed planning, these two Australia pioneers in glass, produced clay maquettes which they then first interpreted as blown-glass components at Santos' Newcastle studio (with Skillitzi's assistance);

then as cast-glass components by Skillitzi in his Adelaide studio. Santos' blown forms were then fabricated together with Skillitzi's kilnformed, cast-glass components, and the works documented.[26]

Their challenge was to complete up to 12 jointly designed-and-made semi-functional glass sculptures. Titled the Voyager Series, they were displayed in a 1993 exhibition at Melbourne's Distelfink Gallery, and later elsewhere, including Chicago's Art Fair '93. One critic succinctly noted this collaborative venture as 'an unholy alliance — unholy only in the sense of being outrageous or provocative — which will serve to promote community interest in contemporary Australian art/craft and to offer viewers a fresh insight into the achievements of two of Australia's most distinguished artists in glass'.[27]

The two glass practitioners, Skillitzi and Santos, had been aware of each others' glass work since 1971, being two of a small pioneering group of Australians who were dedicated to independent hot glass studios in the early seventies (see Chapter 1). Skillitzi worked with Santos in 1991 through to 1993 and also with the other Sydney pioneer Peter Minson in 1988. The latter collaboration celebrated the Australian Bicentenary through the making of a pair of functional spectacles from fumed lampworked glass, the lenses formed as maps of Australia, and used for Skillitz's performance of street theatre.

Julio Santos was born in Portugal in 1933 at Marinha Grande, a village specialising in glass blowing. At the age of twelve he was apprenticed to the National Fabrica de Vidros at Marinha Grande and later, at the age of twenty one, transferred to the Fabrica Angolana. By 1956, Santos was a fully qualified glass blower, and in 1962 he became Master Glass Blower at the Dorsteenhutte Glass Works of Wolfach in the Black Forest of Germany. He migrated to Australia in 1968 and became Master Blower at Phillips Lighting Industries, Wallsend, New South Wales. From 1976 to 1978 he taught as a part-time teacher of Glass Blowing at the College of Advanced Education, Newcastle. In 1979 he held a one-man exhibition in Newcastle and subsequently has held a number of exhibitions in other Australian centres. From 1979, for several years, he was a tutor in Glass Blowing at Monash University where he helped to establish its glass workshop.

In recent years Santos has very successfully marketed his individual and production blown-glass sculptures, vases, plates, goblets, tumblers, jugs and paperweights throughout Australia. He has also fulfilled many private and corporate commissions with a mastery of the material and elegance of design virtually unsurpassed in Australia. His Newcastle studio is the scene of a two-decade-long odyssey of Venetian-style canework techniques such as millefiori, filligrano, and latticino. Yearly working visits to his homeland Portugal have resulted in making and exhibiting there his lead-crystal wares. Santos has also frequently made glass to other artists' designs (for example, Newcastle's Leonora Glass factory with Les Blakeborough and at Monash University with Bronwyn Hughes and students). Hence a team effort was more natural than in Skillitzi's case who, apart from his co-directors (wife and father) in his own Glass, Earth and Fire Studios, has always favoured an independent practice (see Chapters 1 and 4). In fact, Skillitzi, in almost every respect, is in stark contrast to the highly focused craftsmanship of Santos, who reflects traditional vessel-oriented skills and workshop practices.

By bringing to the project the blowing skills of Santos, together with the conceptual and fabrication and casting skills of Skillitzi, both the artists and their collaborative works found common ground in the imaginative zone of outer space; The United States space exploration missions of Voyager I and II — designed to probe the Solar System and beyond — were the thematic focus; it was a union of a classical mythology and contemporary space science, the contrast between the two practitioners' approaches serving to intensify the outcome.

The resultant glass sculptures vary considerably in the manner they combine blown and other furnace-worked glass components by Santos with lost-wax cast glass by Skillitzi. Among the works Dragon Lady, is a candelabrum suggestive of 'a bejewelled siren beckoning intrepid space mariners to their point of no return like moths to the candle flame'. Solar Clock consists of a (blown) sun placed in the centre of a cast-glass solar elliptical track on which the nine planets, represented by blown and marble spheres were placed to orbit. Saturnalian Confection, is a banquet table centrepiece of three atlas-like sentinel figures made with lost-wax cast glass and supporting a blown-glass ringed planet and its sibling moons. The combination of these two seemingly disparate processes of furnace and kilnforming, can result in a difficult conjunction, but Santos and Skillitzi have successfully achieved sculptural pieces which resolve the differing solid and organic forms, or textural, glossy, opaque and transparent finishes. This is even all the more remarkable given these two practitioners widely differing backgrounds: Santos' traditional European glass-blowing expertise, and Skillitzi's art-school and studio glass grounding.

Summary

Glass blowing has come a long way from the 'misshapen bubble' of the 1970s: today it takes on heroic proportions of scale, its range of incandescent colours seems inexhaustible, and its formal manifestations seemingly inexhaustible. Glass blowing continues to have the potency to engender dialogues of form, history, culture, material and colour; it can be cynical or lampooning; playful or challenging; or it can simply be decorative and useful.

The expressive potential of glass blowing has been, and no doubt will continue to be, extended through its merging with other hot and cold-working techniques: there are many novel combinations yet to be discovered and investigated. Even so, the allure of its links to history, from the Roman period of creativity through to the Venetian tradition, appears to be sustaining and driving much of its vitality today. The dance-like orchestrations associated with glass-blowing, its dependency on the human breath, and the need for practitioners to work together in combining their skills towards a common aim, are all distinguishing features. And it may well be this latter facet of glass blowing, that it is people working together, that glass-blowing as an integral area of studio glass will continue to exert a powerful attraction to seasoned and young glass makers alike.

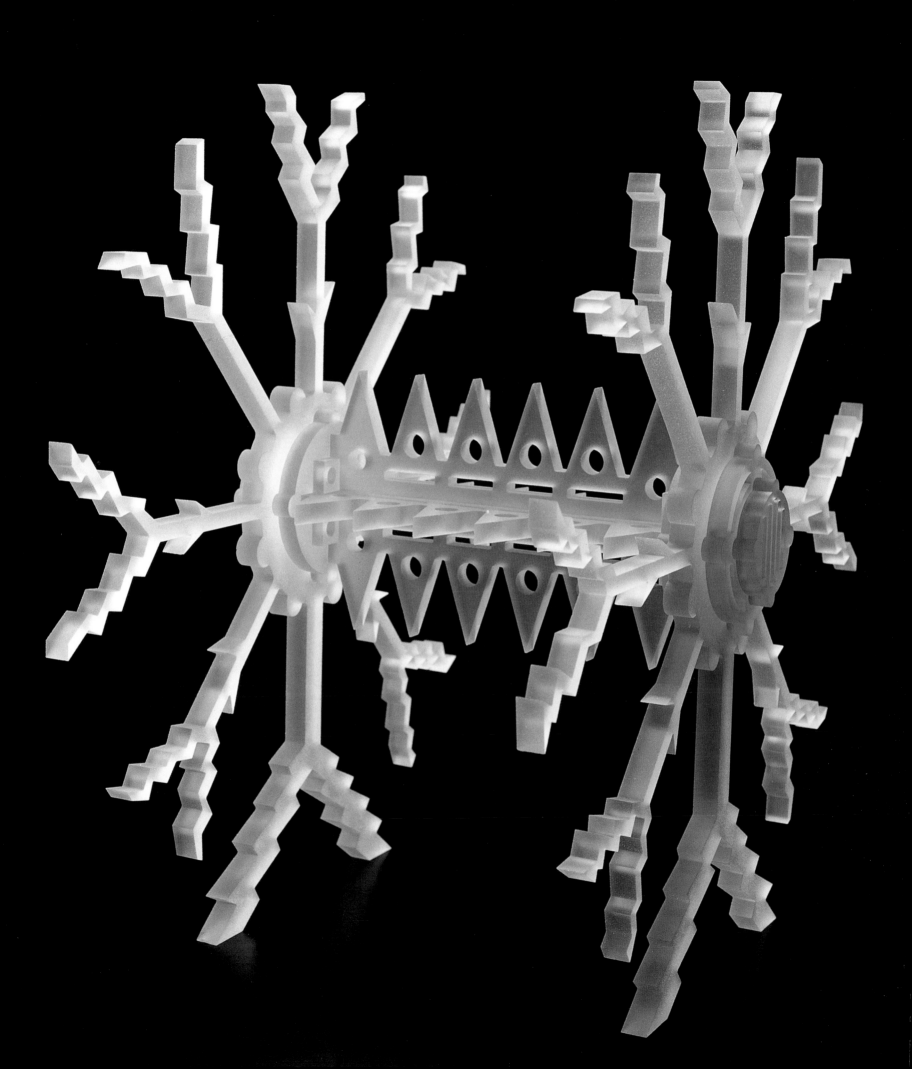

Alternate Glass Practices

'In a sea of anonymous hi-tech, Australia might be seen as an island whose soul has not been seduced by technology and where human energy is still the primary force'.[1]

Although it may be argued that glass blowing and kilnforming constitute the two pillars on which studio glass rests, there are other procedures which extend even further the diversity of expressions glass may be cajoled to bring forth. These include innovative developments in traditional leaded and stained glass, lamp-working, glass engraving, optical glass, laminated glass, and sand-casting to name a few. Although most of these areas overlap with glass blowing and kilnforming — and indeed, are frequently employed in any combination with these approaches — their individual technical and methodological characteristics specify that they are more comfortably located elsewhere, in this instance within the category designated here as 'alternate practices'.

Leaded, stained and kilnformed glass

The traditional practice of leaded and stained glass as applied to religious, domestic and public architecture, and which has its direct lineage from the nineteenth century and even earlier periods, is not the subject of this text.[2] Over the past thirty years, through innovative progression, a small group of glass practitioner's have broadened the area from its traditional parameters, to the extent that it has become more intimately linked to the studio glass movement as a whole. Painting, staining and kilnforming techniques and processes have not only been incorporated into the traditional environmental and architectural format, but these are now regularly used in making sculptural and exhibition works. The transfer of processes from the area of kilnformed glass in particular has, as Marc Grunseit notes, 'allowed practitioners to express their textural urges in three dimensions'.[3]

Four practitioners in particular, David Wright, Klaus Zimmer, Gerhard Emmerichs, and Cedar Prest, have been primarily responsible, from an early involvement, in extending the practice of leaded and stained glass in Australia, through the incorporation of kilnforming and other processes; all four have pursued this aim independently, and all have affirmed and imparted a sense of individuality in their art and their approaches to it.

Among these, David Wright (b. 1948), has been especially singular in his fusion of technological approach and stylistic development. An architectural graduate, Wright came into traditional leaded and

Plate 54 (opposite)
Rob Knottenbelt (b. 1947)
Dervish, Diatom Series #2, 1992
plate glass, high-speed waterjet carved to computer programme;
50 x 50 x 32 cms
photo: Robert Colivin

Plate 55
Patricia (Paddy) Robinson (b. 1944)
Birth Block, 1992
negatively-carved, laminated glass;
24 x 20 x 20 cm

stained glass in 1965 'as a naive without any formal training'; he was not constrained by conventional approaches and attitudes. Although his early work was figurative, by the early 1970s, he had found the usual leaded techniques too cumbersome to permit the translation of the kinds of details he was then developing; this drew him into experimenting with kilnformed glass, particularly texturing techniques. At this point in time, the American Hot Glass Movement had yet to have an impact in Australia: in any case Wright had deliberately isolated himself from the revival of stained and leaded glass work then occurring. With contemporary German glass infiltrating Australian work, he believed that a strong sense of individuality could only emerge if his work was not unduly influenced by this source. In 1976, he toured Europe thinking that glass work there would have much to offer a young practitioner, only to return to the 'freshness Australia offered because of its lack of precedence … the dead weight of tradition is absent here'.[4] Nor was a long apprentice-ship necessary before one could establish a studio as was the case in Europe. With such a liberal foundation, Wright has been unrestricted in his exploration of technique, colour and idea.

Wright's background training as an architect instilled a design basis from which his work emerges, especially in its successful integration with the architectural environment. In addition, his interest in creativi-ty, birth and science has directed and infused his work since its onset; early images came from microscopic studies of nature, the delicate transparencies of fungal threads, and the interconnectedness of life. Commission work for church windows in the early 1970s allowed him to initiate his lifelong interpretation of this creation theme 'into a more human philosophical sense'. At this point embryonic forms began to emerge as part of a characteristic imagery. For Wright, humankind's growing scientific understanding was not diminishing any sense of wonderment of creation. The latter theme has been interpreted by Wright into a symbolic language which contextualises science and its ongoing technological development. This is a specific visual language constituted through the careful layering of intricately-textured glass, which seeming-ly fuses medium with form: idea is bound to technique.

Wright's cellular imagery is not restricted to the architectural panel: he also makes small-scale works which fit the exhibition format because he enjoys the challenge of the shift in scale, but more importantly, because architectural commissions can take six months to a year to be designed and executed He notes, that 'as an artist it takes too long for the concept for the work to be realised. I find that this inhibits the flow of ideas, whereas small-scale work permits a faster turnover …'. Wright's recently-finished commission for two glass panels fitted in the office of the coronary unit of the Austin Hospital in Melbourne, was described as offering 'consolation not only at a sensual but at a symbolic level — a place where the discrete *techne* of the world intermingle in a burbling combination: architecture, woodworking, glassmaking, coronary surgery, plumbing'.[5] Wright's approach has been demonstrated in the United States: he was invited to teach in the Pilchuck Glass School in 1992, and is currently a member of Pilchuck's International Advisory Panel.

Klaus Zimmer has had a life-long involvement with glass as his medium of artistic expression in Australia. Born in Germany in 1928, Zimmer studied design at the Master School of Arts and Crafts in Berlin between 1947 and 1952, following this with painting and printmaking in the 1960s in Australia. Bill Gleeson, who taught experimental and stained glass at the Royal Melbourne Institute of Technology, intro-duced Zimmer to glass as an art form in this period when he was pioneering the use of fusing methods in flat glass. In 1974, Zimmer established the first flat glass tertiary course in Australia at Monash University, becoming the foundation senior lecturer; this determined his subsequent practice with glass. In 1976 he exhibited his first one-person show which consisted of 40 autonomous glass panels; by 1985 he had already contributed to 30 glass exhibitions.[6]

Zimmer has maintained strong links with his European background through regular study trips to this region, including studies under Ludwig Schaffrath (b. 1924) in Germany, and with Patrick Reyntiens in the United Kingdom; he also acted as an assistant for Johannes Schreiter (b. 1930). This contact kept his work strongly aligned to the German School of leaded and stained glass. Early in his development as a practitioner in this area, Zimmer extended the application of conventional stained glass techniques to embrace contem-

Plate 56 (opposite)
Graham Stone (b. 1950)
Fossil Record, 1991
etched, kiln-formed and layered glass;
80 x 50 x 10 cm
photo: Robert Calvin

porary studio glass approaches such as slumping, fusing abrading, etching, and sandblasting. He considered that proficiency in these techniques was necessary before he could express artistic ideas; even as early as 1963, Zimmer was working with laminating and fusing techniques. As well. he has directly transposed his fine art background into the glass medium; his earlier style therefore has a strong visual imagery reminiscent of his earlier printmaking.

From the late 1970s, Zimmer's technical repertoire continued to be extended and perfected, although technique was never an end in itself: suitable processes being chosen in order to match the content of each work. For Zimmer, lead is 'a dead material and you have to work to bring it alive'. His conviction that glass 'should work twenty-four hours a day, and not die during the night when the light fades', led to his development of a special surface structuring which includes lead-ornament, or, as he calls it, lead embroidery. Other techniques like multiple glazing, fusing, etching, painting, staining and lustre of the surfaces, have been gradually integrated into more recent work, the latter especially 'to further enliven the surface'. Zimmer sees himself making collages, and using the lead 'to draw, treating this component, together with glass and light, as freely as possible, but disciplined'.

Innovative techniques and processes are freely employed by Zimmer in his personal autonomous panels, but less so on his major commissions as these need to be accessible to a wider audience. The detailed working of lead, colour, form and graphic imagery, produces an intimate language of complex composition which invites close inspection from the viewer. The 1988 bicentenary cycle of stained glass windows in St Michael's Uniting Church, Melbourne, is considered to be Zimmer's most accomplished work: it engagingly employs a monumental, post-modernist, language which similarly integrates the glass with the architectural environment; Biblical, metaphorical and symbolic levels are combined to achieve visual communication. Virtuosity of design, technique and the visual interpretation of idea unify all categories of his work.[7]

Zimmer has continued to maintain his links with Europe: in July 1994, he was invited to give a workshop in glass at the Central School of Art in London, where he demonstrated the making of miniature panels incorporating his lateral processes. His influence on Australian flat glass has occurred through three areas: his teaching and establishment of the flat-glass design course; his extensive commission and exhibition work; and from 1983, the establishment of his Australia Studios. The latter was conceived as a place where young practitioners could develop their techniques and designs in a supportive setting; its past members include Gerhard Emmerichs, Christopher Bingley and Gisela Hunter.

Cedar Prest is similarly a pioneer of the architectural glass movement in Australia, devoting herself for the past thirty years to the development of 'a distinctively Australian glass style'. Prest's training began in the art and craft of ecclesiastical glass under the English post-Coventry masters, Patrick Reyntiens and Lawrence Lee, in the mid to late 1960's; in 1973, she furthered her study with the leaders of the modern movement in Germany, including Ludwig Schaffrath. A chief tenet upheld by this movement considered that 'the textures of the stained glass are of greater importance than its pictorial effect', a view which influences Prest's work.[8]

As with the two aforementioned Australian pioneers in this area, Prest's approach has been a focussed one: she has combined her European grounding with a freely-adaptive attitude, striving to develop an

impressionistic approach in her ongoing aim to integrate Australian imagery and stained and leaded glass. She has consistently challenged the limitations of flat glass, and since the early 1980s, has been developing techniques whereby light is concentrated in blown, fused, moulded or rolled glass. In this manner, line and image is achieved through the interplay of light, as well as through the varying thickness of the lead. Prest is particularly interested in the surface play of light on the glass and uses texture, opal, paint and selected glasses to achieve particular moods. In this manner her designs manipulate the light in particular settings to provide an atmosphere appropriate to the use of the building.[9]

Each of Prest's projects aim to 'celebrate being Australian where we are'. Inspiration therefore comes largely from the landscape, especially the rich diversity and uniqueness of the flora. Each project evolves after a period of intensive 'communion' with the landscape, and with its local community: only through this means, Prest believes, can 'an authentic sense of place and purpose be developed within the work'.

Her work in communities underlies a philosophy that art should be accessible to all members of any regional or urban group: community art projects, she upholds, 'can demystify stained glass'. To this end, Prest has worked on a number of community projects, including the Araluen Arts project in Alice Springs which involved the Aranda people. A proportion of her commissioned work includes more traditionally-oriented windows for churches and public buildings; however, she also pursues innovative directions, especially in the use of hot-glass work incorporated into windows. The 1993 internal glass wall in the arrivals hall of the Sydney International Airport, was one such project which demonstrates her singular inter-pretation of a brief which asked for a water theme to create a mood 'which would have a calming effect'. Her first innovation was the use of wavy sheets of glass, rather than the usual flat ones: 'wavy glass reflects more light and creates texture and interest'. A second innovation was the merging of the glass with a sand-stone wall base, together with the illusion of waves breaking over the edging.

Prest's urge, to develop an Australian school of glass, extends beyond the design to the material itself. She collaborated extensively with Freedom Glass, a Fremantle workshop and Australia's only coloured glass maker (for leaded and stained glass work). Working closely with the workshop allowed her to develop an extensive range of colours through the addition of cobalt, iron, gold, silver, uranium and other metallic oxides; she sees these hues as representative of the Australian environment, especially the aqueous colours of Sydney Harbour. Prest experimented with the hot glass, slumping, pressing and folding the sheets to pro-duce rich textures and forms, especially ripples and waves. The resultant work, High Tide, East Coast, imagi-natively simulates the effect of an energetic wall of water shimmering with reflected sunlight and breaking against the sandstone edge.

Glass painting in new directions

Traditional flat glass painting has also been taken off the flat glass sheet and developed into a novel artform, making a significant contribution to studio glass. Gerhard Emmerichs (b. 1956), during his fourteen years of practice in Australia, has made a unique contribution by blending German traditional stained glass approaches together with contemporary vision and format.

Emmerichs completed his apprenticeship in the studios of Hein Derix in Germany, eventually becoming a master glass painter after the completion of a course at the State Technical School for the Glass professions, in Hadamar in 1980. In the following year he migrated to Australia and extended his training at Monash University under Klaus Zimmer, where he was somewhat influenced by his teacher's heavily-textured and painterly approach. After a period of experimenting with various facets of flat glass he returned to the traditional techniques of staining and painting as 'they come closest to my ideal of good, spontaneous painting in glass'.[10] From 1987 to 1990, Gerhard Emmerichs was one of six craft practitioners in the cooperative Whitehall Enterprises, which had an output of furniture and other works combining handforged steel, ceramics and glass.

Emmerichs's earlier abstracted imagery was usually applied to flat-glass sheets. The work gradually became distilled into a more impressionistic style which resembled medieval engraving, but with representation that has an Australian mood. More recently, he has incorporated Biblical and personal motifs using a restricted but effective range of golden yellows and sepias as deeply glowing hues. He also uses slumped glass, usually shallow bowls, on which to apply his compositions which frequently incorporate script. The dark imagery of Meeresstille (Silence of the Sea), with its glowing sun, guardian angel, lone vessel and whale — the later submerged in a sea of text — is painted on one such shallow-slumped glass bowl. Emmerichs's imagery has powerful emotional overtones which draws on literary place-markers to source the artist's creative work, in this case a nineteenth-century poet.[11]

Another practitioner who has an innovative approach to stained glass is Gillian Mann. Having shifted from her genre of cast-glass icons in 1992, she now follows a graphic approach to manipulating glass (see Chapter 4). After a year of working on a series of huge narrative woodcuts, she is now translating this development by using traditional stained-glass methods to paint on glass. She uses transparent hand-worked pyrex glass, shaped in circles, half circles, or rectangles; the edges are irregular and the plane of the glass is undulating, while the colour is a delicate stain of silver, transparent red and transparent black. Mann is now exploring the 'abhorrence of violence and the need for compassion and peace'. It is an intriguing direction for this versatile artist which has already shown captivating results.[12]

Painting and staining methods appear to hold considerable innovative potential: Richard Whiteley (b. 1963), is another glass practitioner who is pioneering engaging work in this area. His use of glass has changed considerably over time: initially, he worked with mosaic *pâte de verre* with slumping and assembling to create a series of two-dimensional vessel forms as outlines which interrogated the concept of the vessel. A graduate of the Canberra School of Arts glass workshop, Whiteley subsequently spent seven years in the

Plate 57
Pavel Tomecko (b. 1948)
Opal Dream, 1994
cast solid optical glass,
cut and polished, with opal;
19.5 x 85 x 65 cm
photo: M. Kluvanek

Plate 58
Julio Santos (b. 1933) and
Stephen Skillitzi (b. 1947)
Saturnalian Confection, 1993
blown and cast glass assembly;
50 cm

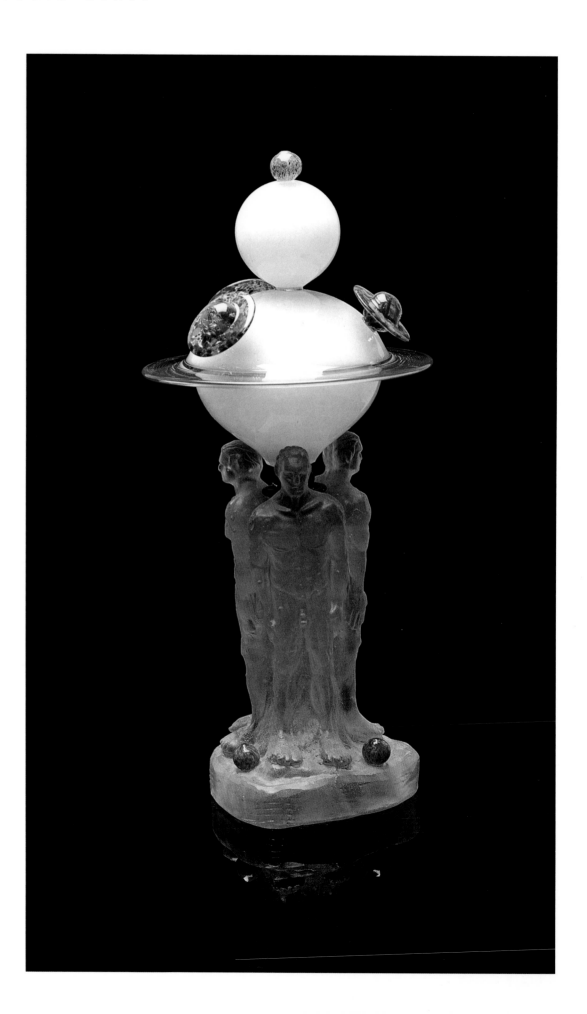

United States from 1988, first at Pilchuck, then studying under various glass masters. In 1993 he obtained a Master of Fine Arts in Sculpture at the University of Illinois, and is currently lecturing in glass at the Sydney College of the Arts.[13]

Whiteley's American experience and study, especially in sculpture, emphasised concept over material: in the past three years he shifted from what he describes as 'a heavy technical approach' to one whereby he employs glass in its simplest or most commonly found forms: uncomplicated blown glass forms or manipulated sheet glass. In doing so the glass has become a component within the work rather than the main constituent element. In one sense Whiteley, who first worked in stained glass before his Canberra and American studies, has now returned to re-investigating the techniques in this area, albeit from a fine arts perspective. He utilises traditional staining to form his images in glass bottles — the latter usually recycled from chemistry laboratories — to investigate scientific rationalism with religious idealism as his piece Madonna and Child expresses, through a combination of glass, glass enamel, rubber and latex. Even though such work clearly has a technical foundation, Whiteley is more interested in privileging idea through cross-disciplinary and conceptual approaches. His work takes a lateral direction to current mainstream studio glass activity, and suggests a new area of investigation is opening up.

Deborah Cocks (b. 1958), as we saw in the preceding chapter, is a versatile glass practitioner working in both enamelling and casting. Although most of her work consists of large slumped and enamelled glass bowls, she also makes limited numbers of enamelled and intricately engraved bowls, as well as some cast, figurative sculptural pieces. After the initial slump firing, bowls are given two, three or more enamel firings: first the under side of the bowl is coated with black-glass enamel, then design is scratched in and various brushes are used to completely or partially remove the enamel, leaving clear or textured areas. After this is fired on, coloured enamels are applied and subjected to the same texturing techniques before refiring. Her imagery usually consists of foliage and figurative forms, especially the chicken, in a whimsical bearing.[14]

Lateral Directions

In contrast to the preceding approaches which are essentially based on a figurative approach which retains some links to traditional architectural or flat-glass painting, is Kazuko Eguchi's unorthodox methodology which places her work within an individual branch of practice. Born in Japan, Eguchi (b. 1946) first studied fine arts at the Kyoto City University of Arts, later becoming a designer in the Yamamura Glass Company. Apart from a short time later spent in Melbourne, she remained with the firm for some 16 years until 1986. Over this period, her chief task was to design bottles and containers, but Eguchi often left the studio to watch the glass blowers at work in the factories. 'Everything was so dramatic and I am certain that this was where my passion for glass began'. She gained practical experience in glass making through the industrial tradesmen who taught her a love and respect of glass. From 1978, Eguchi eventually came to use glass as an artistic medium and to exhibit her work in Japan.[15]

In 1982 her work, large-scale sculptural pieces, was part of the touring show International Exhibitions in Glass Art (see Chapter 3). In Melbourne at the time, Eguchi chanced to meet Klaus Zimmer, then teaching at the Monash University. Zimmer was impressed with Eguchi's work, encouraging her to enrol in his classes which she did in 1985; Eguchi recollects Zimmer's emphatic comment when he first met her: 'idea is the first'. During this period she was encouraged to develop personal techniques; she also had the opportunity to tour the Australian Outback and experience its characteristic space, light and colour. In 1987 Eguchi migrated to Australia.

Over the past 16 years her techniques have changed considerably, but essentially glass-fusing and a painterly approach to colour constitute her predominant activity. Until 1980, her work consisted of large sized sculptural works using free-blown techniques. From 1980 to 1985, she made large painted installations, the colours being sprayed onto glass sheets which were then slumped. Since studying at Monash, she has developed a distinctive way of combining some of these techniques. After sandblasting large sheets of clear window glass she applies colours to each sheet using a palette knife. With some works, coloured architectural glass imported from Germany is used as the starting point rather than clear glass. Three sheets are then fired, layer on layer, often with chips of glass and pieces of metal foil arranged about, until fused together to produce her coloured glass compositions. An additional innovation is her use of clear glass enamels rather than the standard type; this allows her to effectively layer and overlap colours. The works are always presented in pairs, each consisting of a three-sheet sandwhich, and framed in a Japanese style with vertical wooded slats.

The results are subtle compositions of colour of abstract design that 'express human feeling through connections with nature': water, sky and earth seem to flow over and through each other in the manner emotions merge and change. Her experiences of travelling and bush walking in the Australian bush and landscape have certainly informed the work. Eguchi says that 'there is often imperfection, uncertainty and anxiety within these panels, complete with haunting spaces and uneasy movement'. In their presentation as pairs and in their transparent, watery clarity and soft colour, they symbolise a shifting of psychological levels, between the conscious and subconscious.

Similarly alternative areas of exploration in glass have been opened up by Marc Grunseit (b. 1952). He first studied medicine and worked as a medical practitioner before taking up stained glass in 1982 as a full-time pursuit. Following extensive travels in Europe and the Middle East, studying ancient and modern glass, visiting Cathedrals, galleries, studios and factories, he concurrently undertook study in glass blowing and glass painting and architectural glass design; he opened his Lights of Fantasy Studio in 1983. Since then, he has completed numerous commissions, for domestic, ecclesiastical and public buildings here and overseas. He has also worked on numerous autonomous stained glass panels and screens and kiln-fired glass pieces; the scope of his work ranges from huge architectural installations to delicate hand-sized pieces of kilnformed glass. The designs are eclectic, ranging from his more traditional and ecclesiastical to contemporary abstract and computer-generated imagery, fantasy and fractals.[16]

Although Grunseit was incorporating hot-glass formed components into his panels over the 1980s, it was not until the late 1980s, when the recession forced him to expand his traditional leaded and stained glass work, that he crossed the line into the former area. His training in hot-glass techniques allowed him to apply painted and kilnformed patterns which he derived from rock formations or other elements of the environment. Since 1993, he has been making panels using hot-formed glass components entirely, although

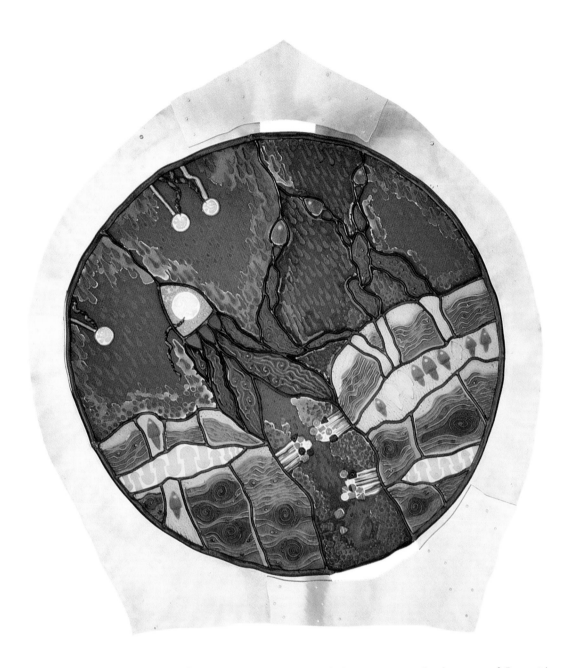

Plate 59
David Wright (b. 1948)
Birth Journey From the River's Mouth, 1988
fused, slumped and leaded glass;
Wagga City Art Gallery
110 x 120 cm
Photo: Ian Hobbs

these are still leaded together in the traditional manner. Particularly captivating is the derivation of Grunseit's imagery: he works from 'fractal iterations', that is, repetitive patterns with very subtle variations which gradually shift back to the original pattern. Using fractal geometry and a programmed computer he produces abstracted designs from which he develops the glass imagery.

It was in 1993, when he delivered a paper at the Ausglass conference critically analysing contemporary architectural stained glass, concluding that he succinctly stated his position in regard to the application of computers to glass art: '… in a sea of anonymous hi-tech, Australia might be seen as an island whose soul has not been seduced by technology and where human energy is still the primary force'.

Alison McMillan (b. 1947), is another practitioner who has combined a number of disparate techniques and processes in the making of leaded and stained glass panels. After completing her studies in the flat-glass course established by Klaus Zimmer at Monash University in 1980, she set up her own studio at Trentham, in Victoria's Central Highlands where the forest provides much of the inspiration for her work.

The design of her work has also, to some extent, been influenced by her participation in workshops with the German stained glass designers, including Ludwig Schaffrath, Johannes Schreiter and Joachim Klos (in 1981, 1986 and 1989 respectively). McMillan's work contains an element of figurative symbolism but this is not overt, and necessitates scrutiny by the viewer. She employs traditional techniques of painting and staining glass, but is also experimenting with fusing in order to broaden colour and textural qualities in the stained glass work: sandblasting, lustre and engraving are also frequently used. McMillan also makes functional forms, especially rectangular bowls, by slumping glass which is then painted and sometimes combined with sandstone feet. A particularly unusual aspect of her work is the incorporation of fused fragments of studio-blown glass by the master-blower Julio Santos, as well as antique glass. These provide a means of composing complex and rich compositions which embody historical associations.[17]

Challenging architecture glass

Maureen Cahill (b. 1947) works in an entirely differing area of glass work to the preceding practitioners. One of the pioneers of the glass movement in Australia, as a practitioner and educator, Cahill's work, in the past two decades, has changed dramatically from small intimate hand-held mosaic glass blocks to large-scale public architectural glass installations spanning up to 35 metres. Although she has exhibited smaller-scaled glass work, she is best known for her permanent installations in public spaces (see Chapter 1).[18]

Cahill has been an innovator in glass from the start of her career: her studies in London and Cairo led her into an investigation of early Egyptian core-vessel technology; kilnformed glass subsequently became the basis of the glass course she instituted at the Sydney College of the Arts in 1978. At this time her own work, mosaic glass cubes exhibited in 1979, highlighted colour interaction through spatial relationships and light refraction within the solid forms.

The plinth-determining scale of work as determined by the gallery setting, led Cahill to realise that she needed to move away from this site and into the public, architectural, arena. The latter was a considerably more challenging environment, forcing an extension of her interpretations of the medium, as well as a re-evaluation of scale, purpose and concept.

Photographic depiction of Cahill's work fails to demonstrate the scale, of the work, reducing it to a two dimensional image which contradicts the main intention: that is, the creation of volume through the spatial relationship between forms and subsequent changes of images. The latter may be actual, transmitted and illusionary, as produced from a repetition of forms within the architectural setting. Willy-Willy, for example, is installed in Parliament House, Canberra, a space where the suspended glass forms act as lenses, depending upon the changes in light during the day, and producing a play of changing shadows. Willy-Willy, an Aboriginal name for a sudden spiralling wind storm or whirlwind, evokes the energy of wind through the interplay of light and shape. This and other large suspended glass architectural installations are distinct from Cahill's earlier installations which were smaller, and hence displayed in designated gallery spaces. The present works are integral parts of the architecture, considered in collaboration with the architect from an early development of planning.

Plate 60 (opposite)
Klaus Zimmer (b. 1928)
Peking Spring, 1991
fused lead ornamenting
onto lustred-glass surface,
with lead-embroidered edges;
18 x 21 cm

Other on-going works of varying scales are addressing limitation and delimitation as focal points, as well as various aspects of visual disorder; the ambiguity of spatial meaning is further explored by the arrangement of light sources and placement of the glass elements, which once again, act as lenses that, as she puts it, 'alter the formal state of being through transmitted, evolving images'.

Cahill cuts her pieces of sheet glass into the desired shape, then reforms them in the kiln over steel moulds: slumping is the predominant kiln work. In her earlier, mid-1980s, gallery pieces, especially the Kite series, she slumped coloured sheets of triangular-shaped glass to signify Indian Hindu philosophy: red for female, blue for male and clear for the infinite. Slumping permits Cahill to explore a variety of ideas and their relationship to glass: volume, fragility, rigidity, formal composition, architectural references, and illusion. More recent works, although devoid of colour, are still primarily concerned with spatial relationships where light is the catalyst and glass is the vehicle for the concept.

Laminating, computer-based and other approaches

Glass does not necessarily need to be melted, fired or hot-treated to be manipulated into an expressive art form. This does not mean that leading and staining or other flat-glass working approaches as previously described are the only other alternatives to kiln or furnace-working. There are an increasing number of other, cold-working techniques, sometimes in combination with hot-working approaches, which provide alternative ways of handling and manipulating this medium.

Since his initiation into glass in the mid-1970s, Robert Knottenbelt has created a considerable body of work closely linked to the scope of the visual arts and craft movement, and to broader social issues generally. His early involvement and work in studio glass has already been disclosed elsewhere (see Chapters 1 & 3). Throughout the past twenty years, in common with most glass practitioners, he has worked in two very distinct areas of glass practice; production work which stems from two formative years of ceramic study at the School of Design, University of South Australia; these functional, blown-glass tablewares, sold under his studio name Britannia Creek Glass, and which reflect his two-year traineeship at the Jam Factory. Otherwise, his other area of glass, exhibition work, has been developed through his own efforts.[19]

However, he considers exhibition work to be a more important aspect of his glass, one which emerges from a deeper part of his persona and from concerns he considers were first consciously realised in his childhood. His exhibition work has been eclectic: it began with poetry, performance and multimedia constructions in the late 1970's, and from 1987, moved to computer-generated plate-glass sculptures — his present and most enduring form of expression. In terms of contemporary studio glass practice it entailed the exploration of a new technological approach, forcing Knottenbelt out of his hot-glass studio base into computer software and industry, to develop entirely new ways of dealing with glass.

Knottenbelt points out that, within the 5,000 year-long history of glass-making, heavy float glass has only been manufactured in the last 80; and until the development of computer-aided design and manufacture coupled to high-pressure water cutters, 'it had been impossible to cut intricate internal sections out of glass'. After his first attempt, he realised that the technique provided 'a completely new area of work in glass with form, linear crispness, scale impossible to achieve in any other way'; A final stage of sand-blasting and

Plate 61 (opposite)
Maureen Cahill (b. 1947)
Willy Willy, 1988
suspended glass installation,
Parliament House, Canberra
laminated and slumped glass,
with stainless steel;
each glass unit 100 cm;
display space 12 x 8 x 8 m

Plate 62
Cedar Prest (b. 1940)
High Tide, East Coast, 1993
Sydney International Airport
leaded, hot-rolled and kiln-cast glass,
with sanstone base;
600 x 800 cm
photo: Richard Woldendorp

acid-etching gives the work an alluring satin and translucent finish.[20] On the other hand, he also discovered that unlike its molten state, 'glass is different as a supercooled fluid, and on occasions cranky'. But he mastered the technique to go on to produce a extended series of sculptures through the articulation of intricately-cut architectonic shapes which are interlocked into complex patterns.

Over the past seven years, Knottenbelt's computer-programmed and water-jet carved plate glass sculptural works have evolved in a manner akin to that of natural selection: from simpler to more complex and sophisticated forms, diversifying from one species into a number of variants; the process is in tandem with Knottenbelt's developing craftsmanship and conceptual mellowing. Hence, although his 1988 Totemic Fish Contemplating a Persimmon — the second work produced with this technique — embodies the proven spatial, interlocking format, its complexity of angles and robust rectilinear alignment gradually gave way to the delicacy and astonishing intricacy of his more recent Diatom series.

As with all of this genre of works, they may be read on two levels: through the formal visual idiom, and concurrently, by decoding its cryptic vocabulary. The first emerges from their apparent sculptural delicacy as denoted by the works' spatial geometry, at once fragile and splendid, luminous and crystal-like; as organic metaphors they underscore the skeletal silicone origins of living diatoms — an extension of microscopic life into a monumental scale. In this manner, beauty, fragility, and life in general, is exaggerated and world anxiety for the greenhouse effect is effectively spotlighted; Knottenbelt has frequently talked about the role diatoms play in scientific studies of environmental research, past and present. Aside from these social qualms, there is yet the second, covert or ambiguous meanings embodied by these sculptures. In this there is room to project our own metaphors and emotions which may be as numerous as the myriad labyrinthine pathways of light the works delineate: literary, personal, totemic, primordial, all are pertinent to the beholder.

As Knottenbelt elaborates: 'Each piece hopefully lives its own ideal life, and although linked occasionally through subject matter, rarely returns to earlier works'. Hi-tech, yet quintessentially organic; symbolic, yet apparently real, Knottenbelt's work presents an iconography relevant to humanity at the end of a technological millenium, or even perhaps, one for an emerging new age.

An entirely different technique, but similarly beginning with sheets of glass, leads to the work of Patricia (Paddy) Robinson (b. 1944). She takes sheets of window glass which she cuts, glues and carves to produce striking sculptural work with a strong emotive feel. She was attracted to glass because of its clarity and refractive light-transmitting properties; these enabled her to express her interest in change, ambiguity, 'and the deceptive outward appearance of things which often contain other more subtle realities'. Robinson considers the multiplicity of images possible in optically-changeable images, as a metaphor for 'the multiplicity of roles we find ourselves in'. She finds this particularly relevant to the way female roles are played out today — hence most of her work is female in content and even more in intent. Robinson has taken on the role of 'the story-telling of the generation history — one which changes with the telling'. This 'serial nature' of the human story, motivates her sculptural work which is frequently autobiographical in nature.[21]

Robinson is also interested in the tactile qualities of the medium — the feel, softness and warmth of glass — as a part of the story which looks at the notion of human generation and maternity. For these reasons, the scale of the work is an important consideration and is therefore often life-sized: this, she believes, permits her to establish direct links with the viewer.

Born in Northern Ireland, Robinson trained at the Belfast College of Art with the glass painter Edward Marr. She came to Australia in 1965 and now lives in Sydney where she has pursued her impressive sculptural work in tandem with architectural stained glass since 1988. Her involvement in the latter has been considerable, and includes working with people such as Stephen Moor, as well as contact with John Hutton: the latter encouraged her original interest in glass engraving and carving. She also studied for three years with Anne Dybka, who fostered her interest in these techniques. Of these people Robinson says: 'All three strengthened me in my figurative exploration'.

Although Robinson employs a number of glass carving techniques, as well as the more traditional stained glass methods, her preferred sculptural technique is to laminate float glass together and then carve it:

Plate 63
Giselle Courtney (b. 1960)
Underwater Bracelet, 1994
lampworked, borosilicate glass,
sandblasted, painted and electroformed;
21 x 5 cm

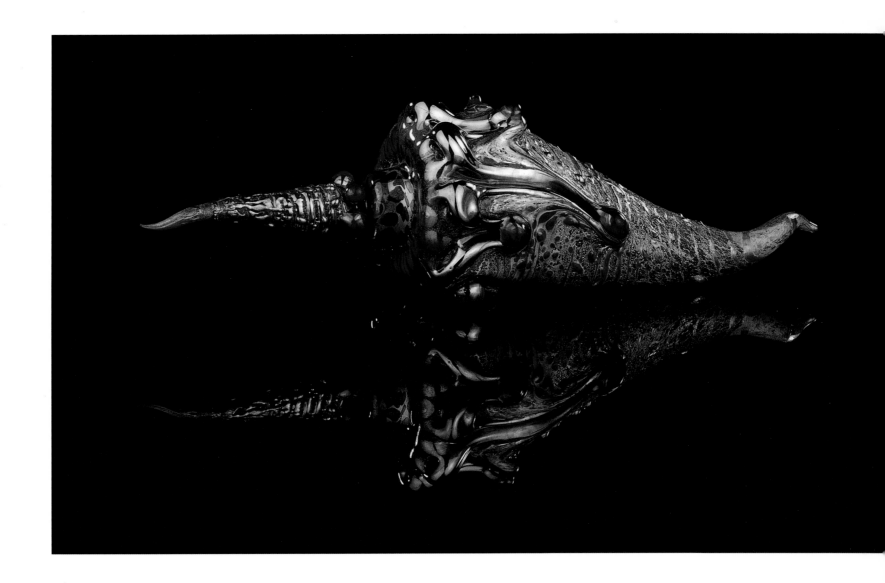

Plate 64
Richard Clements (b. 1950)
Shell Bottle, 1993
lamp worked, borosilicate glass
with metal clouring;
23 x 10.5 cm
photo: Uffe Schulze

she is also able to negatively carve images to create intriguing multiple optical illusions, such as Birth Block, where a life-sized child seemingly emerges from a watery womb of glass.

Another practitioner who similarly utilises clear plate glass for making laminated sculptural works is Sergio Redegalli, although his more recent work employs fusing techniques (see Chapter 4). Soon after graduating, he was commissioned to construct a free-standing sculpture for World Expo 88. Cascade was essentially a glass wave of monumental proportion which required 12 tonnes of glass; it was later relocated to the Adelaide Botanic Gardens. Since then he has made a number of such sculptures which consist of horizontal layers of roughly-cut glass, often also combining negatively-carved imagery to produce internal cavities of the human form.

Included among the handful of glass engravers working in Australia are Alasdair Gordon, Annete Kalnins, Cecil Renfield, Patricia Robinson, Anne Dybka and Tony Hanning. Of these, the latter two in particular are, and continue to be, the most closely allied to the studio glass movement.

Tony Hanning (b. 1950), is involved both in terms of his particularly active participation at conferences and through his on-going commentary on Ausglass members and issues, as well as in his approach and the character of his engraved work (see also Chapters 2 & 3). Hanning first worked as a public gallery director for ten years, during which time he also painted. In 1981 he left to take up painting full time, but found himself drawn to Nick Mount's hot glass studio (they had gone through art school together), where he began to experiment with forming images on glass. He eventually found an approach which suited his intent through the sand-blasting and engraving of cased, blown-glass vessels.[22]

His representative interest developed from a focus on the way glass carries light. 'A painter can describe light allegorically, but with glass, the artist says "this is the light. You are here". So I paint with light'. His concerns are not dissimilar in many respects to a painter or graphic artist; he is attracted to the notion of creating an illusion of depth on the hard surface of glass, which he sees as part of the three dimensional form in itself. Hanning's early paintings represented reflections in water, and played with the idea of the 'fallibility of the canvas to create space no matter how well it was painted'. The three-dimensional glass vessels on which his images appear, similarly, play a major part in what he describes as 'a formalist game where "reality" and "metaphor" come together as "reflections" on a three-dimensional form … I create a place to go to … I like to escape into my pieces'.

His pieces often make visual references to the processes involved in their making: a sphere, for example, may appear to be wrapped in ribbon which is in the process of being unravelled to reveal an underlying layer; within his illusionary imagery there are frequent references to the three-dimensional space seemingly created by sculpture and architecture. These effects are produced by skilled carving away of successive layers of coloured glass within the form. Themes generally revolve about the urban environment: streets, city-scapes, sky, clouds and human figures parade about in a surreal panorama worthy of Salavador Dali. 'streets … [are] like a stage where anything can happen'. Living in the Australian bush, Hanning prefers to leave his illustrated streets empty: 'the city is full of diversions designed to keep you away from yourself … the cities are empty husks …'. Tuz is a prime example: a spherical-form glass vessel carved to show a faceless nude who offers herself blindly to an empty, sky-backed room; another view has her unravelling as a ribbon into the sky.

Anne Dybka's (b. 1921) work has a similarly well-defined personal approach. Her work not only exemplifies the engraved crystal-glass tradition, but also has been extended into new directions. Born in England, Dybka studied drawing and painting under the German Expressionist Martin Bloch, and Fine Art at the London Polytechnic. She migrated to Australia in 1956, joining Guy Boyd's pottery in Melbourne and specialising in Majolica painting. She later became an artist and designer at Crown Corning where she was responsible for numerous classic Australian designs on commercially-made glassware. During this period she experimented with fusing, bending and cased glass, but ultimately became fascinated with glass engraving. In 1973 she opened her own studio in the Rocks, Sydney, where she currently works, continuing her development of clear or subtly-coloured glass engraved to include pierced work, free-standing glass carving and cameo glass.[23]

Dybka's wheel-engraved lead crystal tends to be traditionally-worked and demonstrates a consummate craftsmanship in the design and in its execution, manipulating light to enhance texture and tone. Subject matter ranges widely from depicting Shakespearean characters in solid blocks of crystal glass, to native flora and fauna in a realistic style. Her main innovation is in the manner some of the works are arranged and displayed. For example, Dybka frequently displays glass pieces in combination with holograms as an integral aspect of the work. She also cuts a profile of the engraved work along bowl rims to produce a sculptural effect. Other illusionary effects are obtained through novel combinations of techniques: Salmon Leaping a Waterfall is a large three-panel, plate-glass, installation with an internal light source; the middle and rear panels have been double-wave slumped, the front panel has wheel-engraved imagery of ferns, palms and birds, while the middle panel is illustrated with leaping salmon. Because the rear panel is green-flashed then ground and cut to produce a waterfall effect, the assembled work masterfully combines illusionary and real depth, to simulate the translucency of water and layered habitat of a rain-forest and pool scene.

Illusion, as we have seen, is a frequently sought after element within the diverse field of studio glass: Graham Stone (b. 1950), has developed his own, singular, means of pursuing his imagery and its illusionary nature. Since 1976, Stone has worked almost exclusively with kilnformed glass, often incorporating fused, etched or painted imagery, with vessels, sculpture, wall panels and architectural work as the main applications. Essentially self-taught, although he acknowledges David Wright assisted him early on with technical problems, Stone is best known for his wall panels which feature etched imagery of stylised prehistoric life-forms. These are presented in a layered composition suggestive of a schematic fossil record: unicellular algae, zooplankton, Ginkgo leaves, curled fern fronds, gymnosperms, flowing plants, insects, reptillia, dinosaurs, and human embryonic and other primitive forms, are variously layered across the panel. A recurring device has been that of symmetry 'and the variation that persists within apparent uniformity'. He explores subtle contrasts and even when intricate detail is called for, tries to avoid superfluous elements so that the work appears 'as simple and clean as possible'.[24]

By layering the glass panels, the etching is given soft shadowing and depth, a technique which, together with the neutral colour hues, enhances the imagery and achieves his intention to integrate it with the form. The layering technique is complex and involves two panels of glass: a clear sheet over a two-way mirrored sheet; both are etched, the clear panel on both sides, the mirrored panel with fewer images on its coated front surface. This arrangement with its reflections of images seemingly suspended in a third layer between the two panels, generates a spatial illusion (not apparent in photographs), which depends on movement and the viewing angle. In this manner, Stone effectively evokes an illusion of suspended, though shifting, time, and hence a sense of wonderment at 'the marvels of the natural world, Australian history and images which seek to evoke the evolution of time'. By depicting the numerous forms of living organisms, from dinosaurs to amoeba, as all being the same size in the Fossil series, he underscores 'their equal value in the interwoven story of life'. For Stone, 'Australia is uniquely vast, ancient and biologically distinct — a continent of sand'.

Stone's Fossil Series developed from a collaborative community project in 1988 with David Wright, when the need to trace early European and Aboriginal history of the project location was extended back to its pre-history. Currently, he has extended this time travel to the period preceding the emergence of life itself, to its chemical stirrings. The Event Horizon and Fossil series will eventually be linked together with other portrayals of various eras culminating in the Australian flora of the present.

Optical glass: tradition and innovation

Pavel Tomecko (b. 1948), who styles himself as a glass sculptor, is the only glass practitioner in Australia (aside from his wife), who works entirely with optical glass with a grounding in the traditions of Czechoslovakian glass. Born in Czechoslovakia, Tomecko studied glass making at the Academy of Fine Arts in Bratislava, Slovakia, then headed by Professor Vaclav Cigler. Dan Klein places the latter in same the generation of glass artists as Stanislav Libensky and René Roubíček, with Cigler as one whose 'interest in optical cutting stems from a commitment to the principles of kinetic art'. With Cigler as his mentor for some ten years, Tomecko says he 'realised the creative possibilities of optical glass'. Between 1973 to 1982, he lived and worked as a freelance glass artist in Bratislava, participating in numerous national and international glass and sculpture exhibitions. He developed his essentially geometric style, eventually gaining international recognition. Other works tend to have a figurative or natural form influenced by the modernist sculptor Constantin Brancusi.[25]

Tomecko eventually managed to quit Czechoslovakia, arriving in Australia in 1982 where the only Australian he knew was Stephen Skillitzi: a one-time visitor at his Bratislava studio. For three years Tomecko was employed by the Jam Factory to set up a glass cutting and polishing workshop, assist in the design of new production line, and train apprentices. Later, through an introduction from Skillitzi, he formed a partnership with Stanislav Melis (see Chapter 1), the head of the workshop, designing and producing optical glass sculptures. It was at this time that Tomecko developed a technique to integrate optical glass with Australian opal, creating a unique class of work. Since 1985 he has worked on his own making optical glass sculptures, many incorporating opal. 'Opal is the most precious stone Australia has … combined with the clarity of optical glass and grinding and polishing techniques, it displays everything that is Australian — wide horizons, value and beauty'.

Tomecko points out how optical crystal glass 'allows us not only to view the outside of the form but to view the inside and often multiple shapes and facets at the same time'. Optical glass is, however, technically and aesthetically difficult to work with — its clarity requires exceptionally long hours of skilful manual precision, with even minor mistakes unacceptable. In a simplified description of this process, a basic form is designed, a mould made and the glass cast and allowed to anneal. From this point, a small piece can be completed by cutting, grinding and polishing in less than a day; large complex, exhibition, works take months to finish. For Tomecko, 'the purity and clarity of optical glass is so high that we are really looking at light rather than the sculpture itself'. In addition to light, he considers an important requirement is that the viewer has 'an open and inquiring mind … my sculptures in 3-D offer the view of a 4th dimension'. In this manner, an 'almost infinite complexity of reflected shapes, as well as the vista of enormous space, within a limited volume offers insights into the human mind and physical existence'.

With their prismatic forms, clarity, technical daring and seemingly perfect finishes, Tomecko's work certainly emulates the effects sought by his teacher, Cigler: reflective, refractive, illusionary and metaphoric, all operating to open up the viewer's psychological space.

Aside from his gallery and exhibition pieces, Tomecko also produces much commission work, mostly sculptural trophies including those for the Design Council Award, and corporate and architecture design

Plate 65 (opposite)
Anne Dybka (b. 1921)
Salmon Leaping a Waterfall
Three plate-glass panel installation,
middle and rear panels
double-wave slumped,
front and middle panels wheel-engraved
with plant, bird and salmon imagery,
rear panel green-flashed with
ground and cut waterfall effect;
82 x 50 x 44 cm

awards. In 1991 he married and formed a partnership with Daniela Marthova, also a glass sculptor and designer who specializes in contrasting colour work. Marthova studied glass sculpture under Askold Žačko, also at the Academy of Fine Arts; as well as their individual pieces, she and Tomecko are currently also working collaboratively.

Lamp-working

Lamp-working is sometimes referred to as flame or bench-working, and unlike conventional glass blowers who use molten glass from a furnace, blowing is executed using tubes or rods of imported glass pyrex or borosilicate glass heated with an oxy-welding flame of oxygen and propane. A small group of practitioners in Australia are exploiting this area as a specialty practice and include: Stanislav Melis lamp-works small bottles using coloured soda-glass rods in a manner similar to many Venetian glass workers; Peter Minson, working in the Outback of New South Wales, continues his over 25 years-long commitment to lamp-work

Heart of Glass:
Poesis *and* Praxis

*'why shouldn't I be seduced by it? I want to make
stunning things in glass … its terribly un-art, but if they
want to lump me in the craft category that's okay'.*[1]

This story of studio glass in Australia has ventured to bring a sense of order through a survey of its historic origins, profiles of chief players, the make-up of its institutions, the detailing of key themes, and a portrayal of the creative end results of the makers' endeavours. Various chapters highlighted a perspective of contemporary studio glass as a cultural practice, one which extends from its community base to embrace individual practitioners, their physical manipulation of the medium and their artistic activity; while others examined the social activity which exposes, links and interprets their work in the exhibition and conference arenas.

To the extent that this account has attempted to portray the diversity of studio glass, the picture which has resulted has included a number of evident contradictions. We see a glass community apparently cohesive yet striving to re-unite its members; a community which is conservative in outlook, but adventurous in its creativity; openly celebratory of its individual and collective achievements, yet genuinely concerned for its future directions; and, while one group of practitioners openly revels in the material qualities of glass, others decry its evident seductiveness.

In addition to these incongruities, the resultant portrayal has also underscored additional themes, issues and trends. These are examined in an attempt to provide a further clarification of the dynamics of this group, its creative activities and the cultural meaning of studio glass. It specifically looks at the language of glass as it is articulated by individual practitioners, especially in relation to its essential material and metaphorical properties, its history and its crafting. Similarly, the cyclical shifting of emphasis from fine art to craft values is a long-lasting issue which demands scrutiny.

This window into Australian studio glass also challenges a shifting of the gaze towards the not-so-far horizon, in to attempt to anticipate impending trends. A potential starting point from which to pursue this undertaking is suggested by the frequent instances encountered in the preceding text, of contact and interchange between the practices of ceramics and glass.

The glass rush

Technical and stylistic influences between the two practices have occurred more frequently from clay to glass than the reverse. This is based in part on the large number of practitioners who have made the shift

Plate 68 (opposite)
Mies Grybaitis (b. 1968)
Therapeutic State, 1993
lost wax cast figure with
blown and etched 'bubble';
24 x 8.5 cm

into glass from clay: a consequence of the number of tertiary courses which combine clay and glass studies.

A perusal of ceramics practice over the past thirty years and its comparison to studio glass since the early 1970s, reveals a strong resemblance in their patterns of development, especially over the past decade. However, one critical difference is the fifteen-year lead ceramics has had over glass. A close examination of their concurrent patterns of development is therefore instructive.

The 1960s and early 1970s are generally recognised as the formative years of ceramics in Australia. The latter part of the 1970s through to the mid-1980s saw a 'clay rush', that is a flood of adherents to this area of studio craftwork. Until the early-1980s, clay remained the pre-eminent medium of expression for the crafts movement in this country, given its considerable edge over studio glass. Ceramics' energetic progression, when charted and represented through a linear model with its beginnings in the early 1960s, shows that this area took off from a base of strongly-defined Anglo-Oriental principles which sought to re-evaluate pre-industrial pottery aesthetics through the exploration of medium, function and craftsmanship (see Chapter 2). By the early 1970s, the 'artistic' liberation of the medium through the influence of popular trends in the fine arts, saw ceramics branch into two streams: the former traditional approach; and an 'anything goes' movement.

A decade later the momentum which the clay rush had achieved, showed signs of slowing down; much of the treatment of clay as a medium for sculptural, commentarial or conceptual expression, had become mannerist, formal and superficial: the emulation of art trends, the repetition of visual imagery, the specious use of post-modernist strategies, and the endless parodying of function could only go so far. Not unexpectedly, a sense of impotence and confusion heightened the looming predicament of the ceramics movement. Subsequent re-evaluation of the medium and a return to origins, in a traditional, artistic and personal sense, led to a renewed explorative attitude and sense of values which have lately re-invigorated contemporary clay. The strongly identifiable genres of clay practice in the 1990s each have their band of followers determined to reinforce values and extend the identity of their particular ceramic idiom.

The experience of the early 1980s, would suggest that the studio glass movement has closely followed a similar pattern to that of clay. From this premise, the latter half of the 1980s may therefore be viewed as the decade of an analogous 'glass rush'. The course of progression from the late 1980s, suggests the emergence of a crisis similar to the one experienced by ceramics. If the pattern for studio glass continues to emulate that of ceramics, then it is predictable that a temporarily restraint on the momentum which glass has achieved so far, may also be expected. As well as a loss of impetus, further effects of an impending crisis may include a decline of originality, and a sense of confusion concerning identity and bearing within the movement. Some commentators suggest that these signs are already visible. In the words of American art critic William Warmus: 'Stagnation, exhaustion and lack of direction are words applied in the 1990s … to studio glass'. And the Czechoslovakian glass curator Sylvia Petrová has observed in the movement 'occasional crises and feelings of futility and exhaustion …'. Similarly, Helmut Ricke's originally unfavourable assessment of Australian studio glass, although subsequently retracted, nevertheless has also reinforced the perception that, in the early 1990s, the glass movement had begun to

Plate 69 (opposite)
Warren Langley (b. 1950)
Spirit of Mars, 1989
Puzzling Evidence Series, 1993
kiln cast and fused float glass
and applied colour;
80 x 66 x 25 cm

reveal some anxious moments. Tony Hanning's passionate paper at the 1993 conference, even interpreted Warmus' and Petrová's comments, perhaps somewhat extremely, as 'trying to tell us that glass is dead'. Hanning had already criticised the movement a year earlier when, referring to the 1992 Tenth Australian Glass Triennial, he lamented the lack of originality: 'There is nothing here that we have not seen before …' (Chapter 3).[2]

Although our proximity to studio glass activity may distort any accurate present-day reading of the situation, the indications suggest that, as the glass rush advances and becomes increasingly complex and diverse, its practitioners may find themselves in a similar quandary to that which once threatened studio ceramics. Certainly, the glass movement's values, identity and sense of bearing are in the process of being re-defined, as has been made evident in more recent Ausglass forums (Chapter 2). Another area where signs may be gleaned, and the pattern of development of studio glass practice clarified, is within the critical literature.

Glass and criticism

There is general consensus that contemporary glass lacks the critical discourse which has developed around the other traditional craft media, particularly ceramics, jewellery and textiles. While it is observed that adequate critical appraisal of glass was lacking during the formative years of Australian studio glass, a cursory examination over the mid to late 1980s, reveals the conventional arts-versus-craft rhetoric as dominating discourse in glass.

Since the end of the 1980s, new attitudes, as embodied by post-modernism, have led to the progressive scrutiny, dismantling and broadening of critical perspectives in the visual arts and crafts by encouraging the use of interdisciplinary approaches. For the crafts, modernist discourse with its focus on technique, tradition, skills, medium, form, function and ornament, has been enriched with alternative viewpoints and interpretations derived from anthropological, semiotic, literary, social and cultural theory generally. It has been a gradual shift towards the material culture stance.[3] This change in tact has not occurred without some resistance: Sue Rowley for one has pointed out how, following the formative period of the craft movement in Australia in the 1960s, 'the need to consolidate the institutional base for the crafts in the early 1970s … tended to suppress critical frameworks that would rock the boat so recently launched'. This tendency is still prevalent. Alternative criticism has often been conceived as threatening to the professional status of makers, the recognition of their work through exhibitions, to market success, and to institutional viewpoints generally.[4]

This failure, to address the crafts movement at a consistently critical level beyond an institutionalised or modernist perspective has until recently, been particularly applicable to studio glass practice. It was not until the early 1990s that critical texts informed by a variety of alternative theoretical constructs emerged to probe glass practice: Nola Anderson's historical analysis, as noted early in this text, was among the first. It especially highlighted how writing 'interprets the events of history, and is based on various assumptions which in turn affect the criticism brought to bear on the medium'.[5]

Plate 70
Jan Blum (b. 1948)
Trollop, 1990
blown glass, matches, wood, paint;
40 x 25 cms

This dearth of glass criticism has not simply been an Australian phenomenon: in 1992, the American critic Vincent Carducci, surmised that 'the most important factor insulating studio glass from the rest of the art world is a paucity of critical and scholarly writing on art glass when compared to other media [and] this lack prevents a healthy discourse taking place'. It was not until 1989 that Brian Hirst writing in the Ausglass journal, voiced membership concern for critical evaluation, appealing for the development of 'some kind of aesthetic related to the medium ... if glass is to develop as we anticipate'.[6]

The resistance of the material

One of the chief reasons often stated for this apparent difficulty of developing a critical context for glass, is the inherent individuality of the glass medium itself: it is this crucial point too, which leads us into an understanding of certain trends and the potential conditions which may lead to a crisis in glass practice.

Over the past fifteen years or so, critics, curators, writers and practitioners have repeatedly pointed out the distinctive qualities of glass: its clarity of colour, its manipulation of light, its crystalline density or its seeming organic fluidity, and its symbolic contradictions and associations; but more frequently, they warn of the 'dangers' of the medium's natural and sensual beauty which is often seen as 'seductive'. It is a perspective which constitutes glass as a kind of irrepressible genie, one which can dazzle and mislead any would-be master. Yet there are other commentators who celebrate these qualities. What is it about glass that attracts these charges and contradictions? It is intriguing that, whereas this caution is customary for glass, it is not the case for other craft media — a further indicator of the singular characteristics of glass.

Constant references to the unique and seemingly seductive qualities of glass emerge as a strong,

Plate 72 (opposite)
Robert Wynne (b. 1959)
Gender, 1993
Plate glass with blown, iridised,
sand-blasted
and fabricated glass on sandstone;
48 x Diam. 39 x 11 cm

Plate 73 (left)
Nick Mount (b. 1952)
Plate, 1993
blown with incalmo join;
Diam. 44 cm
photo: Alex Makeyev

proficiency appeared to approached a zenith in the late 1980s, the originality of representative strategies which aim for the expression of material, function, form, aesthetics, ideas and meaning lost some of their edge. Although various symptoms suggestive of such a condition are about, they are not necessarily prevalent across the whole field of glass practice: kilnforming, is one area which has especially maintained its strong impetus and vitality of expression — to date. Whereas glass blowing, which was perhaps less creative in the late 1980s, appears to be entering a period of greater vitality.

The glass practitioner today is surely faced with an enormous range of techniques, tools and processes with which to manipulate the medium. But the delight in novel technique and the free-fall out-look of the 1980s, has lately given way to a more studied approach which blends technique, skill, inherent associations and medium with the glass practitioner's conceptual intention. Each craft medium has its own language made up of a vocabulary derived from its unique properties: its potential textures, colours, forms, aesthetics, traditions, and its particular set of historical and cultural associations. If the medium is the message, how and what is the vocabulary and language of glass as manipulated and interpreted by contemporary practitioners?

Lately, there has been a greater realisation of the metaphorical power of glass — sometimes referred to as its 'inner being', or even, its 'heart'. This is engendered through the emotive connections people have with the medium: the mental processes linked to glass, its symbolic embodiments and ritualistic associations. These add up to produce what may be referred to as its psychodynamics: the mental processes and responses that we have in association with glass. In effect, they derive from both its unique light-affecting properties in combination with deep-seated culturally and historically-determined mean-ings. Yet despite the fact that these are the source for understanding the medium's enduring potential for metaphorical or other expressions, this psychodynamic facet of glass has yet to be comprehensively examined at depth.

Plate 74
Judi Elliott (b. 1934)
Black Box, 1994
kiln cast and fused glass;
69 x 53 x 1.5 cm

A more complex, but ultimately clearer, understanding of this process argues that every craft involves both *poesis* and *praxis*. Whereby the former refers to 'the content and meaning of art' and the latter as 'that which relates to the means of technical realisation'. These in turn, conflate into theory and practice, which are 'combined in the single process of technology'. From this analysis of the origins of terminology, the glass maker may be considered as 'both poet and practitioner'.[18] Glass practitioners themselves have frequently raised the question, grappling with the idea of the interaction of medium with technical process and idea. Nola Anderson has argued for a similar view she refers to as an 'ideology of making', whereby technical processes are not simply seen as ways of getting things done, but that 'They are part of the artist's aesthetic'.[19] Beyond this understanding, further query currently seeks to reveal to how this process may be reconciled with the value attitudes of the visual arts and crafts, or with broader cultural theory generally.

Glass practitioners have shown that they are committed in their investigations of their medium's properties, its historical technology and emotive potential. There is no doubt, for example, that the succession to kilnforming rather than glass blowing was — in addition to the tendency for people to follow trendsetters — prompted by the allure of mastering what was a new, extended, vocabulary for glass expression. To the researcher, kilnforming has the additional attraction of the measured pace it imposes on the practitioner, hence facilitating the study and translation of its particular physical and metaphorical terminology; similarly, the systematic approach to kilnforming processes allows the practitioner to set his or her own pace, and hence determine to a very controlled degree, the outcome. The direct manipulation of glass or clay, also engenders feedback, through the actual technique, into the underlying motivation and idea for the work. The actual process of making therefore permits the practitioner to develop his or her idea through technique or hand-skills, that is, the intimate interaction of medium and hands.[20]

Ann Robinson's work illustrates this process. By varying the thickness of the vessel walls, and through the relationship of sharp-angled repeat motifs, this practitioner, like many others, manipulates the transmission of light through the thick-walled cast glass: 'Glass changes with the light of the day, its not static but a living thing. I find that glass used in this manner becomes an emotional material'. Over a period of months, Robinson works on moulds, developing the pattern and form as it eventually appears when cast; 'its a developmental, meditative, approach'. In this manner, ideas develop gradually, not in quantum leaps, the casting process itself often suggesting subsequent changes or modifications for later pieces. She emphasises the 'hands on' importance of being involved as a maker, not simply acting as a designer: 'it's the process of making that suggests the progression'.

This experiential perspective and its relationship to the eventual outcome of the work, has yet to be systematically investigated, yet it is at this convergence, of *poesis* and *praxis*, where the unravelling of the process will most likely occur.[21]

The current tendency for the glass practitioner is to concentrate on becoming versed in one or a select number of technologies which are then applied towards the refinement of a personal idiom, generally realised through series development. Medium, idea and technique are now seen to be of equal significance in achieving a particular 'look', one which is recognised as the 'signature style' of the maker. Klaus Moje agrees that there is a tendency to develop one's own style: 'I have my niche ... so have others, this is the way you overcome your own limitations, through constant involvement and refining of one's abilities you reach a master stage, then you may jump into a new area'.[22]

However, these are the words of glass masters who have arrived at their position after years of experience. The difficulty of making purely original work is generally acknowledged, especially given the memories and cultural baggage of previous generations, and the media-saturation of today's global village. How does the practitioner achieve a balance between the influences of traditional models and the pressures of innovation, hence avoiding outmoded imagery or self-conscious pastiches? We may approach an understanding of this query through comments made by the art theorist and historian Herbert Read, who considered originality to be revealed in the artist's 'unique and private vision of the world'.[23] This concept may be reworked to consider that something is original if it provides a new perception, a new way of looking at the world. Within this definition we see that elements from pre-existing or old models of representation may be reworked within a new configuration in order to achieve a new perception. Through personal insight or perception a particular angle of the familiar may be grasped, hence

Plate 75
Paul Sanders (b. 1963)
Archaisian Fragment, 1993
slumped glass with post-kiln fired
patination,
concrete;
27 x 41 x 12 cm

permitting a re-working of the ordinary into the extraordinary, or at least providing an alternative view. The work therefore becomes transformed into an original if it is not too esoteric, if is adaptive, if it somehow takes into account previous models; and further, if it challenges, if it is accessible, and if it permits a glimpse into the maker's private vision. These are the hallmarks of successful works in glass.

A clearer idea of originality may be derived through an examination of how new perception comes about. It is not necessarily achieved through rational thought, but rather constitutes a process of penetrating awareness. The practitioner somehow, through a process balancing critical and intuitive faculties, arrives at a perception of what might be, subsequently translating inner vision into the glass medium through the aforementioned routine of feedback and technique; it is at this point that the interactive process of *poesis* and *praxis,* as described, comes to the fore.

Another perspective of this process derives from the Jungian model. This contends that humanity's perception of the external world is strongly coloured by a collective unconscious, a mythological world of powerful emotions and experience, primitive and passionate. It is this very inner world which is also the source of an imagination which 'promotes the discovery of symbolic achievements and satisfactions'.[24] It

Plate 76
Peter Tysoe (b. 1935)
Yulara, 1993
cire perdue, cast glass;
32 x 15 x 40 cm

has been frequently observed that, as a consequence of our insecure existence and perhaps, anxiety, there is a urge to achieve a firmer grasp of reality, to gain satisfaction, emotionally and economically, and to impose order onto the external world. Art and science are the creative means by which a closer and truer relation with reality may be achieved. As a ritualistic activity, creativity directed at the production of art 'can act as a bridge between the inner world of the subject and the external world'. The split between inner and outer world is present to varying degrees in all of us, and it is from the impulse to resolve this split, and it is because of the need to bridge this gap that creative energy is considered to stem.[25]

This model of creativity portrays it as an integrative one which seeks to re-organise inner experience, and which becomes, through craft practice, manifested in the work. Glass practitioners have their own way of putting their views on the matter forward, and perhaps not so surprisingly, these often match the preceding: Stephen Procter, for example, maintains that 'creative work is very much a dialogue between the physical and the spiritual, the work itself providing the meeting point. Creating is the means for exploration, towards a greater understanding'. David Wright similarly asserts: 'the artist makes a work and in doing so expresses a new sense of self, the viewer in a successful relationship with the work creates a changed view of him or her self within the world'.[26]

This creative process and its outcome has been repeatedly revealed in the numerous examples of the work of glass practitioners described and illustrated throughout the text. The following summation of some of these practitioners and their specialty idiom, serves to illustrate the means, as well as emphasise the integration of *poesis* and *praxis*, of inner vision and craftsmanship — although it is not generally articulated as such: Stephen Skillitzi's figurative works embody a narrative complexity which highlights selective emotive elements, as emphasised through the lost-wax casting method and his use of electroforming techniques; Gillian Mann's stylized female genitallia are formed in a particular quality of *pâte de verre* reminiscent of plasticine, in order to symbolise profanity and creation; Nick Mount's blown and frosted torsos exaggerate the female form to imbue it with a palpable, sensual appeal with classical hints; Brian Hirst's integration of painterly panels and mould-blown vessels, are carved, engraved and lustred to generate discourses on ancient themes and contemporary making processes; Paul Sanders post-kiln fired coloured glass fragments, balanced on solid bases, celebrate the process of glass making and its historical connotations; Helen Aitken Kuhnen's kiln-cast glass lights unify strength, translucency and crystalline monumentality with functional design; Katsuko Eguchi's fused and painted abstract glass compositions manifest emotional states through allusions to natural landscape features and their qualities of light transmission; Mikaela Brown's blown figurative goblets portray imagery which entertains, concurrently evoking festive memories, otherwise satirising aspects of daily life; Tony Hanning's engraved pieces refer to their making, and present an illusionary imagery symbolic of life's predicaments. Rob Knottenbelt's computer-directed, plate glass sculptural works, are complex yet lyrical works, portraying aspects of environmental concern together with personal allegory; and Pamela Stadus' sand-cast work combines shadowy figures, a depth of clarity and intense colours to contrast reality and illusion, and elicit a disposition of vulnerability and memory.

Based on the preceding argument, unless practitioners have sourced their intellectual and emotional experience, and effectively linked these through their craftsmanship, there is a risk that studio activity in glass — or other media — will result in superficial or mannerist works.

The way of glass

The anthropologist Claude Lévi-Strauss' model of the *bricoleur* is particularly useful in explaining the considerable diversity of much current work: it is also one which dovetails in with the previous notions of the artist's inner world, the dynamics of creativity, and role playing and representation. The anthropological idea of the *bricoloeur* also provides a means of explaining the condition of contemporary culture and culture-makers. Just like the junk collector, the *bricoloeur* searches about and reclaims bits and pieces, in this case of jettisoned culture, re-assembling these discards of routine images or symbols, into new representations. If successfully applied, *bricolage* becomes a strategy whereby symbolic representations of reality are selected and integrated to produce a work of alternate or new meaning. The successful use of *bricolage* to create an original work, therefore stems from the interplay and eventual balance between intuitive and critical faculties.

Warren Langley's comments on his methodology gives some insight into this process: 'Glass is a material which is my vocabulary. This is what I'm at ease with just as a painter is at ease with his oils. This is the material I talk best with … If I want to achieve an effect I know what to do to the material. My

Endnotes

PREFACE

1. Yoko Ono, *Interview Magazine*, 1981 (inside cover). Quoted in full in Elizabeth McClure, 'Idioms of the Antipodes', *Glasswork*, Nov 1992, No 13, p.10

2. William Warmus, 'The Completion of Studio Glass', in *Design Visions*, Art Gallery of Western Australia, 1992, p.33; Helmut Ricke, *Neus Glas*, 1992, p.26; Dan Klein, *Glass: Contemporary Art*, 1989, p.29.

3. Interview, S. Skillitzi, 2 Mar 1994; S. Skillitzi, 'Glass Narrative Questioned', letter to *Crafts NSW*, Summer 1991 p.31, and a more detailed letter in *Ausglass*, summer edition, 1990, pp.22–23; *Crafts NSW*, Autumn 1991 p.20; For a chronological account of glass events see Grace Cochrane, *The Crafts Movement in Australia*, New South Wales University Press, 1992, pp.230–233, and pp.383–391

4. For an interpretive account which examines the manner in which 'a glass narrative' was constructed see Nola Anderson's series of essays *The Glass Narrative, in Crafts New South Wales*: Autumn, Winter, Spring and Summer issues, 1991, and later published in annotated form in: Noris Ioannou, *Craft in Society*, Fremantle Arts Centre Press, 1992, pp.100–114; ibid., p.113

CHAPTER 1: THE SEMINAL YEARS

1. *Ausglass*, Winter, 1992, p.18. Daniel Thomas said this to Tony Hanning during a glass blowing demonstration in Gippsland in 1973. Hanning says that Thomas had 'put his hands over my eyes' when he said this to him as they walked past the demonstrator — who was Stephen Skillitzi. Interview, T. Hanning, 16 Mar 1994

2. Interviews, S. Skillitzi, Feb, 20 Mar and Apr 1994

3. Susanne Frantz, *Contemporary Glass*, Harry Abrams, New York, 1989, p.135

4. Interviews, S. Skillitzi; letter by Skillitzi in *Craft Australia*, 1982, No 2, p.72, and another in *New Glass*, (English Edition), 1990, No 1, p.45: both give a synopsis of the genesis of the Australian studio glass movement pre-1974

5. Interview with S. Skillitzi, 20 May 1994; Noris Ioannou, *The Culture Brokers: towards a redefinition of Australian contemporary craft*, State Publishing, 1989, pp.35–38; Grace Cochrane, *The Crafts Movement in Australia*, New South Wales University Press, 1992, pp.230–233, and pp.383–391

6. Fiona Gavans, 'Discussion Paper on the Glass Situation in Australia', unpublished, Crafts Board of the Australia Council, Sydney, 1978. Although glass practitioners are generally critical of this report considering it uninformed about glass activity which was non-government funded prior to 1974

7. Interviews, S. Skillitzi, 11 and G. King, 13 Apr 1994

8. Michael Taylor, 'Glass Education in the USA', *New Glass*, No 4, 1988, pp.290–291; Interview, R. Whiteley, 17 Apr 1994

9. Interview, M. Cahill, 7 Mar 1994

10. Catalogue, *Contemporary Glass — Australia, Canada, U.S.A. and Japan*, The National Museum of Modern Art, Kyoto, 1981; *The New York Times*, 18 Oct 1981

11. Interview, M. Cahill, 7 Mar 1994. In 1993 the Glass Artists Gallery promoted Australian work to the Chicago International New Art Forms Exposition

12. Noris Ioannou, 'Glass Production at the Jam Factory', *Craft Arts*, 1990, No 19, pp.78–79; Noris Ioannou, 'The Jam Factory Workshop and the Studio Glass Movement in Australia', *Ausglass*, Summer 1990, pp.26–32; Jenny Zimmer, 'New Developments', *Craft Australia*, 1979, No 3, p.23; John McPhee, Contemporary Decorative Crafts in the Collection of the Australian National Gallery', *Craft Australia*, 1982, No 4, p.43; Glenn Cooke, 'The Studio Glass Movement in Australia, *Craft Arts International*, 1989, No 15, p.77

13. Jenny Zimmer, 'Studio Glass Australia. The first decade of exhibitions', *Craft Australia*, 1988, No 4, p.78

14. Ioannou, op cit.,1990, *Craft Arts*, pp.78–79

15. For a historical survey of this institution see Ioannou, op cit., *Craft Arts*, 1990, pp.75–80

16. Ibid., p.80; Interview, P. Tysoe, 9 Mar 1994

17. Interview, P. Tysoe, 5 Apr 1994

18. Interviews, N. and P. Mount, 30 Mar, and 30 Apr, 1994

19. Ioannou, op cit., 1989, pp.36–38

20. Doreen Ehrlich, *The Bauhaus*, Mallard Press, 1991, p.47 and p.147

21. Interview, K. Moje, 29 Mar 1994

22. Ehrlich, op cit., p.10

23. Interviews, K. Moje, 7 and 29 Mar 1994

24. Frantz, op cit., 1989, p.134

25. Interviews: T. Hanning, 16 Mar, and R. Knottenbelt, 3 Mar, S. Skillitzi, 20 May, G. King 13 Apr. B. Hirst 16 Mar, W. Langley, 29 Mar. All 1994

26. Interview, E. McClure, 28 Apr 1994

27. Interview, S. Procter, 18 Apr 1994

CHAPTER 2: THE GLASS COMMUNITY

1. David McNeil, 'An Ausglass Alchemy', *Object*, Autumn, 1993, p.34

2. Ibid.

3. *Ausglass '93*, p.18; Nola Anderson, 'Ausglass Advance', *Crafts New South Wales*, Summer 1991, p.14

4. Interviews: S. Skillitzi, 2 Mar; M. Cahill, 7 Mar; R. Knottenbelt, 3 Mar, W. Langley, 29 Mar. All 1994

5. Interview, T. Hanning, 16 and 22 Mar, and B. Hirst, 1994

6. Interview, G. King, 13 Apr 1994

7. Interview, T. Hanning, 22 Mar 1994

8. Nola Anderson, 'Ausglass '85', review, *Craft Australia*, 1985, No **, p.92

9. Noris Ioannou, *The Culture Brokers: towards a redefinition of Australian contemporary craft*, State Print, Adelaide, 1989, pp.33–44

10. Ibid., pp.33–44; Grace Cochrane, 'crafts in the eighties', *Ausglass*, Winter, 1989, pp.12–14; Jenny Zimmer, 'Throwing the Baby Out with the Bath Water', *Ausglass*, Summer, 1990, pp.6–9

11. *Ausglass 1989 Conference Report*, 1989, p.11

12. Anderson, Nola, 'Ausglass Advance', *Craft Australia*, Summer,1991, pp.14–17, and p.17

13. Ibid., p.15

14. Ausglass Conference Synopsis, and Sylvia Kleinert, 'An Historical Context', in *Ausglass Magazine*, Post Conference Edition, 1991, p.5

15. Noris Ioannou, *Ceramics in South Australia 1836–1986*, Wakefield Press, Adelaide, 1986, pp.332–335

16. *Ausglass*, 1991, p.8 and p.9

17. *Ausglass*, 1991, p.72

18. Noris Ioannou, *Craft in Society*, Fremantle Arts Centre Press, 1992, p.10

19. B. Hirst, 27 Mar 1994; Grace Cochrane, handwritten report to Ausglass Committee, April 1994

20. *Ausglass*, 1991, pp.73 and 74

21. T. Hanning, 22 Mar 1994; *Ausglass* Post Conference Edition, 1991

22. McNeil, op cit., p.34

23. *Ausglass Conference and International Summer School '93*, Canberra School of Art Press, 1993, p.41 and p.43

24. *Neues Glas/New Glass*, (Germany),1992, p.26

25. *Ausglass Conference '93*, pp.9–13, and p.44

26. *Ausglass*, 1993, p.110

27. Interviews: W. Langley, 29 Mar., and S. Skillitzi, 7 Apr 1994; *Ausglass*, 1993, p.117

28. *Ausglass*, 1993, p.58, 62, 63

29. *Ausglass*, 1993, pp.23–28

30. Donald Kuspit, 'Glass Heart: Stylistic Issues in Contemporary Glass', *Glass*, No. 53, 1993, pp.30–35

31. *Ausglass '93*, pp.56–57

32. Interview, W. Langley 29 Mar 1994

33. Tony Hanning, 'The Real Value of Australian Glass', *Ausglass*, Spring/Summer, 1993, p.5; Bronwyn Hughes, Editorial, op cit., p.28

CHAPTER 3: ON THE PLINTH

1. Harvey Litteton, quoted by Finn Lynggaard, in *Ausglass '93*, p.45

2. Noris Ioannou, 'The Craft Exhibition: Workshop, Medium and Text'. in N. Ioannou (Ed.,) *Craft in Society*, 1992, pp.213–214

3. For a detailed chronological survey and analysis of Australia's first decade of

exhibitions in studio glass, from 1974 to 1984, see Jenny Zimmer, 'Studio Glass, Australia. The first decade of exhibitions', *Craft Australia*, 1988, No 4, pp.74–89

4. Peter Ward, 'Through a glass brightly', *The Australian*, 2 May 1979; Interview, W. Langley, 3 Mar 1994

5. Ward, op cit.; Jenny Zimmer, 'New Developments', *Craft Australia*, 1979, No 3, p.22

6. Michael Young, 'Glass Sculpture', *Craft Arts*, No 16, 1989, p.75; Nola Anderson, *Crafts NSW,* Summer 1991, p.15

7. Noris Ioannou, *Ceramics in South Australia 1836–1986: from folk to studio pottery*, (Wakefield Press), 1986, pp.332–333; Peter Ward, op cit.

8. Peter Emmett, *Art Works Glass*, catalogue, Crafts Council of NSW, 1985 (unpaginated)

9. Catalogues of the *First Contemporary Australian Glass Exhibition* (1981), and *Third National Glass Biennial*, 1985, Wagga City Art Gallery.

10. Ibid., 1985 catalogue, p.2

11. Catalogue of *4th National Studio Glass Exhibition,* City Art Gallery, 1988, pp.4 and p.7

12. Ibid., p.9; *Ausglass*, Spring/Summer, 1991/92, p.2; Interview, B. Hirst, 17 Mar 1994

13. Noris Ioannou, 'Breaking a glass tradition', *The Advertiser*, 22 Apr 1992, p.13; Catalogue, *10th Anniversary Australian Glass Triennial*, City Art Gallery, 1991

14. Tony Hanning, 'The Wagga Show and the Language of Glass', *Ausglass*, Winter, 1992, p.16

15. Interview M. Cahill, 7 Mar 1994

16. Interview, J. Le Lievre, 15 Mar 1994

17. Noris Ioannou, *The Culture Brokers*, State Print 1989, pp.35–39

18. Jenny Zimmer, 'Glass from Australia', *Craft Arts*, No 2, 1985, p.54

19. Jenny Zimmer, *Stained Glass In Australia*, Oxford University Press, 1984

20. Earlier exhibitions included USA Glass, and Adventures in Swedish Glass, shown in 1975 and in 1978 respectively, in Adelaide: Interview S. Skillitzi, 29 Apr 1994

21. Jenny Zimmer, 'Ausglass 11' *Craft Australia*, 1983, No 2, p.117; Marc Grunseit, '"Big" is in, but where's the meaning?', *Object*, Autumn, 1993, p.32

22. M. Cahill, 7 Mar 1994

23. Dan Klein, *Glass: Contemporary Art,* 1989, p.83

24. *World Glass Now '88*, Hokkaido Museum of Modern Art, 1988

25. Robert Bell, 'Design Visions: International Directions in Glass', *Ausglass '93*, p.7

26. *Ausglass '93*, p.45

27. Author's notes on Kevin Murray responding to panel discussion, 'Whose Compass/Which Direction?' at *Ausglass '93*

CHAPTER 4: KILNFORMING

1. Geoffrey Edwards, 'Like a Dome of many-coloured glass', *World Glass Now*, Hokkaido Museum of Modern Art, (Catalogue), 1988, p.166

2. Interview, K. Moje

3. Nola Anderson, 'Processes and Idea', *Craft Australia*, 1988, No 3, pp.93–96

4. *Craft Australia*, 1988, No 3, p.72; Interview, S. Skillitzi, 29 Apr 1994

5. Catalogue, *Kilnformed Glass: An International Exhibition*, Crafts Council Gallery of the ACT, 1988

6. The analysis was compiled by Stephen Skillitzi who used a *New Glass Review*, 1991, No 2, pp.74–93, to survey the categories of 100 illustrated works submitted to the Corning Museum New Glass Review No.12. It would be worthwhile doing a more statistically-acccurate assessment using a larger sample size

7. Interview S. Skillitzi, 15 Mar 1994; edited CV notes

8. Interviews, A, Robinson, 31 Mar and 29 Apr 1994

9. Interview, B. Hancock, 1 Apr 1994

10. Interview, P. Tysoe, 4 Apr 1994

11. Interview, R. Morrell, 11 Apr 1994

12. Interview, W. Langley, 29 Mar 1994

13. Interview, S, Redegalli, 13 Mar 1994

14. Interview, M, Kalifa, 4 Apr 1994

15. My thanks to E. McClure for this information. Interview, 28 Apr 1994. What appears to be the world's oldest man-made glass was recently discovered at Nippur in Iran (Mesopotamia). The glass beads date at approximately 2,600 years before Christ. *Ausglass*, Spring/Summer, 1993, p.6

16. Interviews, J. Bohm-Parr, Mar 1993 and 26 Apr 1994

17. Interview, A. Crynes,13 Apr 1994

18. Interview, R. Buddle, 12 Apr 1994

19. Interview, J. Candy, 19 Apr 1994

20. Interview, I. Mowbray, 20 Apr 1994

21. Interview, Paul Sanders, 11 Apr 1994

22. Interview, John Elsegood, 12 Apr 1994

23. Interview, G. King, 13 Apr 1994, and edited CV notes

24. Interview, J. Elliott, 29 Apr 1994; re-edited profile notes compiled by Jane Riley

25. Re-edited profile notes by V. Vilmanis

26. Elizabeth McClure, 'Idioms of the Antipodes', *Glasswork*, Nov 1992, No 13, p.12

27. Ibid., p.14

28. Interview, L. Ryan, 28 May 1994

29. Interviews, G. Mann, 31 Mar and 8 Apr 1994

30. Sallie Portnoy, edited CV notes

31. Interview, D. O'Connor 7 Apr 1994

32. Interview, Deborah Cocks, 12 Apr 1994

33. Personal observations by author during residency in Canberra School of Art. September, 1993. See *Oz Arts*, No 10, 1994, pp.104–107

CHAPTER 5: BLOWN GLASS

1. Interview, D. Wreford, 16 Apr 1994

2. Interview, B. Hirst, 27 Mar 1994

3. Interview, N. Mount, 30 Mar 1994; N. Ioannou, *The Culture Brokers*, State Print, Adelaide, 1989, pp.36–38

4. Jenny Zimmer, 'mesmerising glass worth reflection', review in *The Age*, 28 Sept, p.17

5. Bronwyn Hughes, 'Whose Compass/Which Direction', *Ausglass '93*, p.18

6. Interview, G. Nash, 6 Apr 1994

7. *Ausglass 1989 Conference Report*, 1989, p.11

8. Interview, C. Heaney, 12 Apr 1994

9. Interview, C. Pantano, 25 Apr 1994

10. Interview, Dick Marquis and Dante Marioni, Feb 1994. See *Object*, Issue 1, 1994, p.2

11. Interview, N. Wirdnam, 29 Apr 1994

12. Interview, K. Rowe, 29 Apr 1994

13. Interview, B. **, 27 Apr 1994

14. Interview, E. Kelly, 27 Apr 1994

15. Observations by author, Sept, 1994, Canberra School of Art. See *Oz Arts*, No 10, 1994, pp.104–107

16. Interview, J. Cowie, Mar 1994; edited CV notes

17. Interview, S. Chaseling, 27 Apr 1994

18. R. Wynne, edited CV notes

19. P. Delaney, edited CV notes

20. Interview, D. Wreford, 16 and 29 Apr 1994

21. Interview, S. Procter, May 1994; edited CV notes

22. Stephen Procter, 'Artist Introduction', *Ausglass '93*, p.37; notes taken by author from talk given by Procter at that conference

23. Interview, E. McClure, 27 Mar and 28 Apr 1994

24. Interview, S. Ogishi, 29 Apr 1994; edited CV notes

25. Interview, J. Blum, 18 Apr 1994

26. This section is based on extracts edited from notes by J. Santos and S. Skillitzi, and interviews with the latter

27. Geoffrey Edwards, 'Skillitzi and Santos: An Unholy Alliance', *Craft Arts*, No 27, 1993, p.107

CHAPTER 6: ALTERNATE GLASS PRACTICES

1. Marc Grunseit, 'What is Australian Stained Glass', *Ausglass '93*, Canberra School of Art Press, 1993, p.35

2. For histories of this area see: Jenny Zimmer, *Stained Glass in Australia*, Oxford University Press, 1984; Beverley Sherry, *Australia's Historic Stained Glass*, Murray Child, Sydney, 1991; Peter and June Donovan, *A Guide to Stained Glass Windows in and about Adelaide*, Donovan and Associates, SA, 1983

3. Grunseit, op cit.

4. Interview, D. Wright, 18 Apr 1994

5. Kevin Murray, 'The Importance of Sang-froid', *Craft Victoria*, Vol 23, No 222, 1993, p.9

6. Interview, K. Zimmer, 19 Apr 1994; Ken Lockwood, 'Art Forms in Glass',

Craft Arts, No 1, 1984, p.43

7. Interview, K. Zimmer, 19 Apr 1994; Patrick Hutchings, 'Textures of Light', *Craft Arts*, No 16, 1989, pp.84–89

8. *Contemporary German Glass in Australia 1981*, exhibition catalogue, Goethe Institute and Crafts Board of the Australia Council, 1981, p.36

9. Interview, C. Prest 17 Mar 1994; N. Ioannou, 'A Sense of Place', *Oz Arts*, No 5, 1993, pp.38–41

10. *Glass From Australia*, 1984, catalogue biography, p.66

11. Interview, G. Emmerichs, Jan 1993

12. Interview, G. Mann, 8 Apr 1994

13. Interview, R. Whiteley, 17 Apr 1994

14. Interview, D. Cocks, 22 Mar 1994

15. Interview, K. Eguchi, 19 Apr 1994; edited CV notes

16. Marc Grunseit, 'What is Australian Stained Glass', *Ausglass '93*, Canberra School of Art Press, 1993, p.35

17. Edited CV notes

18. Interview, M. Cahill, 5 Mar 1994; edited CV notes

19. Interviews: R Knottenbelt, Jan, Feb, Mar, May, Apr 1994

20. Rob Knottenbelt, Cutting Glass with Water', *Artlink*, Vol 7, No 2, 1987, pp.86–87

21. Interview, P. Robinson, 20 Apr 1994; edited CV notes

22. Interview, T. Hanning, 16 Mar 1994; edited CV notes

23. Interview, A. Dybka, 21 Apr 1994; edited CV notes

24. Interview, G. Stone, 20 Apr 1994; edited CV notes

25. Edited CV notes; Dan Klein, *Glass A Contemporary Art*, Collins, 1989, p.98; Laurie Drake, 'Artistic Refractions in Optical Crystal', *Craft Arts*, Oct 1985, p.50

26. Interview, S. Skillitzi, Apr 1994

27. Interview, R. Clements, 21 Apr 1994

28. Interview, G. Courtney, 26 Apr 1994

29. Interviews, P. Stadus, 21 Apr and 9 Jun 1994

30. Interview, K. Williams, 22 Apr 1994.

CHAPTER 7: HEART OF GLASS

1. Interview, Ann Robinson, Mar 1994

2. Sylvia Petrova', Individual Glass in Europe — Its Myths, Legends and Reality', *Design Visions*, catalogue, Art Gallery of Western Australia, p.28; 1992 *Ausglass Conference '93*, p.17; Tony Hanning, 'The Wagga Show and the Language of Glass', *Ausglass*, Winter, 1992, p.16

3. Sue Rowley, 'Warping the Loom: Theoretical Frameworks for Craft writing', in N. Ioannou (Ed.), *Craft in Society*, pp.167–168

4. Ibid.

5. Nola Anderson, *Crafts NSW*, Autumn 1991, p.22

6. Vincent Carducci, 'Seasons of Glass: Michigan Invitational Catches Glass at a turning Point', *American Craft*, Aug/Sept 1992, p.69; *Ausglass*, winter, 1989, p.9

7. Frantz, Susanne, *Contemporary Glass*, Harry Abrams, New York, 1989, p.53

8. Ibid.

9. Libensky, Stanislav, 'Glass in Europe: Some observations', in *International Directions in Glass Art*, Australian Consolidated Press, 1982, p.19

10. Janet Koplos, 'Criticism', Glass, (New York), Spring 1994, No 55, p.30; Anthony Storr, *The Dynamics of Creation*, Penguin, 1972, p.289

11. Interviews: T. Hanning, and K. Moje, 29 Mar 1994

12. Interviews: M. Cahill and R. Knottenbelt, 7 and 25 Mar 1994

13. Atsushi Takeda, 'Diversification of Glass Art', *World Glass Now '85*, Hokkaido Museum of Modern Art, 1985, p.161; Meza Rijsdijk, panel discussion, *Ausglass '93*, p.20

14. Interview, P. Tysoe, 12 Apr 1994

15. Interview, W. Langley, 29 Mar 1994

16. Dan Klein, *Glass A Contemporary Art*, Collins,1989, p.29

17. Sue Rowley 'Throwing Stones at Glass Houses: Craft criticism Looks at Glass', *Ausglass '93*, Canberra School of Art Press, 1993, p.56

18. Michael Tawa, *'Poesis* and *Praxis*: Craft, Modernity and the Techne of Architecture'. In Ioannou (Ed.), op cit., 1992, pp.275 and 277

19. Nola Anderson, 'Process and Idea', *Craft Australia*, 1988, No 3, pp.93–96; and Nola Anderson, 'Kilnforming Techniques', *Craft Australia,* Spring, 1988, p.94

20. N. Ioannou, 'Residency at the Canberra School of Art', *Oz Arts*, 1994, pp.104–106; Interview, A. Robinson, 30 Mar 1994

21. Interview, A. Robinson, 30 Mar 1994

22. Interview, K. Moje, 7 Mar 1994

23. Janice Lally, 'The kitchen Chair as Theatre: An Eclectic Approach for Aesthetic Evaluation', Noris Ioannou (ed.) *Craft in Society*, 1992, p.91

24. Anthony Storr, *The Dynamics of Creation*, Penguin, 1972, p.234 and p.205

25. Ibid., p.176

26. *Ausglass Conference and International Summer School '93*, p.36 and p.79

27. Interview, W. Langley, 29 Mar 1994

28. Interview, A. Robinson, 30 Mar 1994

29. Christopher Lasch, *The Culture of Narcissism,* Abacus, 1979, p.90

30. Ibid., p.97

Biographies

HELEN AITKEN-KUHNEN

1952   Born in Melbourne, Australia

Education

1970   First Year Diploma of Art, Frankston Technical College, Vic
1975   Diploma of Art, Gold and Silversmithing 1, Royal Melbourne Institute of Technology, Melbourne
1977   Guest Student, Fachhochschule Düsseldorf, Düsseldorf, Germany
1978   Graduate Diploma, Middlesex Polytechnic, London
1978–81   Gold and Silversmithing workshop with Herbert Schulze and Johannes Kuhnen, Düsseldorf

Related Professional Experience

1980   Design contract work, Ideal-Standard, Bonn, Germany
1981–84   Gold and Silversmithing workshop with Johannes Kuhnen, Kalorama, Vic
1981–   Part-time Lecturer, Royal Melbourne Institute of Technology, Melbourne
1983   Visiting Lecturer, Riverina Murray Institute of Advanced Education, Wagga Wagga, NSW
1984   Gold and Silversmithing workshop with Johannes Kuhnen, Michelago
1986   Associate Diploma, Glass, Canberra School of Art, Canberra
1988   Visiting Lecturer, Otago Polytechnic, Dunedin, NZ
1990   Visiting Lecturer, Fachhochschule Düsseldorf and Idar-Oberstein, Germany
1993   Visiting Lecturer, Fachhochschule Düsseldorf

Exhibitions

1979   Middlesex Polytechnic Degree Show, London
       Palais Wittgenstein (city gallery), Düsseldorf
       Schüler und Lehrer der Fachhochschule Düsseldorf
       Workshop exhibition, Düsseldorf
1980   Centenary Exhibition, Meat Market Craft Centre (Meat Market), Melbourne
       'Jugend gestaltet', Handicrafts Fair, Munich, Germany
       Armschmuck Competition, Schmuckmuseum, Pforzheim, Germany
       'Jugend gestaltet', World Craft Council Conference, Vienna
       Gallery Decus, Nürnberg, Germany
       Workshop exhibition, Düsseldorf
1981   Gallery Orfevre with Frank Bauer, Düsseldorf
       State Award Exhibition, Bielefeld, Germany
       Easter Exhibition, Meat Market, Melbourne
       Bracelet Exhibition, Makers Mark, Melbourne
       'Contemporary German and Dutch Craft', Frankfurt
       Diamond Valley Art Award, Melbourne
       Email Travelling Exhibition, Australia
1982   International Jewellery Art Exhibition, Japan
1983   'Das Tablett', International Competition, Germany
       Enamel Exhibition, Distelfink Gallery, Melbourne
1984   TASTE group exhibition, together with Carlier Makigawa, Lyn Tune, Kate O'Sullivan, Makers Mark, Melbourne
1985   Easter Exhibition, Meat Market, Melbourne
       'Eltham Art Award', Eltham, Vic
       '20th Century Jewellery', Electrum Gallery, London
1986   Easter Exhibition, Meat Market, Melbourne
1987   Easter Exhibition, Meat Market, Melbourne
       Contemporary Jewellery Gallery, with Johannes Kuhnen, Sydney
       'Glass in Public Spaces', Westpac Gallery, Arts Centre, Melbourne
1988   'Glass from Canberra', E.A. Joyce and Sons, Hobart
       '12 Gold and Silversmiths', Solander Gallery, Canberra
       'Kiln Formed Glass', Crafts Council of the ACT, Canberra
       Fluxus Jewellery Gallery, with Johannes Kuhnen, Dunedin, NZ
       Fingers Jewellery Gallery, with Johannes Kuhnen, Auckland, NZ
       Fourth National Studio Glass Exhibition, Wagga Wagga, NSW
1989   'Pâte de Verre Jewellery', solo exhibition, Sydney
       'Schmuckszene '89', Contemporary Jewellery Gallery, Munich

1990   Gallery Neon, with Johannes Kuhnen, Brussels, Belgium
       'Pave', with Johannes Kuhnen, Düsseldorf
1991   Australian Contemporary Jewellery Biennial
       '20 Years Electrum', Electrum Gallery, London
       'Cast of Shadows', Jam Factory, Adelaide
       'Australian Contemporary Design in Jewish Ceremony', Jewish Museum, Melbourne
1992   'New Design Visions', Art Gallery of Western Australia (AGWA), Perth
       'Contemporary Australian Jewellery', Museum of Art, Kyoto, Japan
1993   'Directions: Glass Jewellery', Crafts Council of the ACT, Canberra
       Ausglass (Australian Association of Glass Artists) Members Exhibition, Drill Hall Gallery, Australian National University (ANU), Canberra
       'Glass 3 x 3', Beaver Galleries, Canberra
       Gallery Gold and Silver, with Johannes Kuhnen, Melbourne
       'Art of Adornment', touring exhibition of contemporary Australian jewellery

Public Collections

Gallery Orfevre, Dusseldorf
Victorian State Craft Collection, Meat Market, Melbourne
National Gallery of Victoria (NGV), Melbourne
Victoria State College Collection, Melbourne
Kunstgewerbemuseum, Berlin, Germany
Australian National Gallery (ANG), Canberra
AGWA, Perth
Wagga Wagga City Art Gallery (WWCAG), NSW

Publications

1979   *Schmuck und Gerät*, Palais Wittgenstein, City Culture Department, Düsseldorf
1980   *Jugend gestaltet*, Munich Company for the International Handicrafts Fair
1981   *Manufactum*, State Award of Nordrhein Westfalen, Bielefeld
       Contemporary German and Dutch Crafts, Frankfurt Museum für Kunsthandwerk
       Email International, Kunstverein Coburg
1983   *International Jewellery*, art exhibition, Japan
       Vogue Australia, July
1984   *Craft Australia Year Book*
       TASTE (group exhibition), Makers Mark, Melbourne
1985   Peter Dorman and Ralph Turner, *The New Jewellery Trends and Traditions*, Thames and Hudson, London
       Craft Australia Year Book
1986   Barbara Cartlidge, *Twentieth Century Jewellery*, Abrams, London
       'Light Effects', *Craft Australia*, Spring
1987   *Vogue Living*, November
       Glass in Public Spaces, catalogue
1988   *Craft Australia*, No. 14
1989   'Kiln-formed Glass from Australia', *Craft Arts*, No. 15
       Neues Glas, 1/89
       Ornament, Spring
       Schmuckszene 89, catalogue
       Art Aurea, 2/89, p. 84
1990   *Art Aurea*, 1/90
1991   *First Australian Jewellery Biennial*, catalogue
1992   *Design Visions*, Art Gallery of Western Australia
       Oz Art, 5/92, p. 57
       Object, Summer, p. 19

RUTH ALLEN

1969   Born in Auckland, NZ

Education

1988   Bachelor of Arts (Visual) — one year, Sydney College of the Arts, University of Sydney, Sydney
1988   Hot Glass workshop, Dante Marioni, Whanganui Summer School of the Arts

1989–93   Bachelor of Arts (Visual), Canberra Institute of the Arts (CITA),
          Canberra
Workshops
1989–93   CITA, Canberra
          Neon, Neil Roberts; Blown Glass, Makoto Ito; Lampworking, Giselle
          Courtney; Lampworking, Peter Minsen; Blown Glass, Yoshihiko
          Takahashi; Blown Glass, John Leggot; Glass Technician, John Croucher;
          Sandcasting, Fiona Taylor; Signature Canes, Klaus Moje; Cast Glass,
          Anne Robinson; Glass Painting, Kazumi Ikemoto; Sulphides, Stephen
          Paul Day; Painting, Richard Whitely; Cutting, Stephen Proctor; Bead
          Making, Brian Kerkvliet
1992   Haystack Mountain School of Crafts, Maine, USA: Venetian Goblet
          Making workshop, Lino Tagliopeitra and Dante Marioni
1992   Pilchuck Glass School, USA: Solid Off-Hand Hot Glass Manipulation
          workshop, Pino Signoretto
Related Professional Experience
1992–93   Ausglass Conference Committee
1993   Selection panel, Fondi Travelling Scholarship
Teaching Experience
1990   Demonstration, Jam Factory Craft Workshop, Adelaide
1991   Demonstration, Glebe St Fair, Glebe, NSW
1993   Demonstration, Tokyo Glass Art Institute, Tokyo
1993   Teaching Assistant, Richard Royal/Hiroshi Yamano, Ausglass
          Workshops, Canberra
1993   Teaching Assistant, Richard Royal/Oiva Toikka, Pilchuck Glass School,
          USA
1994   Demonstration, Slide talk, Sydney College of the Arts
1994   Demonstration, Slide talk, CITA, Canberra
Solo Exhibitions
1992   'Fettishes', Nolan Gallery, Canberra
1993   'Pinnacles', Drill Hall Gallery, Canberra
Selected Group Exhibitions
1988   ANZ Glass Prize, Glass Artists' Gallery, Sydney
          'Kiss My Glass', Sydney College of the Arts
1991   Ausglass Members Exhibition, St Andrews College, University of
          Sydney
          'Wearable Glass', Glass Artists' Gallery, Sydney
1992   Christmas show, Glass Artists' Gallery, Sydney
1993   'Sunday Brunch', David Jones, Canberra
          Nationwide student exhibition, Contemporary Art Space, Canberra
          'Women Under Glass', The Door Exhibition Space, Fremantle, WA
          Gallery Artefact, Tokyo
          Kiranis Gallery, Tokyo
1994   'As One', Shotaru Gallery, Tokyo
          'Made in Japan', Glass Artists' Gallery, Sydney
Awards
1992   Fondi Travelling Scholarship
          Work/Study Scholarship, Haystack School of Craft, USA
1994   Nominated Saxe Award, Pilchuck Glass School, USA
Commissions
1992   Captain Classie's Chalice, Achievement Trophy, *Canberra Times*
1994   Junko Design: Restaurant accessories
Memberships
1988–94   Ausglass Society Member
Publications
1991   Jewellers and Metalsmiths Group of Australia, *Wearable Glass*, Glass
          Artists' Gallery
1992   'Spring has Sprung', promotion for Arts, *Canberra Times*
          'Crafting a Scholarship from Glass', *Canberra Times*
1993   *Graduating*, ANU magazine
1994   *State of the Arts*, April–June, p. 11

CLARE BELFRAGE
1966   Born in Melbourne, Australia
Education
1988   Bachelor of Arts, Hot Glass Major, Chisholm Institute of Technology
          (CIT), Melbourne

Workshops
1988   *Pâte de Verre* workshop conducted by Liz McClure, Meat Market,
          Melbourne
1990   Glass Blowing workshop conducted by Lino Tagliapietra, Dante
          Marioni and Richard Marquis, Sunbeam Glass Studio, Auckland, NZ
1992   Organised and participated in collaborative demonstration workshop
          with Nick Mount and Nick Wirdnam, Jam Factory Glass Workshops,
          Adelaide
1993   Demonstration, Hot Glass workshop, Rich Royal, Meat Market,
          Melbourne
Related Professional Experience
1990–91   Assistant (Michael Hook), Resolution Glassworks, Melbourne
          Self-employed glass blower, Meat Market, Melbourne
          Assistant (Rob Knottenbelt), Brittania Creek Glass Studio, Melbourne
1991   Guest Lecturer, Monash University
1991–92   Resident Designer (Traineeship), Jam Factory Craft and Design Centre,
          Adelaide
1992–93   Currently self-employed glass artist working from Nick Mount's glass
          studio
          Adelaide Vice-President, National Executive, Ausglass
Exhibitions
1987   'Australia Glass Designers', David Jones, Melbourne
          'Show Your Colours', Craftlink, Melbourne
1988   'Beauty and the Feast', graduate exhibition, Melbourne
1989   'In House', Meat Market, Melbourne
          ANZ Glass Prize, Glass Artists' Gallery, Sydney
1990   'Masterworks', Parnell Gallery, Auckland, NZ
1991   'Melbourne Makers', Glass Artists' Gallery, Sydney
          'Feasts', Rituals Gallery, Unley, Adelaide
1993   'Origins & Originality', Ausglass Members Exhibition Canberra
          Alice Craft Acquisition, Alice Springs, NT
Currently working on solo exhibition for the Jam Factory Craft and Design
          Centre, SA
Awards
1989   ANZ Glass Prize, Highly Recommended, Sydney
1990   ACI National Glass Award, Finalist, Melbourne
1993   Department for the Arts and Cultural Heritage
Memberships
Associate Member, Crafts Council of South Australia
Ausglass
Collections
Museum of the Northern Territory, Darwin
Numerous private collections

JAN BLUM
Born in 1948
Education
Rozelle School of Visual Arts, Sydney
Bachelor of Arts, Sydney College of the Arts
Graduate Diploma, Visual Arts, Sydney College of the Arts
Hotglass and Lampworking, Pilchuck Glass School, USA
Experimental and Furnace Glass, Pilchuck Glass School, USA
Teaching Experience
1986–87   Assistant to Cherry Phillips and Susan Stinsmhuelen, Ausglass, Vic
1987   Freelance Lecture, Sydney College of the Arts
1988   Keynote Lecture, Ausglass '89, 'Women in Glass', Melbourne
1988   Assistant to Ginny Ruffner, Ausglass, Vic
1989   Glassworking, Bondi Evening College of Adult Education, Sydney
1989   Cock's and Blum's Glass Workshop, Fusing and Slumping Techniques,
          Leichhardt, Sydney
Exhibitions
1984   Christmas Show, Glass Artists' Gallery, Sydney
1985   Students Show, Glass Artists' Gallery, Sydney
1985   'Pertinent Points', Crafts Centre, The Rocks, Sydney
1985   Sydney College of the Arts Exhibition, Pier 2, Walsh Bay, Sydney
1986   Christmas Show, Gates Gallery, Neutral Bay, NSW
1986   Grand Opening Show, Glass Artists' Gallery, Sydney
1986   'Contemporary Craft', James Hardie Showcase, Sydney

1987 Graduate Diploma Exhibition, Glass Artists' Gallery, Sydney
1987 Gay Mardi Gras Art Exhibition, Nidus Gallery, Sydney
1987 'Jan Blum's Naughty Bits', Glass Artists' Gallery, Sydney
1988 'Glass Australia', Gas and Fuel Glass Award, Meat Market, Melbourne
National Womens Art Award Exhibition, Gold Coast, Qld
Fourth National Studio Glass Exhibition, WWCAG, Wagga Wagga, NSW
1989 Australian International Crafts Triennial, AGWA, Perth
North Coast Glass Workers, Epicentre, Byron Bay, NSW
1989 Diamond Valley Art Award, Melbourne
1990 'Designed and Made', Queen Victoria Building, Sydney
1991 'Challenging the Medium', Ausglass exhibition, Blaxland Gallery, Sydney
'Glass Art From Australia', Galerie Rob Van Den Doel, The Hague, Holland; Galerie Art Duverre, Luxembourg, Belgium
'Chicago International New Art Forms Exposition (CINAFE)', Navy Pier, Chicago
1992 Tenth Anniversary Australian Glass Triennial, WWCAG, Wagga Wagga, NSW, touring to Jam Factory, Adelaide; Tasmanian Museum and Art Gallery, Hobart; Queen Victoria Museum and Art Gallery, Launceston; Blaxland Gallery, Melbourne
'Guests from Australia', Jahresmesse Kunsthandwerk Museum für Kunst Gewerbe, Hamburg, Germany
1993 'The Travelling Conch Show', solo exhibition, Glass Artists' Gallery, Sydney
Sculptures in Glass and Glass Lights, Beaver Galleries, Canberra
1994 Australian Glass Show, Contemporary Art Niki, Tokyo

Grants and Awards
1986 Workshop Travel Grant, Crafts Board, Australia Council, to attend Pilchuck Glass School, USA
1987 Scholarship Award, Pilchuck Glass School, USA
Workshop Development Grant, Visual Arts/Crafts Board, Australia Council, for Glass Access Studio 'Cocks and Blum's Glass Workshop'
1991 Ansett Airlines Sculpture Prize, Byron Shire Art Show (collaborative)
Pat Corrigan Artist Grant, freight costs to Chicago
NAVA Marketing Grant Scheme for NSW Artists, freight costs to Germany

Public Collections
WWCAG, Wagga Wagga, NSW
Ebeltoft Glasmuseum, Denmark
Musee des Art Decoratifs, Lausanne, Switzerland
ANG, Canberra
Queensland Art Gallery, Brisbane
Represented in numerous private collections nationally and internationally

Selected Publications
1986 *Craft Australia*, No. 1, Autumn
Craft Arts, No. 8, October/December
1987 *Craft Australia*, No. 4, Summer
Sydney Morning Herald, November
Ausglass Magazine, October, cover story
1988 *Craft Arts*, February/April
'Arts and Entertainment', *The Age*, Melbourne, 29 June
1990 *Australian Collectors Quarterly*, February/April
Craft Arts, No. 20, cover, pp. 63–9
Neues Glas, September
1991 *Interiors Magazine*, Vol. 5, No. 2 pp. 29–30
Sydney Morning Herald, 1 January, p. 12
International Craft, ed. Martina Margetts, Thames and Hudson, London
1992 *Art Museums Association of Australia*, January
1993 *Canberra Times*, 27 January
Dr Joachim Kruse and Dr Clementine Schack von Wittenau (eds.), *Who's Who in Contemporary Glass Art*, Waldrich Verlag, Germany

JUDITH L. BOHM-PARR
1953 Born in Adelaide, Australia

Education
1986–89 Bachelor of Arts (Visual), Major Glass, CITA, Canberra
1993 Creative Design, Cairns, Qld
Instructional Skills, TAFE, Cairns, Qld

Related Professional Experience
1974 Stained Glass workshop, NT
1982 Glass workshops, Darwin, NT
1987 Venetian Hot Glass workshop, Dante Marioni, CITA, Canberra
1988 Assistant, International Master Glass Symposium, CITA, Canberra
1990 Artistic Co-ordinator, Batemans Bay Carnivale, NSW
Adult Education Lecturer, Glass workshops, Batemans Bay, NSW
Part-time Lecturer, Sydney College of the Arts
1991 Lecturer, Glass workshops, Queensland Potters Association (QPA), Brisbane
1991–92 Artist-in-Residence, QPA
1992 Glass lectures and workshops, Gateway TAFE College, Brisbane
Artworks Workshops, Griffith University, Brisbane
Gallery Assistant, The Potter's Gallery, Brisbane
Lecturer, Glass Workshops, QPA, Brisbane
1993 Established studio and glassworks, Cairns
Lecturer, Glass workshops, Cairns

Exhibitions
1984 'A Touch of Glass', solo exhibition, Esplanade Gallery, Darwin
1988 'Made in Canberra', Contemporary Art Space, Canberra
1989 'Spitten Chips', Contemporary Art Space, Canberra
'Old and New and What's Next', Crafts Council of the ACT, Canberra
'Capital Art', Contemporary Art Space, Canberra
'Le Salon Du Succes Fou', CITA Graduating Students Exhibition, Canberra School of Art
'Young Glass', CITA Glass Workshop Graduation Exhibition
1990 'Skupturales Gefab', Gallerie 'L', Hamburg, Germany
Pâte de Verre, Glass Artists' Gallery, Sydney
'Glass', Kingston Gallery, Canberra
Craft Council of the ACT Members Exhibition, Canberra
Alice Springs Acquisition Award, NT
Surry Street Gallery, Darlinghurst, NSW
Studio Alternburg, Braidwood, NSW
Kunsthaus am Museum, Cologne, Germany
Hanover Art Fair, Germany
1991 *Pâte de Verre* and Cast Glass', Kurland/Summers Gallery, Los Angeles
'Challenging the Medium', Blaxland Gallery, Sydney
Hanover Art Fair, Germany
Galerie 'M', Kassel, Germany
Tenth Australian Glass Triennial, WWCAG, Wagga Wagga, NSW
National Craft Acquisition Award Exhibition, Gallery of the Northern Territory, Darwin
Gallerie 'L', Hamburg, Germany
Caloundra Arts and Crafts Festival, Qld
'Selected Solo — Pâte de Verre', McWhirters Artspace, Brisbane
'Quotes from Spring', Crafts Council of Queensland Gallery, Brisbane
'Edibles and Drinkables', The Potters' Gallery, Brisbane
Queensland Potters' Members Exhibition, The Potters' Gallery, Brisbane
1992 'Contemporary Kilnformed Glass', Contemporary Craft Gallery, Portland, Oregon
'International Directions in Glass', Second Australian International Crafts Triennal, AGWA, Perth
Pâte de Verre, solo exhibition, Margaret Francey Gallery, Brisbane
'The Third Dimension and More', Metro Arts, Brisbane
'Museum für Kunst und Gewerbe Hamburg — Jahresmesse', Galerie L, Hamburg, Germany
1993 'Poolside Glass', Sheraton Mirage, Port Douglas, Qld
'Far North Queensland', Radisson Palms, Port Douglas, Qld
Diamond Valley Art Award, Melbourne
Donald and Carol Wiiken Collection, University of Michigan, USA

Awards and Grants
1989 Acquisition Award, Emerging Artist Support Scheme, ANU
1991 Glass Award, Caloundra Arts and Crafts Festival, Qld
1993/94 $10,000 Arts Queensland Professional Development Grant

Commissions
1992 Retailers Association of Qld: Fashion award trophy
Numerous private commissions in Queensland, NSW and NT

Collections

1989   ANU, Canberra
1991   Queensland Art Gallery, Brisbane
        Private collections, Germany
        Daniel Greenburg Collection, USA
1989–92 Private collections in Australia, USA, Germany
1992   AGWA, Perth
        WWCAG, Wagga Wagga, NSW
        Donald and Carol Wiiken Collection, Chicago

Publications

1989   *Pâte de Verre*, a final year thesis, CITA, Canberra
1990   *Southern Star*, 13 July, p. 8
1991   *Neues Glas*, 3/91, p. 55
1992   *Contemporary Kiln-formed Glass*, Bullseye Glass Co., Oregon, p. 18
        Design Visions, AGWA, p. 57
        Craft Arts International, No. 24, p. 100
        Brisbane Review, 11 June, p. 4
        Brisbane Review, 14 May, p. 7
        Brisbane Review, 13 February, p. 5
1993   *Cairns Post*, 3 June, p. 5
        Cairns Post, 19 June, p. 36
        Cairns Post, 3 June, p. 5
        Cairns Post, 19 June, p. 36
        Artfile, p. 483
        Oz Arts, pp. 52–5

MIKAELA BROWN

1966   Born in Sydney, Australia

Education

1982   Advanced photography course, Australian Centre for Photography, Sydney
1983   Higher School Certificate, North Sydney Girls High School, Sydney
1984–87 Bachelor of Arts (Visual), Glass Major, Photo-media Sub-major, Canberra School of Art
1993–   Master of Arts (Visual), Glass Workshop, Canberra School of Art

Selected Workshops

1985–87 1985 Ausglass Conference
        Neon, Neil Roberts
        Photo-images on Glass, Michael Keighery
        Design, Joechem Poesgen
        Venetian Glass Blowing, Dante Marioni
1988   Advanced Hot Glass workshop with Flora Mace and Joey Kirkpatrick, Pilchuck Glass School, USA
1989   1989 Ausglass Conference, Melbourne
1990   Italian Glass Workshop with Lino Tagliapietra, Richard Marquis and Dante Marioni, Auckland, NZ
1991   1991 Ausglass Conference, Sydney
        Solid Off-Hand Glass Sculpture workshop, Loradano Rosin and Louis Scafali, Pilchuck Glass School, USA
        Correll Furnace Building workshop, University of Illinois, Champaign-Urbana, USA
        Toured American Glass teaching programs, studios, museums and galleries
1992   Signature Cane workshop, Klaus Moje, Canberra School of Art
        Hot Glass workshop, John Leggott, Canberra School of Art
1993   1993 Ausglass Conference, Canberra School of Art
        Furnace and Technology workshop, John Croucher, Canberra School of Art
        Theory of Glass workshop, John Croucher, Canberra School of Art

Related Professional Experience

1988–90 Trainee Glassblower, Jam Factory Workshop, Adelaide
1989–91 Taught Beginners' Glassblowing workshops, Jam Factory, Adelaide; Meat Market, Melbourne
1990–91 Artist-in-Residence, Hot Glass Workshop, Meat Market, Melbourne
        Presented a Goblet Making demonstration and slide show, University of Illinois, Champaign-Urbana, USA
        Presented a Goblet Making demonstration and slide show, San Jose State University, California
        Blew glass, San Jose State University, California
1992–93 Workshops Co-ordinator, Ausglass/Canberra School of Art International Summer School
        ACT State Representative, Ausglass
1993   Taught visiting Japanese 3 day glass workshop, Canberra School of Art
        Taught first year students (six week block), Canberra School of Art
        Member of Ausglass Conference working party
        Presented slide show, University of Illinois, Champaign-Urbana, USA

Solo Exhibitions

1990   'Tantalising Goblet Show', Focus Gallery, Meat Market, Melbourne

Selected Exhibitions

1985   Ausglass Members and Students Exhibition, Sydney College of the Arts
1987   Graduate Show, Canberra School of Art Gallery
        'Various Hammers', Final year show with Richard Whiteley, Glass Department, Canberra School of Art
        'Wearable Glass', Glass Artists' Gallery, Sydney
1988   'New Work, New Artists', Glass Artists' Gallery, Sydney
        'Glass from Canberra', E.A. Joyce and Sons, Hobart
1989   'Wealth of Talent', Jam Factory Gallery, Adelaide
        Diamond Valley Art Award, Melbourne
        Ausglass Members Show, University of Melbourne
        Feature artist, Jam Factory City Style, Adelaide
1990   'Goblet Extravaganza', joint exhibition with painter Bob Marchant, Ken Done's Moore Park Gallery, Sydney
        'The Cup That Cheers', Seasons Gallery, North Sydney
1991   'The Decade Show', Canberra School of Art Gallery
        'Appreciating the Medium', Glass Artists' Gallery, Sydney
1992–93 'Pilchuck Glass Exhibition', Seattle
1993   Ausglass Student Exhibition, Contemporary Art Space, Canberra
        'Sunday Brunch', David Jones, Canberra
        'Small Works', Glass Artists' Gallery, Sydney
        'Eggs and their Cups', Remo, Sydney
        'Women Under Glass', The Door Exhibition Space, Fremantle, WA

Awards and Scholarships

1988   Pilchuck Glass School Scholarship, to attend Advanced Hot Glass workshop with Flora Mace and Joey Kirkpatrick, Seattle
1990   ACI Glass Packaging National Glass Award
        Six Months access to the hot shop, Meat Market, Melbourne
1991   Pilchuck Glass School Scholarship, to attend 'Solid Off-hand Glass Sculpture' workshop with Loradano Rosin and Louis Scafali
        Queen Elizabeth II Silver Jubilee Trust Fund, for travel to the USA to attend Pilchuck Glass School
1992   Young Achiever Awards, The Canberra Milk Arts Award

Commissions

1993 Florist of the Year Trophy, Canberra
Canberra Milk: Trophies for Canberra Raiders Football Team
Michael Delaney, Chief Executive, Canberra: Service trophy
ACI, Melbourne: Diploma Milk Trophy

Memberships

1992–93   ACT State Representative, Ausglass

Collections

Interflora
Motor Traders Association
Australian Submarine Corporation
Axel White, General Manager, Adelaide
Jam Factory Craft Collection, Jam Factory Craft and Design Centre, Adelaide
University of Illinois Glass Department, Champaign-Urbana, USA
San Jose State University Glass Department, California
Private collections in Australia, Italy, Japan, Singapore, Sweden, USA

Publications

1990   'Jam Factory Production Glass', *Craft Arts*, September
1992   'Idioms of the Antipodes', *Glasswork*, No. 13, November
        'Glass Gifts', *Vogue* Australia, No. 12, December
Numerous exhibition reviews

ROGER BUDDLE

1940   Born in Adelaide, Australia

Education
1982   Flat Glass Techniques course, Paul Kempen, Adelaide
1991   Glass Painting Techniques workshop, Paddy Robinson, Sydney
1991–   Bachelor of Design, Ceramics and Glass, University of South Australia
Related Professional Experience
1982–89   Part-time Flat Glass work
1989–91   Full-time Flat Glass work
Selected Solo Exhibitions:
1990   Studio 20, Blackwood, SA
        Crafts Council of South Australia, Foyer Exhibition
Selected Group Exhibitions
1993   'Designing Ways', Studio 20, Blackwood, SA
        Ausglass Student Exhibition, Canberra
        'Noahs Art', Crafts Council of South Australia Member's Exhibition
        National Craft Acquisition Award, Darwin
        Alice Springs Craft Acquisition Award, Alice Springs
1992   Lombard Art Gallery, Exhibition at the Adelaide Zoo
1991   Ronald Adams Victor Harbor Gallery
        Lombard Gallery, Exhibition at the Adelaide Zoo
1990   Lombard Art Gallery, Stepney, SA
        National Craft Acquisition Award Exhibition, Darwin
Memberships
Ausglass
Crafts Council of South Australia (accredited member)
National Association for the Visual Arts
Arts Law Centre of Australia
Publications
1993   *New Glass Review 14*, Corning, New York

MAUREEN CAHILL
Education
1968–72   Painting Diploma, ESTC National Art School, Sydney
1973   Experimental glasswork in home/studio
1974–77   BA (Hons) Glass, Stourbridge, UK
        Exchange student visit, Reitveld Academy, Amsterdam
        Studied ancient glass techniques, Egypt
        Study tour of Europe, visiting various workshops, collections, factories
        and studios
1983–88   MA (Visual Arts), NSW Institute of the Arts
Related Professional Experience
1977   Established Glass Department, Sydney College of the Arts
1977–   Lecturer in Charge, Glass Studios, Sydney College of the Arts
1978   Instigator and coordinator, First National Glass Conference, Sydney,
        where Ausglass was formed
1984   Judge, Philips First New Zealand Glass Award, Auckland, NZ
        Exhibitor and attendee, Glass '84, Tokyo
1982–83   Instigator and co-founder, Glass Artists' Gallery, Sydney
Currently   Director of Glass Artists' Gallery, Sydney
Exhibitions
1977   Stourbridge Graduate Glass Show
1979   'Australian Glass', Springwood Gallery, NSW
1980   Meat Market, Melbourne
1981   'Contemporary Australian Glass', WWCAG, Wagga Wagga, NSW
        Contemporary Glass Exhibition, Australia, Canada, USA, Japan
        National Museums of Modern Art, Kyoto and Tokyo
1982   'Hot, Flat and Slumped', Fine Arts Gallery, Tas
        Opening Exhibition, Glass Artists' Gallery, Sydney
1983   Second National Glass Biennial, WWCAG, Wagga Wagga, NSW
        'Contemporary Australian Glass', Gallery Alpha, Maroochydore, Qld
        'Australian Selected Glass Exhibition', Jam Factory, Adelaide
        'Wearable Glass', Glass Artists' Gallery, Sydney
        Christmas Show, Glass Artists' Gallery, Sydney
1984   Meat Market, Melbourne
        'Glass '84', Tokyo; Kobe, Japan
        Phillips New Zealand Glass Award, Auckland City Art Gallery, NZ
        'Wearable Glass', Glass Artists' Gallery, Sydney
        'Constructions', Crafts Council Gallery, The Rocks, Sydney
        Christmas Show, Glass Artists' Gallery, Sydney

'Glass from Australia and New Zealand', Hessisches Landesmuseum,
        Darmstadt, Germany; Romont, Switzerland; Chartres, France
1985   'Exposition', Glass Artists' Gallery, Sydney
        'Wearable Glass', Glass Artists' Gallery, Sydney
        Ausglass Members Exhibition, Sydney
        Third National Glass Biennial, WWCAG, Wagga Wagga, NSW, and
        touring
1987   'Glass in Public Spaces', Westpac Gallery, Arts Centre, Melbourne
1988   Major Architectural Commission, Parliament House, Canberra
1990   Glass Sculpture, The Blaxland Gallery, Melbourne
1991   'Fabrications', Reptilia Salon, Sydney
        'CINAFE, Navy Pier, Chicago: architectural installation work
        represented in video presentation by Crafts Council of Australia in
        association with Austrade
Awards and Grants
1974–77   Crafts Board, Australia Council Grant for overseas study
1987–89   Crafts Board, Australia Council Grant for research: Architectural glass
        applications in public spaces
Commissions — Major Architectural Commissions
1987–88   'Willy Willy' Glass Installation, House of Representatives Advisers
        Waiting Space, Parliament House, Canberra
1987–88   Suspended Light in collaboration with Helge Larsen, House of
        Representatives Stairwell, Parliament House, Canberra
1988–91   'Seaclouds', Glass Installation, Condux Building, Sussex Street, Sydney
1989-90   'Shoreline', Glass Installation, World Congress Centre, Melbourne
1992-93   'FanFair', Glass Installation, Mirah Silver, Indonesia
Selected Publications and Citations
1990   'Glass in Architecture', World Conference of Glass Education,
        Barcelona, Spain
1991   'Freeform Glass in Public Spaces', *Ausglass Magazine*, Post Conference
        Edition
1976   *Glass Review*, microfiche, Corning Museum of Glass, New York
1981   *Glass in the Modern World*, Tankosha, Kyoto
1982   *Craft Australia*, Winter
1984   *Financial Review*
1984–85   *Craft Australia Year Books*
1985   *Vogue Living*
1986   *Courvoisier's Book of the Best*,
1986–87   *Craft Australia*
1988   *Expressing Australia Art*, Parliament House
        Progressive Architecture
1989   Dan Klein, *Glass: A Contemporary Art*, William Collins, London
        Australia Business Collectables,
1992   Nola Anderson, *Craft NSW: History of Contemporary Glass*
        Grace Cochrane, *The Craft Movement in Australia: A History*, Sydney
        University Press
Collections
Powerhouse Museum of Applied Arts and Sciences (Powerhouse Museum),
Sydney
WWCAG, Wagga Wagga, NSW
Janos Collection, New York
Queensland Art Gallery, Brisbane
Tasmanian Art Gallery, Tasmania
NGV, Melbourne
Ebeltoft Glasmuseum, Denmark
Auckland Museum, NZ
Numerous private collections

ROBYN CAMPBELL
1964   Born in Australia
Education
1990–93   Bachelor of Arts (Visual), Institute of the Arts, ANU — Major Glass
        (Workshop Head: Klaus Moje 1990–92, Stephen Proctor 1992–93),
        Sub-major Printmaking (relief and etching)
Workshops
1987   Glass Painting, Fusing and Slumping, Deb Cocks and Bridget Hancock
        (Australia)
1990   Lamp Working, Giselle Courtney (Australia)

Lost-wax Casting, Ann Robinson (NZ)
1991   Sandcasting, Fiona Taylor (Australia)
Glass Fusing, Klaus Moje (Australia/Germany)
Cutting and Polishing, Pavel Tomecko (Australia/Chechoslovakia)
Glass, Furnace and Kiln Technology, John Croucher (NZ)
1992   Printmaking using Glass Plates, Brian Hirst and Basil Hall (Australia)
Murrini Cane Making, Klaus Moje (Australia) and John Leggot (NZ)
Pâte de Verre, Christina Kirk (UK)
Lamp Working, Peter Minson (Australia)
1993   Glass Technology, John Croucher (NZ)

Related Professional Experience
1988-89   Travel and work in Europe and the Middle East
1992–93   Co-ordination and co-curator (1 of 2), 1993 Ausglass Nationwide
Student Exhibition, Galleries 1 and 2, Canberra Contemporary Art Space,
Braddon, ACT
1993   Teaching Assistant for Katsuya Ogita (Japan) and David Reekie (UK) in
the Kiln Forming Workshop at the 1993 Ausglass Summer School
1994   Visiting Lecturer (4 weeks), Glass Casting workshop, CITA, Canberra,

Group Exhibitions
1993   'Surfacing', Glass Artists' Gallery, Sydney
1993   'Interval', Canberra School of Art Graduating Student Exhibition,
Canberra School of Art Gallery, Canberra
1993   'Surfacing', Glass Graduate Exhibition, Glass Workshop, Canberra
Institute of the Arts
1993   'Women Under Glass', The Door Exhibition Space, Fremantle, WA
1993   'Origins & Originality', Ausglass Members Show, Drill Hall Gallery,
Canberra
Ausglass Nationwide Student Exhibition, Contemporary Art Space,
Canberra
1992–93   'Sister Trust Exhibition', Contempory Art Space, Canberra

Commissions
1992   Motor Traders Association, Canberra: untitled

Collections
1994   Becky and Jack Benaroya (USA), private collectors belonging to The
Collectors Circle, which is affiliated with The American Craft Museum
of New York

JUDITH CANDY
Education
1972–74   National Art School, Sydney
1987   Diploma of Teaching, studied Glass as liberal study, South Australian
College of the Arts and Education (SACAE), Adelaide
1988–   Bachelor of Education, studied Glass as liberal study, SACAE, Adelaide
1992   Study tour of India and Nepal to further research glass techniques and
bronze casting
Studied Bronze Casting, University of South Australia
Established Studio
1993   Bachelor of Design, Glass, University of South Australia

Demonstrations and Workshops
University of South Australia Design School:
1993   Ian Mowbray
Nick Mount and Clare Belfrage
1991   Richard Morrell
Tim Shaw
1990   Vikki Torr
Ian Mowbray
1989   Meza Rijsdijk

Related Professional Experience
1992   Tutor, Drawing, University of South Australia
Part-time Lecturer, Glass Studies, University of South Australia
1994   Working from own studio

Exhibitions
1987–93   Various student and local group exhibitions
1991   'The Glass Bowl', Distelfink Gallery, Melbourne
1992   'Out Of The Fire', Graduate Exhibition, Artspace, Festival Centre,
Adelaide
1993   ACI Glass Award, Meat Market, Melbourne
'Designing Ways', Studio 20, Blackwood, SA

'Bowls to Behold', Distelfink Gallery, Melbourne
'Life Is But A Dream', Ceramics Conference, Barr Smith Library,
Adelaide University, SA
1994   'American Collectors Show', Glass Artist's Gallery, Sydney

Memberships
Ausglass
Crafts Council of South Australia

Collections
Dale and Doug Anderson, New York
Numerous private collections

Publications
1994   *Prospectus*, University of South Australia

SCOTT CHASELING
1962   Born in Tamworth, NSW, Australia
Education
1980   Bachelor of Arts (Fine Arts), Sculpture, studied 2 years, SACAE,
Adelaide
1982   Sculpture Certificate, North Adelaide School of the Arts and Craft
1983–86   Trainee Glassblower, Jam Factory Craft Workshop, Adelaide
1989   Pilchuck Glass School, USA
1 (Graduate Workshop)
2 (Hot Glass Sculpture, Pino Signoretto, William Morris)
1990–91   Post Graduate Degree, Hot Glass, Canberra School of the Arts

Related Professional Experience
1980   Member Contemporary Arts Society
1982–85   Member Experimental Arts Foundation, SA
Royal Art Society of South Australia
1984   Sculpture studio, Central Art Studios, SA
1986   Constructed Hot Glass Studio at the Canberra School of the Arts
1987   Assistant to Dante Marioni Workshops (SA, ACT), visiting artist from
the USA
1988   Constructed Hot Glass studio with Christopher Wright
1989   Assistant to Dante Marioni, Seattle
Assistant to Dale Chihuly and Lino Tagliapietra, USA
1991   Temporary supervisor of Hot Glass Workshop, Meat Market, Victoria
1992   Constructed Hot Glass studio, ACT

Teaching Experience
1986–87   Teacher, Hot Glass, Canberra School of the Arts
1987   Artist-in-Residence, Magill College of Advanced Education, SA
1989   Demonstration, Lubbock Tech., Texas
Workshops, Tulane University, New Orleans; Ohio State University
1991   Workshop, Ausglass Conference, Sydney, NSW
1991   Part-time Teacher, Monash University, Melbourne
1991   Week-end workshops, Access Glass, Meat Market
1993   Teaching Assistant to Richard Royal and Hiroshi Yamano, Ausglass
Conference, Canberra
1993   Workshop, Notojima Glass Studio, Japan
1993–94   Teacher, Hot Glass, Tokyo Glass Art Institute, Japan

Solo Exhibitions
1984   'Glass', Harrington Art Gallery, SA
1985   'Fighting Against Time for a Lighter Side to Glass', Jam Factory Gallery,
Adelaide
1991   'Recent Works', Blackwood Street Gallery, Melbourne
1993   'Difficult Loves', Art Stop, ACT
1993   'Offering Cups', Karanis Gallery, Shibuya, Tokyo, Japan

Duo Exhibitions
1988   'Chaseling-Wright Glass' with Christopher Wright, Theatre 62,
Adelaide Festival Of Arts
1994   'As One' with Ruth Allen, Shotoru Gallery, Tokyo
1994   'Made in Japan' with Ruth Allen, Glass Artists' Gallery, Sydney

Selected Group Exhibitions
1982   'A Sculptured Show', Royal Art Society, SA
1983   'Glassworks', Australian Craft Gallery, Qld
'State of Craft', Mount Gambier, SA
'Artists in St Peters', Adelaide
1984   'Australian Glass 84', Darmstadt, Germany
'Three Cone-Binations', MGM Gallery, Melbourne

1981–84 Bachelor of Fine Art, CIT, Melbourne
1981–88 Tutor in Glass Painting and Design, CIT, Melbourne (now Monash University)
1988 Australia Council Artist Development Grant

Exhibitions
1981 'Contemporary German and Australian Glass', Meat Market, Melbourne
1981–88 'Australian Crafts', Meat Market, Melbourne
1982 'Directions', Glass and other media at Victoria House, London, United Kingdom
1983 'Cut and Run', Victoria craft people in glass, Meat Market, Melbourne
1983–85 Second/Third National Glass Biennial, WWCAG, Wagga Wagga, NSW
1984–86 'Glass from New Zealand and Australia', Hessisches Landesmuseum, Darmstadt, FRG, Chartre (France), Musee du Vitrail, Romont (Switzerland)
1985 'World Glass Now', Hokkaido Museum of Modern Art, Sapporo, Japan
1986 'Survey Two', Ceramics, textiles, glass, Devise Gallery, South Melbourne
'Continuity and Change', Nanjing College of the Arts, China
1986–87 'View Points', Meat Market, Melbourne
1987 'Glass in Public Spaces', Westpac Gallery, Arts Centre, Melbourne
1988 'World Glass Now', Hokkaido Museum of Modern Art, Sapporo, Japan
'Whitehall Enterprises', Linden Gallery, St Kilda, Melbourne
1989 International Craft Triannual, Perth
'Laboutique Fantastique', Adelaide Arts Festival
1990 'Decorex '90', Melbourne
'Garden Art', Adelaide Festival Centre
'Whitehall' Adelaide Festival Centre
1991 'Whitehall', Melbourne Contemporary Art Gallery
'World Glass Now '91', Hokkaido Museum of Modern Art, Sapporo, Japan
'The Alternative Home Show', Blaxland Gallery
1992 'Home is Where the Art is', Adelaide Festival Centre
'Design Visions', AGWA, Perth
'Whitehall', Melbourne Contemporary Art Gallery
1994 'Hock Baroque', Plimsol Gallery, Hobart, and Tasmanian Regional Gallery (touring)

Commissions
1987 Anglican Church, Wonthaggi, Victoria: Window
1988 B and V Council Residence, 46 George Street, Prahran, Victoria: Windows
Scanlon and Theodore, Chapel Street, Prahran, Melbourne: Windows
1989 Mariana Hardwick, Bourke Street, Melbourne: Skylight
1990 Mentone Hotel, Beach Road, Mentone, Melbourne: Skylight
Holy Trinity Church of England, East Melbourne: Crucifix
Simply French Pastry, Toorak Road, South Yarra: Steel and glass gates, picture frames etc
1993–94 St George's Cathedral, Perth: Windows

Collections
CIT, Melbourne, Glass Collection
NGV, Melbourne
Powerhouse Museum, Sydney
AGWA, Perth
Queensland Art Gallery, Brisbane
Hokkaido Museum of Modern Art, Sapporo, Japan
Carusa No Sato, Museum of Glass Arts, Hiroshima, Japan
Victoria State Craft Collection, Melbourne
WWCAG, Wagga Wagga, Glass Collection
City of Box Hill Art Gallery, Vic
City of Footscray Art Collection, Vic
Melbourne CAE Art Collection

Publications
Various exhibition catalogues as well as:
1982 *Neues Glas*, 1/82, pp. 27, 30
1984 *Craft Australia*, Spring, p. 90
Crafts Arts, October/December, p. 44
Neues Glas, 4/84, pp. 213, 239
Jenny Zimmer, *Stained Glass in Australia*, Oxford University Press, pp. 138, 154

1985 *Crafts Arts*, January/March, p. 55
1986 *American Craft Magazine*, February/March, p. 17
Craft Victoria, 4/86, pp. 3, 11
Craft Victoria, 5/86, pp. 8, 14
Artforce No. 53, p. 60
Craft Arts, May/July, p. 91
Craft Australia Year Book, pp. 83, 84
1987 *Craft Victoria*, 4/87, p. 14
Craft Arts, June/August, p. 109
1988 *Interior Design* No. 12, pp. 47, 48, 90–9
Craft Victoria, 3/88, p. 7
Ausglass, Autumn, pp. 15, 16 and cover
Belle, October/November, p. 14
Craft Victoria, 6/88, p. 2, 3
Interior Design, No. 13, p. 60
1989 *Interior Design*, No. 16, pp. 80–1
Belle, February/March, p. 15
Australian House and Garden, March, p. 21
Vogue Living, April, pp. 116–19
1990 *Vogue Living*, June/July, pp. 39–58
Vogue Australia, March, p. 48
Belle Year Book, December, p. 88
1991 *HQ Magazine*, March, pp. 70–5
Vogue Living, June/July, pp. 80–5
Vogue Australia, December, p. 100
1992 Grace Cochran, *The Crafts Movement in Australia*, pp. 315, 380, 390, 400
Neues Glas , 4/92, pp. 12, 17
1993 *Home Beautiful*, January, pp. 74–6
Vogue Entertaining, February/March, pp. 44–51
Vogue Entertaining, June/July, p. 74
1994 *Arts Magazine*, No. 5, p. 55

MARC DAVID GRUNSEIT
1952 Born in Sydney, Australia
Education
1977 MB, BS, University of New South Wales
Self taught
Attended courses, workshops and master classes in the following disciplines:
Architectural Stained Glass Design
Colour and Design
Glass Blowing
Kiln Techniques and Glass Casting
Surface decoration Techniques
1985 Jochem Poensgen Masterclass in Advanced Architectural Stained Glass Design, Sydney
1986 Second International Stained Glass Seminar, Kevelaer, Germany
1988/89 Lutz Haufschild Architectural Glass Design Masterclass, Sydney, as Technical Assistant
1992 Narcissus Quagliata Architectural Stained Glass Design seminar, Reno, Nevada, USA
Solo Exhibitions
1984 'Lights of Fantasy' in conjunction with the Festival of Sydney
1990 Holdsworth Galleries, Sydney
1991 Holdsworth Galleries, Sydney
Selected Group Exhibitions
1984 'Light Sources', Glass Artists' Gallery, Sydney
'Glass Glorious Glass', Craftworks, The Rocks, Sydney
Sheer Magic, ANZ Exhibition Centre, Martin Place, Sydney
1985 Royal Easter Show, RAS Showground, Sydney
Craft Expo 85, Centrepoint, Sydney
Christmas Show, Glass Artists' Gallery, Sydney
1985/87/89 Ausglass Members Exhibitions, Sydney and Melbourne
1986 'Glass on Edge', Glass Artists' Gallery, Sydney
1986–87 Annual Review, Hamilton Design Gallery, Sydney,
1989 'Index 89', Interior design show, Darling Harbour, Sydney
'Designed and Made', Crafts Council of NSW, Sydney
1989 Northern Territory Craft Acquisition, Darwin Art Gallery
1989–90 Australian Craft Show, RAS Showground, Sydney

1990	Lakeside Hotel, Canberra
1991–92	Crafts Council of Australia boutique, David Jones, Sydney
1993	Northern Territory Craft Acquisition, Darwin Art Gallery
	Craft Australia franchise, David Jones, Sydney
	The Bougainvillea Festival Art Exhibition, Framed Gallery, Darwin
	Studio Showcase, Rozelle, Sydney

Selected Commissions

1984	Wolper Jewish Hospital, Sydney: Freeman Memorial Triptych
1984–85	Royal Alexandra Hospital for Children, Sydney: Laminated glass panels for Chapel
1985–86	Mason Residence, Sydney: 13 sq metre Tiffany-style panels, comprising over 5000 pieces of glass; and a subsequent window, 1993
1986	Rubin Residence, Sydney: 8 sq metre panels (see *Australian House and Garden,* June 1988)
1987	Star of the Sea Church, Watsons Bay, Sydney: Pair nave windows
1988	Sydney Town Hall: Pair Bicentennial Commemorative windows for front entrance
	The Prince Henry Hospital, Little Bay, Sydney: Link corridor panels
	Chapel by the Sea, Bondi, Sydney: Pair contemporary Sanctuary windows
1989	North Shore Memorial Synagogue, Lindfield, Sydney: Construction of Rev. Katz Memorial Reredos, 25 sq metre
1989–90	Residence of Danny La Rue, Sydney: Stained glass windows
1990	St Vincents Hospital, Sydney: Painted stained glass for Chapel panel
	Church of St Peter Chanel, Berala, Sydney: Painted stained glass for 12 sq metre window
1992	Wolper Jewish Hospital, Sydney: 10 panel narrative depicting history of medicine

Selected Restoration Panels

1987	'Roslyn', Coogee, Sydney: Entrance, landing and lantern panels
1988	'Neeoola', Randwick, Sydney: Entrance
1990	St Saviour's Anglican Church, Redfern, Sydney: Vestibule window
	St Mary's Anglican Church, Waverley, Sydney: 3 altar windows (built 1864: *Australia's oldest locally made stained glass windows*); and 2 west windows in 1992
1991	University of Sydney: Women's College and Medical School windows
	St Mathew's Anglican Church, Surry Hills, Sydney: North nave window
	Our Lady of the Rosary Catholic Church, Kensington, Sydney: Painted stained glass for earthquake damaged panels
1992–93	St Luke's Anglican Church, Clovelly, Sydney: 3 altar windows and 1 north nave window,
1993	Woollahra Council Chambers, Sydney: Entrance panel

Recent Public Lectures

1992	World Glass Congress, Reno, Nevada, USA with assistance from CCA
1993	Ausglass Conference, Canberra,

Professional Associations

Australian Contributing Editor, *Professional Stained Glass Magazine*, USA
Member Crafts Council of NSW
Member Arts Law Centre
National President, Ausglass, 1989–90
NSW Flat Glass Representative, Ausglass, 1987–88
Represented in the permanent slide library of Crafts Council of Australia

Publications

1987	*Ausglass* Magazine, Winter
	Second International Architectural Stained Glass Seminar Book, Germany
	Craft Arts, July (Co-author)
1993	*Object* (CCNSW) Autumn
	Ausglass Conference Papers

MIES GRYBAITIS

1968	Born in Australia

Education

1987	Watercolour Painting Open Art Course, Canberra School of Art
1988	Life Drawing Open Art Course, Canberra School of Art
1989	Painting (Oils and Acrylics) and Portfolio Presentation Open Art Courses, Canberra School of Art

1990–93	Bachelor of Arts (Hons — Visual Art), CITA, Canberra

Workshops Completed

1991–93	Casting Glass, Ann Robinson
	Glass Cutting and Polishing, Pavel Tomecko
	Glass Painting, Kazumi Ikemoto
	Glass Blowing, Yoshi Takihashi
	Pâte de Verre, Christina Kirk
	Lamp Worked Glass, Giselle Courtney
	Glass Blowing, John Leggott
	Glass Chemistry, John Croucher
	Murrini Cane Making, Klaus Moje and John Leggott
	Glass Painting, Elizabeth McClure
	Sulphides, Stephen Paul-Day
	Sandcasting, Fiona Taylor
	Lamp Worked Glass, Peter Minson
	Fusing Glass, Klause Moje, Kirsty Rae
	Glass Cutting and Polishing, Stephen Procter and Franz Hoeller

Related Professional Experience

1993	Assistant Convener and Technical Assistant, Cold Glass Workshop, Ausglass Conference, Canberra

Exhibitions

1989	The Depo Resturant, Canberra
1991	Glass Workshop Exhibition, Gallery Foyer, Canberra School of Art
1992	Nationwide Student's Exhibition, Contemporary Art Space, Canberra
	Group Show
1993	'Interval', Graduate Exhibition, Drill Hall Gallery, Canberra
	'Surfacing', Glass Workshop Gallery, CITA, Canberra
	'Women Under Glass', The Door Exhibition Space, Fremantle, WA

Publications and Awards

1993	Review by Edward Arrowsmith, Australian*Craftwest* magazine, Summer
	EASS Collection Purchase Award, ANU

BRIDGET HANCOCK

Born in 1959

Education

1979–82	Bachelor of Arts, Adelaide University
	Diploma of Jewellery/Silversmithing, South Australian CAE
	Associate Diploma of Photography, South Australian CAE
1984	Diploma of Education, Sydney CAE
1993–94	Post Graduate Design, University of Technology, NSW

Related Professional Experience

1981	Stained Glass Workshop with Terry Beaston, Tatachilla, SA
1983	Design Workshop with Paul Marioni, Ausglass Conference, Adelaide
	Moved to Sydney to work with Mitch Foley Stained Glass and Restoration
1984	Kiln Worked Glass Workshop with Maureen Cahill, Sydney College of Art
1985	Kiln Casting Workshop with Clifford Rainey, Ausglass Conference, Sydney
1987	Established Turkeyworks Studio with Deb Cocks and Jan Blum
1989	Architectural Design Workshop with Lutz Haufchild, Ausglass Conference, Melbourne
1991	Attended GAS Conference, Corning, New York
	Sand Casting with John Lewis, Pilchuck Glass School, USA

Throughout this time I have developed my own studio practice, incorporating exhibition work, architectural commissions, and a range of kiln worked limited edition glass selling in australia and Asia

Major Exhibitions

1986	'Sculptured Light', Artes Studios,Adelaide Festival of Arts
1987	'Changing Environments', Crafts Council Gallery, Sydney
1989	'President's' Choice, Meat Market, Melbourne
1991	'Cast of Shadows', contemporary lighting exhbition, Jam Factory, Adelaide
1993	Features Artist, Studio Showcase, Sydney
	'Limited Editions', WWCAG, Wagga Wagga, NSW

Awards and Commissions

1986–87	Excellence Award, NSW Library Association
1987	Ultra Art Film Studio, Sydney: Entrance panels

1989   Northbeach International Hotel, Wollongong: 2 x 15 metre panels
        Rokoko Nightclub, Sydney: Light fittings, bar panels and ceiling
        features
        Metropolis Nightclub, Sydney: Installation with 'broken glass' bar
        The Regent, Sydney: Corporate Christmas gifts
1990   Skygarden, Sydney: Glass World, 2 metre diameter
        Hield Residence, Sydney: Balustrade panels, floor tiles, mirror, lighting
        and 16 sq metre window
        Story of Sydney: 3 x 5 sq metre windows
        Horwitz Graham: Cast glass logo
        Tarasin Jewellery: Display torso
1991   Oceanic Hotel, Sydney: Presidential suite wall; foyer vases
1993   Jack Daniels: 8 ball league trophies
1994   Prudential, Brisbane: 1 metre high cast glass vase

Publications
1986   *Vogue Living* No. 3
1988   *Belle* No. 2
        Interior Design No. 13
        Interior Design No. 19
1990   *Country Style* No. 2
        GH Magazine No. 2
1991   *Corporate and Office Design*, Spring/Summer
        Craft Arts International No. 30
1994   Good Living,*Sydney Morning Herald*, 12 April

TONY HANNING
1950   Born in Victoria

Education
1956–69   Certificate of Art, primary and secondary education
1970   Teacher (Art), Yallourn Technical College, Vic
1971–72   Diploma, Visual Arts, GIAE (Monash University)
1972–81   Director, Latrobe Valley Arts Centre
1976   Studied in the UK and Europe; Industrial Patronage of the Arts
1979   Studied USA Community Arts
1984   Studied glass with Paul Marioni in Seattle

Related Professional Experience
1981   Private enterprise partnership: Budgeree Glass
1982   Set up own Studio
1985   Contracted to work on the mini series 'Sword of Honour', Simpson Le
        Mesurier Films
1987   Teaching Assistant, Pilchuck Glass School, USA
1987–88   Studio in Byron Bay, NSW
1989   Toured with exhibition to Washington DC and Seattle
1991–   Teacher, Central Gippsland College of TAFE
Currently   Independent Artist/Teacher

Awards
The artist does not support (indeed opposes) the award/prize system, and has
published articles on the subject.
1984   Australia Council Grant to study in the USA with Paul Marioni

Commissions
The following are commissions for presentation to dignitaries and noted collections:
APEA to Sir Charles Court, Premier of Western Australia
City of Morwell to Mr Nakasone, Prime Minister of Japan
Australian Zionist Association to Mr Chaim Herzog, President of Israel
Bellini Australia to Bellini Italy
New South Wales Premier to the People's Republic of China
Jean DuPont-Blair to Tulane University, New Orleans
Peter McCallum Clinic to Kevin Heinze
Queensland Premier's Department to the Mayor of the City of Nice, France

Collections
NGV, Melbourne
Latrobe Valley Arts Centre, Vic
Powerhouse Museum, Sydney
Devonport Art Gallery, Tas
City of Rockhampton Art Gallery, Qld
Art Gallery of South Australia, Adelaide
Queensland Art Gallery, Brisbane
Tweed Valley Regional Art Centre, NSW

AGWA, Perth
Victorian State Craft Collection, Melbourne
Art Bank
State College of Victoria, Melbourne
Museums and Art Galleries of the Northern Territory, Darwin
Sale Regional Art Centre, Vic
Pilchuck Collection, USA
Wanganui Community College, NZ
Parliament House, Canberra
Parliament House, Sydney
NSW Premier's Collection, Quong Don, China
WWCAG, Wagga Wagga, NSW
Crafts Council of Australia, Sydney
Tulane University; New Orleans

Agents
Margaret Francey Gallery, Brisbane
Flying Stone, Port Douglas
Lauraine Diggins Fine Art, Melbourne
Distelfink, Melbourne
Powell Street Gallery, Melbourne
William Traver Gallery, Seattle
The Glass Gallery, Bethesda, Maryland, USA

Publications
1981   *Craft Australia*, March
1983   *Vogue Living* , March
        Craft Australia, Spring
1984   *Neus Glas* Vol. 4 No. 1, Germany
        Jenny Zimmer, *Stained Glass in Australia*
1989   Dan Klein, *Glass: A Contemporary Art*
1992   Grace Cochrane,*The Craft Movement in Australia: A History*
        The Survey of Glass In The World, Vol. 6, Kyirudu Art Publishing, Tokyo
        Robert Bell, *Design Visions*, AGWA

COLIN HEANEY
1948   Born in Vancouver, Canada
1956   Moved to California
1967   Arrived in Australia

Exhibitions
1983–87   12 exhibitions in Australia
1988   Gold Coast City Art Gallery, Qld
        David Jones Gallery, Sydney
1989   Linda Garland Design, Bali
        Glass Artists' Gallery, Sydney
        Moree Plains Regional Gallery, NSW
        Primavera Gallery, Virginia
1990   New York International Gift Fair, New York
        Bridge Gallery, Melbourne
        Chapman Gallery, Canberra
        Gallery Amelia, Tokyo
        Thomas Goode, London
1991   Tweed Regional Gallery, Murwillumbah
        Manning Regional Gallery, Taree, NSW
        Bond University Gallery, Gold Coast, Qld
        Dubbo Regional Gallery, NSW
1992   David Jones, Brisbane
        World Expo, Seville, Spain
        Crafters Gallery , Mt Tamborine, Qld
        Bay Gallery of Fine Art, Perth
1993   Australian Craftworks Gallery, Sydney
        Distelfink Gallery , Melbourne
        Jens Monk Collection, Hong Kong
        Glass Canvas Gallery, St Petersburg, Florida
1994   Glass Canvas Gallery, St Petersburg, Florida
        Myer Pacific Fair, Gold Coast, Qld
        Distelfink Gallery, Melbourne

Commissions
1989/90   'Colours of Desire', German Expressionist Masters, Art Gallery of NSW
        and NGV

1990 Multi-Sport World Cup Triathalon: Merchandise accompanying touring exhibitions
'Civilisation: Ancient Treasures of the British Museum', ANG, Canberra
1991 National Mohair Design Awards
Multi-Sport World Cup Triathalon
Kooralbyn Valley Resort, Qld
Michel Roux's Waterside Inn Restaurant, Bray, England
Ambria Restaurant, Chicago
1993 Collaboration with Julie Wileman representing Australia, Interflora World Floral Championship, Stockholm

Collections
Tweed River Regional Gallery, NSW
Queensland Art Gallery, Brisbane
Glass Museum, Majorca, Spain
WWCAG, Wagga Wagga, NSW
Ebeltoft Glasmuseum, Denmark
Private collections in Australia, Germany, Singapore, USA, Channel Islands, United Kingdom, Canada, Italy, Bali, Japan, Switzerland, Spain, Hong Kong, Monaco, France

BRIAN HIRST
1956 Born in Victoria, Australia
Education
Diploma of Arts (Visual Arts), Gippsland Institute of Advanced Education
Conferences Attended
1978 Inaugural Ausglass Conference, Sydney College of the Arts
1980 Second National Ausglass Conference, Melbourne
1983 Third National Ausglass Conference, Adelaide
Attended Workshop with Richard Meitner, Holland
1984 Delivered Paper on Professional Practice, 'Crafts: The Country and the City — Options for the Eighties', Crafts Council of NSW, University of New South Wales
1985 Fourth National Ausglass Conference, Women's College, University of Sydney
1987 Glass Art Society Conference, Philadelphia
Fifth National Ausglass Conference, Melbourne
1989 Art Association Conference, Melbourne
Sixth National Ausglass Conference, Melbourne
1991 Contemporary Making — Current Thinking, Seventh National Ausglass Conference, St Andrew's College, University of Sydney
Glass Art Society Conference, Corning, New York
A Symposium and Exposition of Contemporary Glass, Creative Glass Centre of America, Wheaton Village, Millville, New Jersey
'Industry Interface', National Ceramics Conference, Australian Potters' Society, Brisbane
'Interglass Symposium', Czechoslovakia (sole Australian representative)
1993 'Origins & Originality', Eighth National Ausglass Conference, Canberra
Glass Art Society Conference, Toledo, USA
Related Professional Experience
Guest Lectureships:
1980 Glass Department, Sydney College of the Arts
1981 Sculpture Department, Sydney College of the Arts
1986 Glass Workshop, Canberra School of Art
1987 Tyler School of Art, Philadelphia
Reitveldt Academy, Amsterdam, Holland
1988 Glass Department, Sydney College of the Arts
School of Visual Arts, Newcastle University
Professional Development Seminars, Crafts Council of NSW
1989 Glass Department, Sydney College of the Arts
1990 Professional Development Seminars, Crafts Council of NSW
1991 CGCA Art Alliance for Contemporary Glass Symposium, Wheaton Village, New Jersey
Artist-in-Residence, National Ceramics Conference, Brisbane
1992 Glass Etching, Studio One, Canberra
1993 Glass Workshop, CITA, Canberra
Teaching Positions:

1980–81 Glass Department (Part-time position), Sydney College of the Arts
1987–88 Senior Lecturer, Canberra School of Art
Solo Exhibitions
1982 'Glass Connection', Blackfriars Gallery, Sydney
1985 'Glass by Brian Hirst', Distelfink Gallery, Melbourne
1986 'Cycladic Series', Gates Gallery, Sydney
1992 'Object and Image Series', Blaxland Gallery, Sydney
1993 'A Celebration of Glass', Narek Galleries, ACT
'The Two Australians', The Glass Gallery, Bethesda, Maryland, USA
Selected Group Exhibitions
1978 Gippsland Regional Gallery (photography), Vic
1980 Beaver Galleries, Canberra
1981 First National Glass Biennial, WWCAG, Wagga Wagga, NSW
Cooks Hill Gallery, Newcastle, NSW
'Contemporary Glass: Australia, USA, Canada and Japan', National Museum of Modern Art, Kyoto; National Museum of Modern Art, Tokyo
1982 Blackfriars Gallery, Sydney
Distelfink Gallery, Melbourne
1983 Second Annual Glass Biennial, WWCAG, Wagga Wagga, NSW
Lake Russell Gallery, Coffs Harbour
1984 Glass Artists' Gallery, Sydney
'Australian Crafts 1984', Meat Market, Melbourne
'Glass '84 in Japan', Tokyo and Kobe, Japan
'Glass from Australia and New Zealand', Hessisches Landesmuseum, Darmstadt, Germany
1985 'Australian Hot Glass', Art Gallery of the Northern Territory, Darwin
1987 Canberra School of Art Staff Show, Canberra School of Art, ACT
'The Bowl Show', Meat Market, Melbourne
'ACI Collection', Queensland Art Gallery, Brisbane
'Glass '87 in Japan', Japan Glass Artcraft Association, Tokyo
1988 'Glass Australia '88', Meat Market, Melbourne
'Contemporary Craft Survey', Powerhouse Museum, Sydney
ANZ Glass Prize, Glass Artists' Gallery, Sydney
'Form and Function', Meat Market, Melbourne
Fourth National Studio Glass Exhibition, WWCAG, Wagga Wagga, NSW
1989 'International and Australian Glass', NGV, Melbourne
ANZ Glass Prize, Glass Artists' Gallery, Sydney
'President's Choice', Meat Market, Melbourne
1988–91 'A Free Hand: 40 Years of Contemporary Australian Crafts', Powerhouse Museum, Sydney
1990 'Australian Crafts 1990', Meat Market, Melbourne
'Art Glass from Australia', Galerie Gottschalk-Betz, Frankfurt Am Main, Germany; The Glass Gallery, Bethesda, Maryland, USA
1991 'Challenging the Medium', Blaxland Gallery, Sydney
'Appreciating the Medium', Glass Artists' Gallery, Sydney
'Profiled Personalities', National Ceramic Conference, Brisbane
'The Glass Bowl', Distelfink Gallery, Melbourne
'A Touch of Glass', Bellingen River Gallery, NSW
'Ten Guineas Show', Blaxland Gallery, Sydney
Interglass Symposium, 1991 Crystalex
Featured at CGCA Conference Exposition with The Glass Gallery, Bethesda, Maryland, USA
'Art Glass from Australia', Galerie Art de Verre, Luxemberg; Galerie L, Hamburg, Germany
Rob Van Doel, Den Haag, Holland
1992 'Australian Crafts: New Works from the Powerhouse Collection 1989–92', Powerhouse Museum, Sydney
'International Directions in Glass', AGWA, Perth
Third Australian Contemporary Art Fair, Melbourne, with Blaxland Gallery, Sydney
'Glass and Drawing', Gallery Nakama Annexe, Tokyo
'Crystalex Collection', Lemberk Castle, Czechoslovakia
'CINAFE '92', Navy Pier, Chicago, with Glass Artists' Gallery, Sydney
1993 'Coast to Coast', Myer, Perth
'Ten Guineas Show', Blaxland Gallery, Sydney

'The Bowl Show', Meat Market, Melbourne
'The 21st Annual International Invitational', Habitat Galleries, Michigan
'CGCA Glass Weekend', Wheaton Village, Millville, New Jersey
'CINAFE', with The Glass Gallery, Bethesda, Maryland, USA
1994 'World Glass Now '94', Hokkaido Museum of Modern Art, Sapporo, Japan
'Glass Now 16', Tokyo

Awards
1983 Diamond Valley Art Award, Melbourne
1984 Crafts Board of the Australia Council, Grant: 'Electric Furnace Research'
Crafts Board of the Australia Council, Grant to assist with attendance as the Australian Representative at *Glass '84 in Japan*
1988 'Glass Australia '88', Conceptual Award, Meat Market, Melbourne
1989 Visual Arts/Crafts Board of the Australia Council, Grant to attend the Art Association Conference, Melbourne
1991 Ausglass Award 'Appreciating the Medium', Glass Artists' Gallery, Sydney
(Joint Award with Meza Rijsdijk)
Grant to produce work for an exhibition in the USA — CGCA Conference, Visual Arts/Crafts Board of the Australia Council
Ad Hoc Fund Grant to attend Interglass Symposium in Czechoslovakia, Crafts Council of Australia

Commissions
1986 The Bulletin Magazine and Compac Computer Company 'Top Five Hundred Awards': Commissioned to design and produce award trophy
1987 New Parliament House Project, Canberra
Johns Perry Lifts: Light Lenses
1989 Commonwealth Bank Restoration Project, Martin Place, Sydney: Consultancy to restore and manufacture chandeliers, including design research
Park Hyatt on Sydney Harbour, Campbell Cove: Art Incorporate
1990 The Royal Mint, Canberra: Australia Prize Medallions
Banksia Foundation Environmental Awards: Design and manufacture of trophy
The Australian Opera Trophy: Presented to Dame Joan Sutherland at Sydney Opera House
1991 AMP Corporation, Western Australia
Libesa Trading Co., Singapore
The Royal Mint, Canberra: Australia Prize Medallions
Radison Hotel, Potts Point, Sydney: Art Incorporate
1992 Australian Opera Trophy
Park Lane Hotel, Sydney: Art Incorporate
ANA Hotel, Sydney: Graphics,
Louis Pulsen Lightmakers, Sydney: Exterior lighting for Southbank (Expo Site) Brisbane
1993 Royal Australian Mint, Canberra: Australia Prize medallions

Honorary Positions
1982–83 Board Member, Crafts Council of New South Wales
1984–85 Vice President, Ausglass
1989–91 Member of the Executive Committee, Ausglass

Collections
The ANU Collection
Powerhouse Museum, Sydney
WWCAG, Wagga Wagga, NSW
Diamond Valley Art Collection, Melbourne
Gippsland Regional Art Gallery, Vic
Queensland Art Gallery, Brisbane
AGWA, Perth
Victorian State Craft Collection, Melbourne
NGV, Melbourne
Corning Museum of Glass, New York
Kunstmuseum, Dusseldorf in Ehrenhof and Glasmusuem Hentrich
Ebeltoft Glasmuseum, Denmark
Museum of Modern Art, Kyoto, Japan
Guang Dong Province, China

Selected Publications
1982 *Craft Australia*, Winter, pp. 61–2
1984 *Craft Arts*, No. 5, pp. 94–5
1984/85 *Craft Australia Year Book*
1986 Nola Anderson, 'Working in the Space', *Craft Arts*, No. 9
Maralyn Bell, Studio Glass profile, *Craft Arts*, No. 11, Canada, p. 55
1988 *Victorian State Craft Collection Catalogue*
1989 Dan Klein, *Glass: A Contemporary Art*, pp. 27, 206–8
Pottery in Australia, Vol. 28, No. 4, December
1990 'Art Glass from Australia', *Neues Glas*, Autumn
Craft Arts, No. 20, Summer
1991 E. Bilney (ed.), *Decorative Arts and Design from the Powerhouse Museum*, Powerhouse Publishing
1992 Grace Cochrane, *The Craft Movement in Australia: A History*
Tsureso Yoshimizu, *The Survey of Glass in the World*, Vol. 6, Kyuryudo, Japan
1993 Dr Helmut Ricke, 'Australian Design Visions: International Directions in Glass', *Neues Glas*, 1/93

MARC KALIFA
1951 Born in Paris, France
Related Professional Experience
1975 Worked as a Jeweller in Darwin
1977 Relocated to the Sunshine Coast and started making stained glass windows
1978–84 Ran own 'Translucence Studio' producing commissioned work including some large projects for historical monuments
1985 9 months study tour in France, providing the inspiration to switch to a Hot Glass studio
1986–88 Small production of blown glass pieces
1989 Completion of my own Hot Glass studio
Recent Exhibitions
1989 'Escape from Colour', Latrobe Gallery, Brisbane
'Early Mornings', Plumridge Gallery, Brisbane
'Class Glass', Crafts Council of Queensland, Brisbane
1990 'Dancers', L'Unique, exhibition in conjunction with Arts Festival, Adelaide.
'Carnival of Flowers', Classic Gallery, Toowoomba
Australian Craft Show, Sydney
1991 Glass exhibition, Tweed Shire Regional Art Gallery
'Reflections in Colours', Niecon Tower Gallery, Surfers Paradise
'Glass, Glorious Glass', Aldgate House, Blue Mountains
'Wonders of Glass', Margaret Francey Gallery, Brisbane
'Paperchase Paperweight', Potoroo Gallery, Melbourne
'Facets of Australia', The Crafters Gallery, Gold Coast, Qld
Australian Craft Show, Sydney
1992 'Facets of Australia', The Crafters Gallery, Gold Coast, Qld
Australian Craft Show, Sydney
1993 'Terra Australis', Artist-in-Residence, Mulgara Gallery, Uluru, NT
'Dreamers', Forest Gallery, Batemans Bay, NSW
Australian Craft Show, Sydney
1994 'Dreamers', masks and torsos exhibition, part of the fringe festival, L-Unique, Adelaide
'The Great Goblet Show', Glass Artists' Gallery, Sydney
Group exhibition, Golden Canvas Gallery, Sydney
Collections
Tweed Shire Regional Gallery, NSW
Darwin Museum of Arts and Science
Private collections in Australia, USA, France and Japan

ELIZABETH KELLY
1960 Born in Adelaide, Australia
Education
1985–87 Glass Workshop Trainee, Jam Factory Workshops, Adelaide
1988 Certificate in Art, North Adelaide School of Art, Adelaide
1989–91 Bachelor of Visual Art in Glass, Canberra Institute of the Arts

Related Professional Experience

1987 Studio Assistant for Cedar Prest, Adelaide
1990–91 Studio Assistant for Klaus Moje, Canberra
1992 Demonstrator, Glass Studio, Sydney College of the Arts
Studio Assistant, Gordon Glass Studio, Numurkah, Vic
1993 Lecturer, Glass Studio, Sydney College of the Arts
Research Assistant, Hot Glass workshop, Glass Studio, Sydney College of the Arts
1994 Lecturer, Glass Studio, Sydney College of the Arts

Exhibitions

1987 'Pendingo Au Go-Go', Jam Factory Bull-Ring, Adelaide
1988 Fourth National Studio Glass Exhibition, WWCAG, Wagga Wagga, NSW
Art for Aids, Artzone Gallery, Adelaide
1991 Members Exhibition, Craft Council Gallery, Watson, ACT
Double or Nothing, 1991 Graduating Student Exhibition, Canberra School of Art Gallery
'Triphane', an exhibition of three graduating students from the glass workshop, CITA, Canberra
National Students Exhibition, Exhibition Centre, Melbourne
Tenth Anniversary National Studio Glass Exhibition, WWCAG, Wagga Wagga, NSW
1992 'Pellucid Blown Glass Vessels', solo exhibiton, Glass Artists' Gallery, Sydney
'Wearable Glass', Glass Artists' Gallery, Sydney
'Art in Shopfronts', Taylor Square, Sydney
'Fearless', Craftspace Gallery, Sydney
'100 Goblets Exhibition', Gallery Nakama, Tokyo
'Ceramics and Glass', Jaishree Srinivan and Elizabeth Kelly, Crafts Council Gallery, Watson, ACT
1993 'Reflections in Glass', The Pottery Workshop, Hong Kong
'Reflections in Glass II', The Pottery Workshop, Hong Kong
'Small Works', Glass Artists' Gallery, Sydney
'Sunday Brunch', David Jones, Canberra
'Origins & Originality', Ausglass Selected Members Exhibition, Drill Hall Gallery, Canberra
'A Celebration of Glass', Brian Hirst and Elizabeth Kelly, Narek Gallery, Cuppacumbalong Craft Centre, Canberra
1994 'The Great Goblet Show', Glass Artists' Gallery, Sydney

Awards and Grants

1993 Individual Materials Grant, ACT Arts and Special Events
1991 CITA Emerging Artists Support Scheme, ANU Award

Collections

1991 ANU Glass Collection

GERRY KING

Born in 1945

Education

Doctor of Creative Arts, University of Wollongong, NSW
Master of Science, Education, Alfred University, USA
Advanced Diploma of Teaching (Fine Art), Torrens College of Advanced Education, SA
Diploma of Art (Teaching), South Australian School of Art
Certificate Ceramics, South Australian School of Art
Certificate Printmaking South Australian School of Art
Certificate Hot and Flat Glass, Georgian College, Canada

Related Professional Experience

1981–82 President, Ausglass
1987–89 Vice President, Ausglass
1988 Guest Artist, Niijima International Glass Festival, Japan
1991 Visiting Artist, Carrington Polytechnic, NZ

Selected Exhibitions

1979 First Ausglass Exhibition, Jam Factory, Adelaide
1981 First National Glass Biennial, WWCAG, Wagga Wagga, NSW
'Contemporary Glass: Australia, Canada, USA and Japan', Tokyo and Kyoto Museums of Modern Art, Japan
'Australian Craft', Meat Market, Melbourne

1982 Second Ausglass Exhibition, Jam Factory, Adelaide
1983 Second National Glass Biennial, WWCAG, Wagga Wagga, NSW
1984 'Glass from Australia and New Zealand', Darmstadt, Germany
1985 'Australian Hot Glass', Art Gallery of the Northern Territory, Darwin
Third National Glass Biennial, WWCAG, Wagga Wagga, NSW
1987 'Australian Glass', Indigenous Gallery Melbourne
1988 'Australian Kiln Worked Glass', Canberra School of Art
Fourth National Studio Glass Exhibition, WWCAG, Wagga Wagga, NSW
'Ten Years of Australian Glass', Glass Artists' Gallery, Sydney
International Exhibition of Glass Craft, Kanazawa, Japan
1990 'Australian Contemporary Glass', Meat Market, Melbourne
International Exhibition of Glass, Kanazawa, Japan
1991 'Australian Glass', Distelfink Gallery, Melbourne
1992 'International Directions', AGWA, Perth
International Exhibition of Glass, Kanazawa, Japan
'CINAFE '92', Navy Pier, Chicago
1993 'Australian Glass Sculpture', Beaver Galleries, Canberra
'Origins & Originality', Barrack Gallery, Canberra
'CINAFE '93', Navy Pier, Chicago

Solo Exhibitions

1979 Studio 20, Adelaide
1980 Studio 20, Adelaide
1981 Distelfink, Melbourne
1982 Gallery Maronie, Kyoto, Japan
Solander Gallery, Canberra
1987 Studio 20, Adelaide
1988 Solander Gallery, Canberra
1990 Solander Gallery, Canberra
1991 Seibu Gallery, Tokyo
Glass Art Gallery, Toronto, Canada
Masterworks Gallery, Auckland, NZ
1992 City Gallery Of Wollongong, NSW
Gallery L, Hamburg, Germany

Awards and Honours

1974 Phi Kappa Phi
1975 Grant, Crafts Board of the Australian Council
1980 Grant, Department of the Arts, South Australian Government
1988 Cultural Exchange Fellowship, Bank of Tokyo

Public Collections

Contemporary Australian Glass Collection, WWCAG, Wagga Wagga, NSW
State Craft Collection of Victoria, Melbourne
Queen Victoria Museum and Art Gallery, Launceston, Tas
Diamond Valley Art Collection, Melbourne
Queensland Art Gallery, Brisbane
University of South Australia Collection, Adelaide
Ebeltoft Glasmuseum, Denmark
Art Gallery of South Australia, Adelaide
Auckland Institute and Museum, NZ
AGWA, Perth

Publications

CraftWest: various issues
CraftWest National: various issues
Oz Arts: various issues
SA Crafts: various issues
Craft Australia: various issues
Craft Arts International; various issues
Neues Glas: various issues
1982 *Contemporary Glass in the Modern World,* Tankosha, Japan
1984 *Craft Australia Year Book*
Jenny Zimmer, *Stained Glass in Australia*
1986 *Craft Australia Year Book*
1987 *Contemporary Studio Glass: An International Collection*, Weatherhill/Tankosha, New York
1988 D. Richardson, *Art in Australia*, Longman Cheshire, Melbourne
1989 Dan Klein, *Glass: A Contemporary Art*
1992 B. Thompson (ed.), *Forceps of Language,* Crafts Council of Australia, Sydney
R. Bell (ed.), *Design Visions*, AGWA Perth

ROBERT KNOTTENBELT
Born in 1947
Education
1971   Bachelor of Art, University of Auckland, NZ
1973–74   South Australian School of Art
1975 –77 Jam Factory Workshops, Adelaide
1978–80   SAW, Artists Co-operative, Adelaide
1980–82   211 Inc., Artists Co-operative, Adelaide
1984   Britannia Creek Glass, Private Studio, Wesburn, Vic
1988   World Crafts Council International Masters Classes, Canberra School
              of Art
1990   Artist-in-Residence, ATEC, Regency College of TAFE, SA
1993   Lecture, Smithsonian Institute/Australian Embassy, Washington DC
Selected Major Exhibitions
1979   'Ausglass', Jam Factory Gallery, Adelaide
1981   First National Artglass Biennial, WWCAG, Wagga Wagga, NSW
1981   'Contemporary Glass: Australia, Canada, USA and Japan', Museums of
              Modern Art, Kyoto and Tokyo
1984   'Contemporary Australian and New Zealand Glass', Germany; France;
              Switzerland
1985   'World Glass Now '85', Hokkaido Museum of Modern Art, Sapporo,
              Japan
1985   Third National Artglass Biennial, WWCAG, Wagga Wagga, NSW
1987   'Glass in Public Spaces', Westpac Gallery, Arts Centre, Melbourne
1988   'World Glass Now '88' Hokkaido Museum of Modern Art, Sapporo,
              Japan
1989   First Australian International Crafts Triennial, AGWA, Perth
1990–91   'Australian Art Glass', Germany; Holland; Luxembourg
1992   'National Craft Award', NGV, Melbourne
              'Sculptures de Verre Contemporaines', Musee des Arts Decoratifs de la
              Ville, Lausanne, Switzerland
1992   Second Australian International Crafts Triennial, AGWA, Perth
1993   'Two Australians: Brian Hirst and Rob Knottenbelt', The Glass Gallery,
              Washington DC
1993   'CINAFE '93', Navy Pier, Chicago
1994   'World Glass Now '94', Hokkaido Museum of Modern Art, Sapporo,
              Japan
Awards and Prizes
'Glass in Public Places', T and K Glass Prize
1977/80/86/88 Australia Council Grants
1991–92   Australia Council Fellowship
Collections
Kunstmusuem, Dusseldorf, Germany
Musee des Arts Decoratifs, Lausanne, Switzerland
AGWA, Perth
Queensland Art Gallery, Brisbane
Art Gallery of the Northern Territory, Darwin
Powerhouse Museum, Sydney
Parliament House, Canberra
Victorian State Craft Collection, Melbourne
La Trobe Valley Art Centre, Vic
Publications
1981   *Glass in the Modern World*, Tankosha, Japan
1985   *World Glass Now '85*, Hokkaido Museum of Modern Art, Sapporo,
              Japan
1986   Jenny Zimmer, 'Trivial Postcards', *Craft Australia*
1987   Peta Landman, 'Ausglass Melbourne Conference: Public Glass', *Craft
              Australia*
1988   *World Glass Now '88*, Hokkiado Museum of Modern Art, Japan
1989   *First Perth International Triennial*, AGWA, Perth
              Michael Young, 'Glass Sculpture', *Craft Arts International*, No. 16
1990   Judy Le Leviere, 'Australian Art Glass', *Craft Arts International*, No. 20
1991   *Second Australian International Triennial*, AGWA, Perth
1992   Tsuneo Yoshimizu, *The Survey of Glass in the World*, Vol. 6, Kyurydo Art
              Press, Japan
              Grace Cochrane, *The Crafts Movement in Australia: A History*
              Geoffrey Edwards, 'Labryinths of Light', *Craft Arts International*, No. 24
1993/94   *Who's Who in Contemporary Glass Art*

WARREN LANGLEY
1950   Born in Sydney, Australia
Education
1972   Bachelor of Science (Hons), University of Sydney
1972–78   Glass studies in Australia, England and USA
Selected Exhibitions
Solo and group exhibitions throughout Australia, Japan, USA, Canada, Germany,
Switzerland, France, Holland, Spain, Luxembourg and NZ
1986   Robin Gibson Gallery, Sydney
              Traver Sutton Gallery, Seattle
1987   '30 Years of Glass', Corning Museum of Glass, New York
              'Glass '87', Japan, Tokyo
              'Glass Now 1987', Yamaha Corporation, Japan
              Australian Glass Biennial, WWCAG, Wagga Wagga, NSW
1988   'World Glass Now', Hokkaido Museum of Modern Art, Sapporo, Japan
              'Glass Now 1988', Yamaha Corporation, Japan
              International Glass Invitational, Habitat Gallery, Detroit
              International Exhibition of Glass Art, Kanazawa, Japan
1989   International Glass Invitational, Habitat Gallery, Detroit
              Kurland Summers Gallery, Los Angeles
              Painters Gallery, Sydney
1989   Australian Glass Biennial, WWCAG, Wagga Wagga, NSW
              Monica Trujen Gallery, Bremen, Germany
              International Exhibition of Sculptural Glass, Musee de Artes Decoratifs,
              Lausanne, Switzerland
              'Glass Now 1989', Yamaha Corporation, Japan
1990   Galerie D.M. Sarver, Paris
              The Glass Gallery, Washington DC
              'Glass Now 1990', Yamaha Corporation, Japan
1991   Galerie Suzel Berna, Antibes, France
              Sanske Galerie, Zurich
              Nomados del Vidre, Centre Del Vidre, Barcelona, Spain
              Le Verre, Rouen, Normandy, France
              'World Glass Now', Hokkaido Museum of Modern Art, Sapporo, Japan
              'Glass Now 1991', Yamaha Corporation, Japan
              'Australian Glass', Galerie Gottschalk-Betz, Frankfurt, Germany;
              Galerie Rob Van den Doel, The Hague, Holland
1992   Galerie Rob Van den Doel, Chicago
              International Directions in Glass, AGWA
1993   Galerie Rob Van den Doel, Chicago
1994   Galerie D.M. Sarver, Paris
              'World Glass Now', Hokkaido Museum of Modern Art, Sapporo, Japan
Recent Commissions
New Parliament House, Canberra
Darling Harbour Project, Sydney
John Oxley Memorial Sculpture, Brisbane
Regent Hotel, Melbourne
Snowy Mountains Hydro-Electric Authority, Cooma, NSW
Dow Chemical Corporation, Sydney
ANA House, Sydney
Mayfair Building, Sydney
136 Pitt Street, Sydney
Shortland County Council, Newcastle, NSW
Joint Coal Board, Singleton, NSW
Girvan Corporation, North Sydney
St Stephen's Cathedral, Brisbane
Reserve Bank Training Facility, North Sydney
Clemenger Building, Sydney
Peat Marwick Building, Melbourne
Novotel International Hotel, Sydney
Pacific Fair, Southport, Qld
Overseas Telecommunications Building, Sydney
ANA International Hotel, Sydney
Northern Territory Houses of Parliament, Darwin
MLC Centre, Sydney
Joan Sutherland Centre, St Catherines, Sydney
Awards
1983   Australia Council Grant

1984   Emerging Artist Award, Pilchuck Glass School, USA
1988   Silver Prize, International Exhibition of Glass Art, Kanazawa, Japan

Collections
ANG, Canberra
Musee des Artes Decoratifs, Lausanne, Switzerland
International Museum of Modern Glass, Denmark
Corning Museum of Glass, New York
Yokohama City Art Museum, Yokohama, Japan
Musee du Verre, Sars-Poteries, France
CIRVA, Marseilles, France
NGV, Melbourne
AGWA, Perth
Art Gallery of South Australia, Adelaide
Queensland Art Gallery, Brisbane
Art Gallery of the Northern Territory, Darwin
Powerhouse Museum, Sydney
Hobart Art Gallery, Tas
Victorian Ministry of the Arts, Permanent Collection
Art Bank
WWCAG, Wagga Wagga, NSW
Devonport Regional Gallery, Tas
Manly Art Gallery, Sydney
Canberra College of Advanced Education, Permanent Collection
Warringah Shire Council, NSW
Latrobe Valley Art Centre, Vic
CIT, Permanent Collection, Vic
NSW Premiers Collection, Quong Don, China
Rural and Industrial Bank Collection, Perth
Safeco Corporation, Public Collection, USA
Toho Corporation, Public Collection, Japan

Represented
Christine Abrahams Gallery, Melbourne
Kurland Summers Gallery, Los Angeles
Miller Gallery, New York
Sanske Galerie, Zurich
Galerie D.M. Sarver, Paris
Galerie Rob Van den Doel, Amsterdam
Galerie Suzel Berna, Antibes, France

Selected Publications
1984   *Neues Glas*
        Alan Moffat, *Crafts in Australia*
1985   *Craft Australia*, Spring, pp. 18–24
1987   *Crafts Arts*, February, pp. 30
        Glass Art, Japan, pp. 1–8
        Glass '87 in Japan (catalogue)
1988   *FP Magazine of Art and Design*, March, Japan pp. 38–46
        World Glass Now, Hokkaido Museum of Modern Art, Asahi Shimbun
        (catalogue)
1989   *Design Journal*, October, Korea, pp. 14–15
        Frantz, K. Sussane, *Contemporary Glass, A World Survey From the Corning*
1990   *La Revue de la Ceramique et du Verre*, No. 55, December, France, pp. 42–5
1992   *Craft Arts*, November, pp. 40–5
1993   *Glasswork*, No. 14, February, Japan, pp. 2–12
        All About Glass, Shinshusha Ltd, Tokyo

GILLIAN MANN
1971   Migrated to Australia
Education
1962–67 Undergraduate, Lancaster College of Art and Leicester College of Art,
         England
1967–88 Post Graduate Diploma A.D., Fine Art (Painting), Hornsey College of
         Art, London
Related Professional Experience
Lectures in the Print Workshop, CITA, Canberra
Selected Exhibitions
Exhibited glass in Canberra, Hobart, Perth, Sydney, Wagga Wagga, NSW; USA;
Japan
Exhibited prints and drawings in Canberra, Sydney, Melbourne; Japan; USA;

Canada; Poland; Ukraine; Germany; Belgium; Italy; London; Taiwan
Awards
1985   Commonwealth Teaching Service Overseas Travel Award
1987   Special Award, International Graphics Exhibition, Biella, Italy
1990   The Blake Prize for Religious Art
1994   Professional Experience Programme (Computer Graphics), CITA,
        Canberra
Publications
1988   'New Glass Review 9', *Neues Glas*, 2/88
1994   Liz Murphy, *She's a Train and She's Dangerous: Women Alone in the 1990s*,
        Literary Mouse Press

ELIZEBETH MCCLURE
1957   Born in Lanark, Scotland
Education
1975–79 Diploma of Art, Glass Design, Edinburgh College of Art, Scotland
1979–80 Post Graduate Diploma, Edinburgh College of Art
1980–82 Research Assistant, Sunderland Polytechnic, England
Related Professional Experience
1979   Member of semi-production team (tableware), Dent Glass, Cumbria,
        England
1980   Wedgewood Glass, Kings Lynn, Norfolk, England: Project organised by
        Wedgewood and the Craft Council
1983   Production Assistant (Mike Harris), Isle of Wight Glass, UK
1985–86 Designer, Senami, Tokyo (designing for product and interior ware using
         glass, Japanese lacquer and various other materials)
1987   Freelance glass designer/maker, based at Sunbeam Glass Studio,
        Auckland, NZ
1991   Elected President of 'Ausglass', 1991/93
1991–93 Co ordinator, International Summer School, Ausglass Conference,
         Canberra
1993   Co-designer/Editor, Ausglass Post-Conference Publication
Teaching
1980–81 Part-time Lecturer (studio glass), Department of Extra Mural Studies,
         Sunderland Polytechnic, England
1982–84 Lecturer in Charge (Glass), National College of Art and Design, Dublin,
         Eire
1984–85 Visiting Artist/Lecturer, Tokyo Glass Art Institute, Japan
1984/85 September: Teaching Assistant, Miasa Culture Centre, Japan
1987   Various workshops throughout New Zealand organised by the Crafts
        Council of New Zealand: Southland Community College, Invercargill;
        Otago Polytechnic, Dunedin; Nelson Polytechnic, Nelson; Wanganui
        Regional Community College, Wanganui; Hawkes Bay Community
        College, Nelson; Waikato Polytechnic, Hamilton; Carrington
        Polytechnic, Auckland; Group Workshop for the New Zealand Society
        of Artists in Glass, Auckland
        Visiting Lecturer, Glass Workshop, Canberra School of Art
1988   Commenced as Lecturer (full-time), Glass Workshop, Canberra School
        of Art
        Co-ordinator, Master workshop and symposia, Glass Workshop,
        Canberra School of Art
        Pâte de Verre Workshop, Meat Market, Melbourne
1988–91 Occasional lectures, demonstrations, Department of Cultural
         Conservation, University of Canberra
1989   Demonstrations and production design consultancy, Glass Workshop,
        Fujikawa Craft Park, Japan
1990   Visiting Lecturer, National College of Art and Design, Dublin, Eire
        Visiting Lecturer, Edinburgh College of Art, Edinburgh, Scotland
        Visiting Lecturer, West Surrey College of Art and Design, Farnham,
        England
1992   Acting Head of Glass Workshop, CITA, Canberra
1993   Commenced as Lecturer in Charge of Glass, UNITEC Institute of
        Technology, Auckland, NZ
Exhibitions
1979   Goblet exhibition, British Artists in Glass, Heals, London
1981   Exhibition of Crafts Council/Wedgewood Glass project, ICA Gallery
        (sideshow), London
1982   'In The Pink': Elizabeth McClure glass, Valerie Kirk tapestry, Ceolfrith

Gallery, Sunderland Arts Centre, Tyne and Wear, England

1984 'British Artists in Glass', Shipley Art Gallery, Gateshead, Newcastle upon Tyne, England
'British Artists in Glass', Westminster Gallery, Boston, USA
'Glass': Elizabeth McClure, Mark Abildgaard, Kudan Gallery, Tokyo

1985 'Bin' (bottle exhibition), Savoire Vivre Gallery, Axis Building, Tokyo
'Torii': Elizabeth McClure glass, an exhibition with Urushi furniture by Bushy, Axis Building, Tokyo
'Glass': Makoto Ito, Elizabeth McClure, Craft Yoshikawa, Shikoku, Japan

1986 'Glass Objects', Nakama Gallery, Tokyo
'Glass', Aspects Gallery, London
'British Artists in Glass', Liberty, London
'Glass and Paper', Atrium Gallery, Tokyo
'Nexus', Bushy, Axis Building, Tokyo
'Glass from Japan and USA', Museum für Gestaltung, Basel, Switzerland
Galerie Gottschalk Betz, Frankfurt, Germany
'Elizabeth McClure and Makoto Ito: Glass', Maronnie Gallery, Kyoto, Japan

1987 Glass exhibition, Crafts Council Gallery, Wellington, NZ
Judge and guest exhibitor, Compendium Gallery, Auckland, NZ

1988 'Contemporary British Craft', Miharu Do Gallery, Tokyo
Fourth National Studio Glass Exhibition, Wagga Wagga, NSW

1989 'Form and Function', Meat Market, Melbourne
'Glass' exhibition, Miharu Do Gallery, Tokyo
'Glass' (4 Artists), Despard Street Gallery, Hobart
'Australian Glass 1989', Distelfink Gallery, Melbourne

1990 'Australian Crafts 1990', Meat Market, Melbourne
'Kybosh' (Inaugural exhibition), Canberra
'Light and Living', Glass Artists' Gallery, Sydney
Christmas Show, Glass Artists' Gallery, Sydney

1991 'Challenging the Medium', Ausglass Members Exhibition, Blaxland Gallery, Sydney
'Appreciating the Medium', Glass Artists' Gallery, Sydney
Tenth Anniversary Australian Glass Triennial, Selected group show (touring Australia until September 1992), WWCAG, Wagga Wagga, NSW; Bicentennial Art Gallery, Campbelltown City, NSW; Sale Regional Gallery, Vic; Jam Factory Design Centre, Adelaide; Queen Victoria Museum and Art Gallery, Hobart; Tasmanian Museum and Art Gallery, Launceston, Tas; Blaxland Gallery, Melbourne
'Wearable Glass', Glass Artists' Gallery, Sydney
'10 Guineas and Under', Blaxland Gallery, Sydney

1992 Galerie L, solo exhibition, Hamburg, Germany
'Wearable Glass', Jam Factory Design Centre, Adelaide
'Glas Schmuck' (touring exhibition Germany, until June 1993), Deutsches Goldschmiedhaus, Hanau; Pforzheim Goldschmiedschule; Galerie Monika Borgward, Bremen; Galerie Handwerk, Munchen
'Wearable Glass', Australian Glass Jewellery, ASA Gallery, Tokyo
'Drawings '92', an exhibition by staff of Canberra School of Art, curated by Julie Ewington, School of Art Gallery, Canberra
'Co-incidences: 10 Years On', Elizabeth McClure glass, Valerie Kirk tapestry,
Canberra School of Art
Jahremesse (Australian Craft Exhibit), Museum für Kunst and Gewerbe, Hamburg, Germany

1993 'Origins & Originality', Ausglass Selected Members Exhibition, Drill Hall Gallery, Canberra
Craft Cameo Series, solo exhibition, Bendigo Regional Art Gallery, Vic
'Women Under Glass', The Door Exhibition Space, Fremantle, WA
ACI Glass Award, selected exhibition, Meat Market, Melbourne

1994 Little Jewels, selected exhibition of the Arts Marketing Board of Aotearoa, Wellington, NZ
'Making Marks', solo exhibition , The Glass Gallery, Auckland, NZ
Waitakere City Festival Exhibit with Lopdell Gallery at Corban Wineries Estate,
Auckland, NZ
Royal Easter Show Glass Awards Exhibit, Auckland, NZ

'Australian Glass Exhibition, Contemporary Art, Niki, Tokyo
'World Glass Now', selected group exhibition, Hokkaido Museum of Modern Art, Sapporo, Japan
'Kiln-formed Glass', Masterworks Gallery, Auckland, NZ

Award

1981 Northern Arts Travel Award to visit Corning Glass, Research Centre and various glass centres in USA

Commissions

1985 Architectural work commissioned by Nullhaus Co. (architects/interior designers) for Wacoal Co., Japan, Wacoal Arts Centre, Aoyama, Tokyo Spiral Building, Tokyo: Doors, windows, lighting etc.
' 'mparati', ladies fashion shop, Ebisu, Tokyo: Doors, windows, mirrors

1986 Wu Hospital, Taiwan: Glass brick screen

1987 Hewson-Morrison Architects, Auckland, NZ: 9 large and 45 small interior office screens and panels, sandblasted glass

Public Collections

1982 Shipley Art Gallery, Gateshead, Newcastle upon Tyne, England
Sunderland Museum, Tyne and Wear, England

1987 Auckland City Art Gallery and Museum, NZ

1991 WWCAG, Wagga Wagga, NSW

1991 AGWA, Perth

Publications

1980 *Crafts Magazine*, No. 45, July/August, UK

1982 'The Town That Lives Glass', *Craft Quarterly*, No. 4, Summer, UK
La Revue de la Ceramique et du Verre, No. 4, November/December, France

1985 *British Artists in Glass Newsletter*, June, pp. 9–16
Metiers d'Art. No. 29, June

1986 *Honoho Geijutsu*, February/March, Japan
Aspects Newsletter, March/April, UK
NTT Communication, No. 4, Japan
WWD (Womens' Wear Daily), April, Japan
Interior Design, May, UK
Tokyo Journal, May, Japan
Winds, JAL magazine, June, Japan
Axis catalogue, Vol. 20, June, Japan
Axis magazine, Vol. 20, Summer, Japan

1987 *Across* magazine, No. 1, January, Japan

1988 *Craft Victoria*, Vol. 8, Australia

1989 *Crafts Arts International*, No. 15, March/June, Australia
Glasswork magazine, No. 4, January 1990, Japan

1990 *Unreal City*, Vol. 1, No. 3, December, Australia

1991 'A Conflict of Interests', *Ausglass Magazine*, Post Conference Edition, pp. 53–4
Craft Arts International, No. 21, March/June, Australia
Interiors, Vol. 5, No. 2, Australia

1992 *Craft Arts International*, No. 24, p.100
'Thinking Craft Crafting Thought', *Art Link*, Vol. 12, No. 2, Australia, pp. 41
'Glas Schmuck', *GZ European Jeweller*, No. 6, Germany
Grace Cochrane, *The Crafts Movement in Australia: A History*
Ausglass Magazine, Winter, Australia, pp. 2–3
Kunsthandwerk and Design, No. 6, November, Germany, pp. 26, 28–9
Glas Schmuck/Glass Jewellery, Magistrat der Stadt Hanau, pp. 42, 43
'Idioms of the Antipodes', *Glasswork*, No. 13, November, pp. 1, 10–19

1993 'Painted Glass Vessels', *Neues Glas*, 1/93, pp. 22–9
Ausglass Post Conference Edition, pp. 2, 119–22

1994 'Thursday Arts: Around the galleries', *New Zealand Herald*, 24 February, section 2 p. 3

ALISON McMILLAN

1947 Born in Adelaide

Education

1980 Bachelor or Arts (Ceramic Design)

1987 Diploma of Education

Solo Exhibition

1991 'Alice in Westerland', A-Shed Gallery, Fremantle, WA

Selected Group Exhibitions

1981 'Contemporary Australian Glass', Meat Market, Melbourne

1982/83/85 'Australian Crafts', survey exhibitions, Meat Market, Melbourne
1983 Second National Glass Biennial, WWCAG, Wagga Wagga, NSW
1984–86 'Glass from Australia and New Zealand', Darmstadt, Germany; Chartres, France; Romont, Switzerland
1985 Third National Glass Biennial, WWCAG, Wagga Wagga, NSW
1985/86/88 'Eltham Art Award Exhibitions', Eltham Community Centre, Vic
1986 'Continuity and Change', Sydney Opera House
1988 Fourth National Studio Glass Exhibition, WWCAG, Wagga Wagga, NSW
1989/93 Diamond Valley Art Award, Melbourne
1992 'The Bowl Show', Meat Market, Melbourne
1993 'Origins & Originality' Ausglass Exhibition, ANU, Canberra

Awards
1989/93 Diamond Valley Art Award, Melbourne
1993 Full Scholarship to Pilchuck Glass School, USA

Commissions
1984 Austin Hospital Chapel, Heidelberg, Vic: Stained glass windows and interior design
1988 St Michael's (formerly Collins Street Uniting Church), Melbourne: Collaborated with K. Zimmer in the production of 19 windows for the lower level — these windows are officially known as the 'Bicentennial Windows'
1989 Queens College Chapel, University of Melbourne: Stained glass window in memory of Bernard and Estelle Semmens, made in collaboration with K. Zimmer
1992 St David's Anglican Church, Chelmer, Queensland: 'Ascension Window' in collaboration with Glenn Mack
1993 Canberra School of Art (ANU): Co-ordinated the design and fabrication of the 'Ausglass Window' (incorporating work by all students and tutors in the Conference Glass-painting Workshop)
Numerous private commissions for stained glass

Collections
Ebeltoft Glasmuseum, Denmark
Monash University (formerly CIT), Caulfield, Vic
Diamond Valley Art Collection, Melbourne
Private collections in Australia, China, England, France, Japan, Switzerland, USA

Publications
'The Hibernian Mural', *Pottery in Australia*, Vol. 18, No. 2, pp. 44–5
1980 Photo of Glass Panel, *Craft Australia*, Autumn, p. 34
1982 Wagga Wagga Catalogue Section, *Craft Australia*, Summer, pp. iv, xi
1984 *Glass from Australia and New Zealand,* catalogue, pp. 53, 73, 88
1985 *Third National Glass Biennial*, catalogue, pp. 16, 18
1985 *Craft Arts*, No. 4, Oct–Dec, p. 109
1988 *Fourth National Studio Glass Biennial*, catalogue, pp. 22, 34
Intersection (Journal of the Collins Street Uniting Church), Dec, pp. 2, 3
1989 *Neues Glas*, 1/89, pp. 36, 38, 79
Craft Arts International, No. 16, August/October, p. 80
1990 *Australian Collector's Quarterly*, Feb/Mar/Apr, p. 70
1992–93 *Ausglass Magazine,* Summer, pp. 23–5

KLAUS MOJE
1936 Born in Hamburg, Germany

Education
1952–55 Journeyman's Certificate, training as glass cutter and grinder in the family workshop in Hamburg
1957–59 Master's Certificate, studied at the glass schools Rheinbach and Hadamar

Related Professional Experience
1960–61 Worked in industry and crafts
1961 Joint studio with Isgard Moje-Wohlgemuth
1961–65 Commissions for stained glass windows in churches and public buildings as well as restoration work
1966 First work on container forms in painting and sculptural wheel-cutting
1969–73 Representative of the Arbeitsgemeinschaft des Deutschen Kunsthandwerks at the World Crafts Council and appointment to the Board of Directors
1975 First work in mosaic glass exhibited
1976 Founding member of Galerie der Kunsthandwerker, a continuation of

the Workshop Galerie, Hamburg
1978–82 Member of Jury of Arbeitsgemeinschaft des Deutschen Kunsthandwerks
1979– Guest Lecturer, Pilchuck Glass School, USA (Representative); Arts and Crafts School, Copenhagen, Denmark; Royal College of Art, London; Middlesex Polytechnic, London; California College of Arts and Crafts, USA; Rietveld Academy, Amsterdam, Holland
1980 Sole continuation of the studio in Hamburg
1982 Arrived in Australia with partner Brigitte Enders
1982–91 Founding Head of Glass Workshop, Canberra School of Art, ANU, Canberra
1987–88 Exhibition Co-ordinator, Crafts Council of the ACT, Canberra
1988 Convenor of 'International Masterworkshop in Kilnforming Glass Techniques', Canberra
1988–92 Served on several committees of the Visual Art/Craft Board of the Australia Council
1989 Exhibition Coordinator, 'Kilnformed Glass from Australia', touring USA
1990 International advisory committee, Ebeltoft Glasmuseum, Denmark
1992 Joint studio with Brigitte Enders, Ceramics, Rivett, Canberra
1992 Member of Management Committee, Crafts Council of the ACT
1992–93 Executive member of Ausglass
1993 International advisory committee, Pilchuck Glass School, USA

Solo Exhibitions
1973 The British Craftscentre, London
1979 Contemporary Art Glass Gallery, New York
1980 Retrospective, Museum für Kunst und Gewerbe, Hamburg Germany
1981 Foster/White Gallery, Seattle
Galerie Lietzow, Berlin
1981– Habitat Galleries, Detroit (repeatedly)
Heller Gallery, New York (repeatedly)
1982 Galerie SM, Frankfurt, Germany
1985 Glass Artists' Gallery, Sydney
'John Kuhn, Klaus Moje, Richard Ritter at the Glass Art Gallery', Toronto, Canada
1985– Kurland, Summers Gallery, Los Angeles
1987 Devise Gallery, Melbourne
1987– Habitat Galleries, Miami; Boca Raton Museum, Florida (repeatedly)
1988– Galerie L, Charlotte V. Finckenstein, Hamburg, Germany (repeatedly)
1989– Sanske; Zimmermann Gallery, Zurich (repeatedly)
1991 'Dale Chihuly, Klaus Moje', Ebeltoft Glasmuseum, Denmark
1992 Gallery for Contemporary Art, Niki, Tokyo

Exhibitions
1969 Triennial of European Decorative Art, Stuttgart, Germany
1970 'Werkstoff und Form', Fockemuseum, Bremen, Germany
1973 'Leading German Craftsmen', Rima Vera, Cambridge, England
'Ceramic Art of the World', Calgary, Canada
1974 'In Praise of Hands', World Crafts Council, Toronto, Canada
'Six German Glass Artists', Goethe Institute, Munich, Germany (travelling north); South America; Australia
1976 'Modern Glass Made in Europe, USA and Japan', Frankfurt
1977 Coburg Glass Prize, Kunstsammlungen der Veste Coburg, Coburg, Germany
1978 'Deutsche Glasskuenstler Heute', Interversa, Hamburg, Germany (travelling)
'German Glass Today', worldwide travelling exhibition
1979 'New Glass: A Worldwide Survey', Corning Museum of Glass, New York
1980 'German Glass and Silver', Landesmuseum, Karlsruhe, Germany
'Contemporary Glass: Europe and Japan', Museums of Modern Art, Tokyo and Kyoto, Japan
1981 'Glass '81 in Japan', Tokyo (invitaional)
Pilchuck Glass, Anchorage, Alaska
'Glaskunst '81', Orangerie, Kassel, Germany
1982 'World Glass Now '82', Hokaido Museum of Modern Art, Japan
'International Directions in Glass Art', AGWA, Perth, touring Australia
1983 'Nippon Gendai Kogei Bijutsu', Japan (invitational)
'New Glass in Germany', Kunstmuseum Dusseldorf, Germany

1984	Triennale des Deutschen Kunsthsndwerks', Frankfurt, Germany
	'Glass '84 in Japan', Tokyo and Dobe, Japan (invitational)
	'Deutsche Glaskuenstler', touring Germany
	'Nine Artists in Glass', Snyderman Gallery, Philadelphia
1985	'Material and Form', Metiers d'Art en Allemagne, Paris
	Ebeltoft Glasmuseum, Denmark
	Second Coburg Glass Prize, Coburg Castle, Coburg, Germany
	'World Glass Now '85', Hokaido Museum of Modern Art, Hokaido, Japan (invitational)
	Guest Exhibitor, Annual Show of New Zealand Glass Artists, Auckland, NZ
	Third National Glass Biennial, WWCAG, Wagga Wagga, NSW
	'The Pilchuck Exhibition', Habitat Galleries, Detroit
1986	Ella Sharp Museum, Grandrapid Museum, Krasl Art Center and Midland Center for the Arts, USA
	'Saxe Collection', Oakland Museum, San Francisco
1987	'Form and Function', Meat Market, Melbourne
	'New Expressions with Glass', Hunter Museum, Chattanooga, Tennesee
	Triennale des Deutschen Kunsthandwerks, Frankfurt, Germany; Helsinki, Finland
1988	'Glass from Canberra', Despart Gallery, Hobart
	'Over Here', Canberra School of Art, Canberra
	'World Glass Now '88', Hokaido Museum of Modern Art, Hokaido, Japan (invitational)
	'The New Aesthetics', Habitat Galleries, Detroit
	'European Decorative Arts', Stuttgart, Germany
	'Contemporary Art Glass', Boca Raton Museum, Florida
1989	'Australian Kilnformed Glass', travelling USA, sponsored by the Visual Arts/Craft Board of the Australia Council
	'The Cessel: Studies in Form and Media', Craft and Folk Art Museum, Los Angeles (invitational)
	First Perth International Crafts Triennal, AGWA, Perth
	'The New Aesthetic', Habitat Gallery, Miami; Boca Raton Museum, Florida
1990	International Exhibition of Glass, Kanazawa, Japan
1991	'World Glass Now '91', Hokaido, Japan
	Triennale des Norddeutshcen Kunsthandwerks, Schloss Gottorf, Schleswig, Germany
	'Masters of Contemporary Glass', Naples Museum, Naples, Florida
	'European Glass International', Craft Alliance, St Louis, USA
1992	National Craft Award, Melbourne (invitational)
	'Australian Crafts: New Works 1988–92', Powerhouse Museum, Sydney
	Rufino Tamayo Museum, Mexico City, Mexico
	'New Directions in Glass Art', Second Perth Triennial, Perth, WA
	'International Kilnformed Glass', Contemporary Art Gallery, Portland, Oregon
	'A Decade of Studio Glass', Morris Museum, New Jersey
	'Contemporary International Studio Glass', Monteray, Mexico

Selections and Awards

1956	First Prize in the Competition of German Journeymen
1969	Triennal Stuttgart 'Internationales Kunsthandwerk'
1970	Fockemuseum Bremen, 'Werkstoff und Form'
1971	Hessen State Award for German Decorative Art
1973	Medal, 'Ceramic International', Calgary, Canada
1976	Gold Medal, Bavarian State Award, Munich
1984	Suntory Museums Prize, 'Glass '84 in Japan', Tokyo; Kobe, Japan
1985	Dr Maedebach Memorial Prize at 2.Coburger Glass-preis für Moderne Glasgestaltung in Europa 1985
1989	Selected participant for Third Interglass Symposium, Novy Bor, Czechoslovakia, sponsored by a grant from the Visual Arts/Craft Board of the Australia Council
1990	Silver Prize, International Exhibition of Glass, Kanazawa, Japan
1994	Creative Australia Fellowship

Selected Public Collections

Kunstgewerbemuseum, Berlin, Germany
Kunstsammlungen der Veste Coburg, Coburg, Germany
Corning Museum of Glass, New York
Cooper Hewitt Museum, New York
Glasmuseum Frauenau, Frauenau, Germany
Royal Scottish Museum, Edinburgh, Scotland
Museum of Modern Art, Hokaido, Japan
Kunstgewerbemuseum, Köln, Germany
Kunstmuseum Dusseldorf, Germany
Kestnermuseum, Hannover, Germany
Lobmeyr Museum, Vienna, Austria
Museum für Kunst und Gewerbe, Hamburg, Germany
Grassi Museum, Leipzig, Germany
Ebeltoft Glasmuseum, Denmark
Victoria and Albert Museum, London
Landesmuseum Oldenburg, Oldenburg, Germany
Schloss Cappenberg, Dorftmund, Germany
Museum am Heger Tor Wall, Osnabrueck, Germany
Badisches Landesmuseum, Karlsruhe, Germany
Pilchuck Collection, Pilchuck Glass School, USA
Landesmuseum Schleswig Holstein, Schleswig, Germany
Metropolitan Museum of Art, New York
Wuerttembergisches Landesmuseum, Stuttgart, Germany
WWCAG, Wagga Wagga, NSW
Powerhouse Museum, Sydney
AGWA, Perth
Auckland Museum, Auckland, NZ
Parliament House Collection, Canberra
Queensland Art Gallery, Brisbane
County Museum of Art, Los Angeles
NGV, Melbourne
Musee Art Decorative, Lausanne, Switzerland
ANG, Canberra
Museum Bellerive, Zurich
Shimonoseki City Art Museum, Japan
Detroit Institute of Art, USA
Toledo Museum of Glass, Toledo, USA
Mineapolis Museum of Art, USA
University of Wisconsin Art Collection, USA
Bayerischer Kunstgewerbe-Verein, Germany

Publications

1968	*Gestaltendes Handwerk*, p. 149
1969	*Internationales Kunsthandwerk*, Stuttgart, p. 32
	Kunst und Handwerk, 3, pp. 283;
1970	*Werkstoff und Form*, catalogue, Focke Museum, Bremen, pp. 14–15
1971	*Kunst und Handwerk*, 1, pp. 12–13
1973	*Glas*, museum catalogue, Kunstgewerbemuseum, Köln, no. 717
1974	*In Praise of Hands*, catalogue, World Crafts Council, Toronto
	6 Deutsche Glaskuenstler, catalogue
1975	*Kunst und Handwerk*, 11/12, pp. 380, 381
1976	Schack, *Glaskunst*, pp. 267, 320; *200*
	Modernes Glas, Frankfurt, pp. 63–5, 161–2; no. 79–83
	Glass Art, 5/6, p. 52
	Microfiche, Corning, no. 81
	Hans Dennis, *Vitum, Geschichte und Geschichten um Glas*, Munich, p. 66
	Gottfried Borrmann, 'Modernes Glas aus Amerika, Europa und Japan', *Kunst und Handwerk*, 5/6, pp. 168–79
1977	*Glaspreis*, catalogue, Coburg, p. 91; *128–30*
1978	*Artist Craftsmen and their Vocational Training in the Federal Republic of Germany*, British Crafts Centre, London, pp. 40, 41, 70, 71
	Deutsche Glaskuenstler, Hamburg, cat. no. 30–3
	2.Report, Franzensbad, Vienna, Austria
	'Deutsche glaskuenstler', *Kunst und Handwerk*, 11/12, p. 410; *7*
1979	*New Glass*, Corning, New York, pp. 157–8, 264; cat. no. 152, 153
	Glass Art Society Journal, USA, pp. 18–20
	Recent Purchases Coburg, p. 183; cat. no. 570
1980	*Contemporary Glass*, Kyoto, cat. no. 349–53
	New Glass Review 1, Corning, New York, no. 56
	Kunst und Handwerk in Hamburg, ADK Hamburg, pp. 14, 15
	Glas: Silber, Karlsruhe, pp. 41–5; cat. no. 31–5

Axel von Saldern, Isgard Moje-Wohlgemuth, Klaus Moje, Glas: Monographien zum Kunsthandwerk, bd. 1, Bonn, pp. 1–100

1981 *Glass Modern World*, 42
16 Verriers, Paris
New Glass Review 2, Corning, New York, p. 8; *62*
Triennale Frankfurt, pp. 262, 263; cat. no. 300, 301
Glaskunst Kassel '81, cat. no. 194–6
Preisgekroentes Kunsthandwerk, Frankfurt, pp. 72–9
Werkstattausstellung in der Toepferei Heiner Balzar, Hoehr-Grenzhausen, catalogue
Glass '81 in Japan, catalogue, Odakyu department store, Japan Glass Artcraft Assosiation, Tokyo

1982 *New Glass Review 3*, Corning, New York p. 11; *58*
International Directions in Glass Art, Australia, p, 64; cat. no. 36
World Glass Now, Sapporo, Japan, p. 62, 63; cat. no. 27–9, 195
Glaeserne Kunstwerke, Kassel, p. 12
Helmuth Ricke, *New Glass in Germany*, Düsseldorf, pp. 36, 37, 196–201
Barbara Mundt, *Nostalgy Why?*, Berlin, p. 24; *16*
Glass Now '82, Japan, p. 13
Wolff Uecker, 'Mojes Liebe zur Geometrie', *Art No. 3* Hamburg, pp. 108, 109, 112

1983 *Nippon Gendai Kogei Bijutsu*, Japan, 8, 9
Craft Australia, No. 2, p. 46
B. Lundstroem and Daniel Schwoerer, *Glass Fusing Book One*, Portland, Oregon, pp. 10, 11, 57, 64, 97, 105

1984 Dan Klein, *The History of Glass*, Orbis, London, pp. 268, 269
Zeitgenoessisches Deutsches Kunsthandwerk, Frankfurt, pp. 250–2
Glass '84 in Japan, p. 142
Chr. Sellner, *Die Geschichte des Studioglases*, Theuern, pp. 48, 49
Glass in Miami: American and European Masters in Glass, featuring Klaus Moje, pp. 187–8
Nola Anderson, 'A Symphony in Glass', *Craft Australia*, No. 4, pp. 49–54
Nippon Gendai Kogei Bijutsu, Japan, s9

1984–85 Paul Hollister, *American Craft* , pp. 18–22

1985 *Ernst Museum*, Budapest, Hungaria, p. 31
Kunsthandwerk aus Hamburg und Norddeutschland, pp. 200, *283, 284*
World Glass Now '85, Hokaido, Japan, pp. 218, 219, *320*
2.Coburger Glaspreis, Coburg, Germany, pp. 72–4
Material & Form, Paris; Mainz
Jane Nicholls, *Harpers Bazaar*, No. 3, pp. 13, 44, 46
International Directions, Habitat Galleries, Detroit

1986 'Saxe collection', *Contemporary American and European Glass*, Oakland, p. 62
'Invitational', Ferd. Hampson, Detroit, pp. 45, 46

1987 *Zeitgenoessisches Deutsches und Finnisches Kunsthandwerk*, Frankfurt, pp. 264, 265
Glass Art in Japan '87, pp. 42, 87
Crafts Art, No. 6, Australia, pp. 104; *16*
Craft Australia, No. 3, p. 18; *16*
Glass Now '87, Japan, p. 15
Crafts, No. 3, London, p. 20

1987/88 *Interior Design*, Australia, pp. 20, 22

1988 Auction cat. no. 117, Carola van Ham, Köln, title ill, p. 43
'Bicentennial Arts Guide', *Vogue Australia*, p. 110
World Glass Now, Hokaido, Japan, pp. 166, 167, 244, 245
Auction catalogue, 5, Christies Australia, p. 21
Kilnformed Glass, catalogue, Canberra
'Kilnformed Glass', *New Glass*, No. 4, pp. 294, 295; *59*
Australian Decorative Arts, ANG
Over Here, Canberra school of Art
Marilynn Bell, *Craft Arts*, No. 2, p. 67
Contemporary Art Glass, Boca Raton, USA, *30*

1989 *Material & Form*, Bonn–London–Lincoln–Trier
Auction catalogue, 2, Christies New York, nos. 81, 82
Ben W. Heinemann Sr, *Contemporary Glass: A Private Collection*, p. 94; *85, 65*
Auction catalogue, 5, Christies New York, no. 89

Nola Anderson, *Art Aurea*, 2/89, title, pp. 43, 44, 45
Nola Anderson, 'Kilnformed Glass from Australia', *Craft Arts*, No. 15, pp. 95, 96
Glenn R. Cooke, 'The Studio Movement in Australia', *Crafts Arts*, No. 15, p. 80

1990 Geoffrey Edwards, 'Like an Oriental Calzedonio', *New Glass*, No. 2, pp. 202–9

1991 'Dale Chihuly – Klaus Moje', catalogue (English/Danish), Ebeltoft Glasmuseum, Denmark, pp. 1–66

1992 Shaun Waggoner, 'The Work of Klaus Moje: A New Order', Glass Art, USA, May/June, pp. 4–8
Grace Cochrane, *The Crafts Movement in Australia: A History*, pp. 4, 38, 383, 385, 389, 390, 391
Contemporary Kilnformed Glass: An International Exhibition, cover, pp. 9, 46
All About Glass, Shinshusha Co. Ltd., Japan, p. 214

1993 *The Survey of Glass in the World*, Vol. 6, Tsuneo Yoshimizu, Japan, pp. 80, 232

Published Works

1976 Klaus Moje, 'Material and Medium Glass', *Kunst und Handwerk*, October, p. 364
Klaus Moje, 'Heisser, am Heissesten, Glass Conference, London', *Kunst und Handwerk*, 11 December, pp. 425, 426

1977 Klaus Moje and Isgard Moje, 'Statement Towards WCC — Mexico', *Glass*, 3, p. 39

1979 Klaus Moje and Isgard Moje, in *Gas Journal*, USA, pp. 18–20

1980 Klaus Moje, 'Studio Glass in USA', *New Glass*, 1, p. 18

1981 Klaus Moje, The Glass Art Society, Annual Conference '81 in Seattle/WA, USA', *New Glass*, 3, pp. 110–14

1982 Klaus Moje, 'Willy Pistor: Portrait by Klaus Moje', *New Glass*, 1, pp. 16–19

1984/85 Klaus Moje, 'International Glass Education', Glass Art Society Journal, pp. 127–9

1991 Klaus Moje, 'Education in Glass', *Aussglass Magazine*

RICHARD MORRELL

1953 Born in the UK

Education

1975–76 West Sussex College of Design, UK
1976–79 Bachelor of Arts (Hons) 3D Design, Stourbridge School of Art, UK

Related Professional Experience

1979–81 Tutor in Glass Studies, CIT, Melbourne
1982–88 Artist-in-Residence, Meat Market, Melbourne
1988– Managing own studio, Coburg, Victoria
1991 Artist-in-Residence, University of South Australia
1992–93 External Assessor, Monash University, Melbourne

Solo Exhibitions

1981 Profile Gallery, Melbourne
1983 Beaver Galleries, Canberra
1985 Devise Gallery, Melbourne
1986 Distelfink Gallery, Melbourne
1990/92 Elgin Gallery, Melbourne
1993 Glass Artists' Gallery, Sydney

International Exhibitions

1987 'International Young Glass Artists', Ebeltoft Glasmuseum, Denmark
1991 'World Glass Now', Hokkaido Museum of Modern Art, Sapporo, Japan
1992 Galerie L, Hamburg, Germany
1993 CINAFE, Navy Pier, Chicago

Awards and Prizes

1985 Prizewinner, 'Gas & Fuel' Show, Melbourne
1987 Development Award, Australia Council
1991 First Prize, Ausglass Exhibition, Sydney
1993 Development Award, Australia Council

Selected Public Collections

Ebeltoft Glasmuseum, Denmark
Hamburg Museum of Art, Germany
Toho Corporation Collection, Japan
NGV, Melbourne
Queensland Art Gallery, Brisbane

Powerhouse Museum, Sydney
AGWA, Perth
Victorian State Craft Collection, Melbourne
WWCAG, Wagga Wagga, NSW
Devonport Museum, Tas
Diamond Valley Art Collection, Melbourne
City of Footscray Collection, Vic
Doncaster Municipal Council Collection, Vic

Publications

1981–89	Wagga Wagga Glass Biennial, catalogue
1986	*Form & Function,* catalogue, Gas & Fuel Show
	Craft Arts, November
1987	*International Young Glass Artists,* catalogue
1991	*World Glass Now,* catalogue, Hokkaido Museum of Modern Art
1992	*The Survey of World Glass,* Kyuryodo
1991	*Craft Australia,* Autumn

NICK MOUNT
Born in 1952

Education

1970–71	South Australian School of Art, Adelaide
1972–74	Non-diploma course in Visual Arts, Gippsland Institute of Advanced Education, Vic

Related Professional Experience

1975	Studied glass in USA and Europe with the Assistance of Crafts Board Grant
1976	Tutor, Ceramics Department of Caulfield Institute of Technology; established Hot Glass Studio
1977	Fired up first private studio, named 'One Off', in Gippsland, Vic
1978	Relocated studio to Budgeree, Vic, and renamed 'Budgeree Glass'
1980	Researched glass in California with the assistance of a grant from the Crafts Board of the Australia Council
1984	Moved to Adelaide, South Australia and set up new studio
1985	Teaching Assistant at the Pilchuck Glass School, USA, with Richard Marquis and Therman Statum
1987	Teaching Assistant at the Pilchuck Glass School, USA, with Paul Marioni
1988	Restructuring of Budgeree Glass and relocation into a manufacturing facility in Port Adelaide. Appointed Managing Director of Budgeree Glass Pty Ltd, responsible for design and product development
1991	Began new glass art studio in Norwood, SA
1992	Exhibited in South Australia and Victoria
	Teaching Assistant, Pilchuck Glass School, USA, with Bertil Vallien and Norman Courtney
1993	Teaching Assistant, Pilchuck Glass School, USA, with Danti Marioni and Lino Tagliapietro

Selected Solo Exhibitions

1978	Latrobe Valley Regional Art Gallery, Morwell, Vic
1978	The Crafts Centre, South Yarra, Vic
1979	Art of Man Gallery, Sydney, NSW
1980	Solander Gallery, Yarralumla, ACT
1980	Jam Factory, St Peters, SA
1981	Robin Gibson Gallery, Sydney, NSW
1981	Distelfink Gallery, Hawthorn, Vic
1983	Switchback Gallery, GIAE, Churchill, Vic
1986	Bonython–Meadmore Gallery, North Adelaide, SA
1986	Macquarie Galleries, Sydney, NSW
1992	Beaver Galleries, Canberra, ACT
1992	Artworks Gallery, Nungurner, Vic
1993	BMG Gallery, North Adelaide, SA

Selected Group Exhibitions

1979	Ausglass, Jam Factory, St Peters, SA
1981	'Contemporary Glass', National Museum Of Modern Art, Kyoto, Japan
1982	'Contemporary Glass', University of Tasmania, Hobart
1983	Second National Glass Biennial, WWCAG, Wagga Wagga, NSW
1984	'Australian Crafts 1984', Meat Market, Melbourne
1985	'World Glass Now', Hokkaido Museum Of Modern Art, Sapporo, Japan

1987	'Australian Crafts 1987', Meat Market, Melbourne
1988	'Australian Crafts 1988', Meat Market, Melbourne
1991	'Three Dimensional Art Today', Aptos Cruz Gallery, Stirling, SA
1992	BMG Gallery, North Adelaide, SA
1993	'Small Works', Glass Artists' Gallery, NSW
	'Origins & Originality', 1993 Ausglass Members show, Canberra

Selected Commissions
Australian Wine and Brandy Association Trophy
Turf Journalist Association of Victoria: Trophy for Malboro
South Australian Department of Tourism: 'Blue Ribbon Awards'
Adelaide Art Directors Club Trophy
Adelaide Review White Wine Awards
Portland Aluminium: Gift and Trophy commissions
Hyatt Regency Adelaide: Food presentation glassware
Park Hyatt Sydney: Food presentation glassware

Collections
NGV, Melbourne
ANG, Canberra
Gallery of South Australia, Adelaide
Gallery of Queensland, Brisbane
Victorian Ministry for the Arts, Melbourne
WWCAG, Wagga Wagga, NSW
Powerhouse Museum, Sydney
Parliament House, Canberra

Publications

1984	Alan Moult, *Craft in Australia,* Reed Publishing
1984	*Glass in the Modern World,* National Museum of Modern Art, Kyoto, Japan
1985	*First International Design Year Book,* Thames & Hudson, Europe; Abbeville Press, USA and JAPAN
1986	*Classic Design,* Vol. 11
1988	*Craft Australia,* Summer
1992	Grace Cochrane, *The Crafts Movement in Australia: A History*

IAN MOWBRAY

1955	Born in Queanbeyan, NSW

Education

1978	Leadlight, self taught

Related Professional Experience

1981	Leased workshop at Jam Factory, Adelaide
1983	Started fusing glass
1986	Artist-in Residence, University of South Australia, Underdale Campus
1987	Established Studio in Unley, Adelaide
1989	Established Moto Glass
1990	Temporary Glass Tutor, University of South Australia, Underdale Campus

Selected Exhibitions

1982	Royal Society for the Arts, Adelaide
1983	'Artists in St Peters', Experimental Art Foundation, Adelaide
1984	'National Invitational Glass', Elmswood Gallery, Adelaide
	'Small Works', Glass Artists' Gallery, Sydney
	'Young Australian Glass', Darmstadt, Germany, and touring
1985	'Australian Crafts 1985', Meat Market, Melbourne
	'The Patterned Edge', Craft Centre Gallery, Sydney
	'Two Glass Artists', Glass Artists' Gallery, Sydney
	Third National Glass Biennial, WWCAG, Wagga Wagga, NSW, and touring
1986	'Australian Crafts 1986', Meat Market, Melbourne
	'Art in Architecture', Tall Poppies Gallery, Adelaide
	Eltham Art Awards 1986, Eltham, Vic
	'Group Glass 1986', Hamilton Design Gallery, Sydney
	'Jam Packed', Jam Factory, Adelaide
1987	'Glass Survey', Distelfink, Melbourne
	'Don't Stare: It's Rude', Union Gallery, Adelaide University
	'Australian Crafts 1987', Meat Market, Melbourne
	Beaver Galleries Award, Canberra
1988	'Australian Crafts 1988', Meat Market, Melbourne
	International Exhibition of Glass Craft 1988, Kanazawa, Japan

'Kilnformed Glass', Crafts Council Gallery, Canberra
'Classics', Craft Centre Gallery, Sydney
Glass, Distelfink Gallery, Melbourne
ANZ Glass Prize, Glass Artists' Gallery, Sydney
1989 'President's Choice', Meat Market, Melbourne
       Second New Zealand Crafts Biennale, Auckland Museum, Auckland, NZ
       'Adelaide in Himeji' Art Exhibition, Himeji, Japan
       Jam Factory Gallery, Adelaide
1990 'Pâte de Verre', Glass Artists' Gallery, Sydney
       'Kilnformed Glass', Beaver Galleries, Canberra
       'Personal Visions', Royal SA Society of Arts, Adelaide
       International Exhibition of Glass 1990, Kanazawa, Japan
       'A Taste of Adelaide', Christchurch, NZ
1991 'Challenging the Medium', Blaxland Gallery, Sydney
       'National Glass Show', QPA, Brisbane
       'Gossip', Prospect Gallery, Adelaide
1993 ACI Glass Award, Meat Market, Melbourne
       Diamond Valley Art Award, Melbourne
1994 Travelling South America, to Montevideo, Uruguay; Sao Paulo, Brazil; Buenos Aires, Argentina
       'Australian Glass in Tokyo', Japan

Grants
1988 Workshop Development Grant, Australia Council

Commissions
1982 Sir Samuel Way Law Courts, Adelaide: Leadlight skylight (5 m diameter)
1983 Northfield High School: Window (12 panels)
1984 City Cross Arcade, Adelaide: Fused glass window (2 m diameter)
1986 Northfield High School, SA: Glass Mosaic Wall (4.3 m x 3.8 m)
1989 Regent Arcade, Adelaide: Fused glass panels (9.5 m x 1.2 m)
       Piper Alderman: Fused glass panels (24 x 500 mm x 500 mm)
1991 Concept and designs for eastern wall of proposed Adelaide Magistrate's Court, SA
1992 St Chad Anglican Church: 4 Central lights (1.2 m diameter)
       Nation Line Headquarters: Fused curved glass hob top (4.5 m x 200 mm)
1993 63 Pirie Street: 6 light fittings curved glass, textured and sandblasted (4 x 3.1 m x 215 mm; 2 x 2.3 m x 215 mm)
       Elizabeth Magistrate Court: 4 fused glass windows (1 x 3.2 m x 900 mm; 1 x 3.2 m x 1.2 m; 2 x 2.4 m x 1.2 m)

Public Collections
Diamond Valley Art Collection, Melbourne
Victorian State Craft Collection, Melbourne
Powerhouse Museum, Sydney
Queensland Art Gallery, Brisbane
Art Gallery of South Australia, Adelaide
WWCAG, Wagga Wagga, NSW

Publications
1982 *The Advertiser*, 16 August
1983 *Constructional Review*, August
1984 *Architecture Australia*, January
       SA Crafts, Summer
1985 *Craft Australia*, Winter
1986 *Vogue Living*, Nos. 1 and 10
       'New Glass Review 7', *Neues Glas*, 1/86; *Neues Glas*, 2/86
       Craft Australia, Winter
       SA Crafts Year Book
       Craft Australia Year Book
1987 *Craft Arts*, No. 8
       Ausglass Magazine, June
1989 *Epicurean Diary 1990*, cover photograph
1992 *The Survey of Glass in the World*, Vol. 6
       Oz Arts magazine, No. 3
       'New Glass Review 13', *Neues Glas*

GARRY NASH
1955 Born in Sydney, Australia
1973 Moved to New Zealand

Workshops
1980 Guest Instructor, First New Zealand Glassworkers Symposium
1989 Guest Instructor, Australian Glass Society Conference
1989 Guest Instructor, Fuji River Craft Centre, Japan
1992 Guest Instructor, Northland Polytechnic, NZ

Related Professional Experience
1978 Began working with glass
1981– Glass Artist (full-time), Sunbeam Glassworks
1988 Acquired ownership of Sunbeam. Continue to operate the business with wife Anna Palmer, while pursuing own personal exploration of the glass medium

Selected Solo Exhibitions
1981 Dennis Cohen Gallery, Auckland, NZ
1983 Aigantighe Art Gallery, Timaru, NZ
1984 Glass Artists' Gallery, Sydney
       Compendium Gallery, Auckland, NZ
1985 Show Case Exhibition, Craft Council Gallery, Wellington, NZ
1986 Dowse Art Museum, Lower Hutt, NZ
1987 Cross Creek Gallery, Los Angeles
       Elaine Potter Gallery, San Francisco
       Maurice Littleton Gallery, Washington
       CINAFE, Navy Pier, Chicago
1988 Kurland Summers Gallery, Los Angeles
       Hamilton Glass Gallery, Sydney
       Star Art, Auckland, NZ
       Beaver Galleries, Canberra
1989 Villas Gallery, Wellington, NZ
1990 Compendium Gallery, Auckland, NZ
1992 Dowse Art Museum, Lower Hutt, NZ
       Despart Street Gallery, Hobart
1993 Masterworks Gallery, Auckland, NZ

Selected Group Shows
1980 'Glass 80', Auckland Society of Arts, NZ
1981 'Glass 81', Auckland Society of Arts, NZ
1982 'Fragile Arts', Northern Regional Arts Council, touring exhibition, NZ
1983 Pacific Glass International, NZ
       'Studio Glass', Auckland Museum, NZ
1984 Phillips Studio Glass Exhibition, Auckland, NZ
1985 Dowse Art Museum, Lower Hutt, NZ
       Phillips Studio Glass Exhibition, Auckland, NZ
1986 Glass Artists' Gallery, Sydney
       'World Glass Now', Japan
1987 International Glass Invitational, Habitat Galleries, Michigan
       'Glass Now '87', Japan, touring
1988 'World Glass Now', Museum of Modern Art, Hokaido, Japan
       Hodges Taylor Gallery, Charlotte, USA
1989 'Glass Now '89', Japan, touring
1990 'Glass Now '90', Japan, touring
1992 CINAFE, Navy Pier, Chicago, with Despart Street Gallery Booth
1993 'Glass Now '93', Japan, touring
1994 'Glass Now '94', Japan, touring

Awards
1988 UBS Sutter Craft Award, Bishop Sutter Art Gallery, NZ
1986 QEII Arts Council Award for travel to USA
1983 QEII Arts Council Award for travel to Australia

Public Collections
Auckland Museum, NZ
Dowse Art Museum, NZ
Hawkes Bay Art Gallery, NZ
Manly Art Gallery, Sydney
Smithsonian Institute, Washington
Ebeltoft Glasmuseum, Denmark
Manawatu Art Gallery, NZ

Private Collections
BNZ Bank Collection, NZ
ANZ Bank Collection, NZ
Connections, Borowsky Collection, USA
Glaxo Collection, NZ

DENIS O'CONNOR
1953   Born in Australia
Education
1975   Fine Art Diploma, Newcastle College of Advanced Education, NSW
1976   Post Graduate Art Education Diploma, NCAE, NSW
1980   Guest student, Skolan for Brugskunst, Copenhagen, Denmark, (under Fynn Lynggaard)
Related Professional Experience
1977–81 Lecturer, School of Art and Design, Caulfield Institute of Technology, Melbourne
1985   Lecturer, Canberra School of Art
1987–   Part-time Lecturer, School of Visual and Performing Arts, Charles Sturt University, Riverina Campus, NSW
Awards and Projects
1973   Hunter Valley Drawing Award
1973–76 Design Scholarship, Philips Glass Company, Newcastle, NSW,
1974   Crafts Council of Australia sponsorship to tour QLD, NSW and ACT, with Professor Bill Boysen, USA glass blower
1981   Workshop Establishment Grant, Crafts Board of the Australian Council
1982   Artist-in-Residence, Community Project, WWCAG and Riverina College of Advanced Education, NSW
1982/87/92 Public Lecture series, WWCAG, Wagga Wagga, NSW
1987–   Member of the Board of Trustees, WWCAG, Wagga Wagga, NSW
1989   Invited to conduct Drawing Workshops, Adult Drawing Classes, Wagga Wagga Art Society
1992   Conducted Painting/Drawing Workshop for culturally disadvantaged schools, Charles Sturt University and government-funded 'Country Areas Programs' (CAP), Tumbarumba, NSW
1993   Conducted Visual Arts Workshops 'Major Work and Beyond' for Senior High School students representing Schools from Riverina Region
Collections
Represented in major Australian public and private collections and in overseas collections:
University of Newcastle, NSW
Ministry for the Arts/Craft, Vic
CIT, Melbourne
National College of the Arts, Vic
Her Excellency Lady Cowan
Skolan for Brugskunst, Copenhagen, Denmark
WWCAG, Wagga Wagga, NSW
Manly City Art Gallery, NSW
NGV, Melbourne
Queensland Art Gallery, Brisbane
Ebeltoft Glasmuseum, Denmark
Powerhouse Museum, Sydney
Parliament House, Canberra
Charles Sturt University, NSW
Publications
1984   Jenny Zimmer, *Stained Glass in Australia*
1985   Ken McKenzie, 'Our Glass Studio',*Craft Australia*, Winter
1988   Jenny Zimmer, 'Studio Glass', *Craft Australia*, Summer
1988   *Cultivating The Country*, Oxford University Press
1989   Dan Klein, *Glass: A Contemporary Art*
1990   'Art Glass from Australia', *Craft Arts*,

SETSUKO OGISHI
1954   Born in Japan
1981   Arrived in Australia
Education
Kanazawa College of Arts
Trainee, glass workshop, Jam Factory Craft Centre, Adelaide
Awards
1982–85 Australia–Japan Foundation Grant
1987   Workshop Development Grant from Crafts Boad of the Australia Council
1989   Craft Acquisition Award, Northern Territory Museum of Arts and Sciences
1990   Craft Prize, Hunters Hill (NSW)

Public Collections
Powerhouse Museum, Sydney
Devonport Museum and Art Gallery, Tas
Parliament House, Canberra
Queensland Art Gallery, Brisbane
WWCAG, Wagga Wagga, NSW
Northern Territory Museum of Arts and Sciences, Darwin
Max Watters' Collection, Muswellbrook City Art Gallery, NSW

CHRIS PANTANO
1948   Born in Sydney, Australia
Solo Exhibitions
1985   Gallery of Fine Art, solo exhibition, Singapore
        Enterprise Queensland Exhibition to Japan
1986   'Looking at Glass', Beaver Galleries, Canberra
1988   David Jones, solo exhibition, Brisbane
1990   Distelfink Gallery, Melbourne
1992   Mulgara Gallery, solo exhibition, Ayers Rock
1992   'Facets of Australia', glass exhibition, Crafters Gallery, Mt Tamborine, Qld
1993   CINAFE, Navy Pier, Chicago
        Guest Artist/Exhibitor, Noosa Art Show, Qld
        Exhibitor, Australian Fine Craft Designers Gallery, Adelaide
1994   Exhibitor, SOFA, Chicago
Awards
1985/86/87 Caloundra Arts Festival Glass Award
1988/90/93 Australian Woolshed/Sheraton Award
1990   Maroochy Bicentennial Award
Public Collections
1986   Parliament House, Canberra: 3 pieces
1992   Queensland Art Gallery, Brisbane: 2 pieces
1993   Art Gallery of the Northern Territory, Darwin: 1 piece
        WWCAG, Wagga Wagga, NSW: 1 piece
Publications
1986   *Craft Arts*, No. 7
1987   *Neues Glas*, 4/87
1990/91 *Queensland Homes*, Summer
1992   *Queensland Homes*, Winter
        'Art File 1', *Craft Arts International*
1994   *Noosa Blue*, Autumn
        Craft Arts International, No. 32

SALLIE PORTNOY
Born in 1954
Education
1978–79 Ceramics with Robert Archambeau, University of Manitoba, Canada
1979–80 Nova Scotia College of Art & Design, Canada, Ceramics with John Reeve
1981   Ceramic workshops with Gwynn Hansen, Piggot and Joan Campbell
1984   Ceramics with Dorothy Hafner, Parsons School of Design, New York
1987   Independent study with Michael Keihgery, Glass Department, Sydney College of the Arts
1987   Glass Surface Design with Ann Wolfe, Pilchuck Glass School, USA
1988–89 Bachelor of Arts in Ceramics, City Art Institute, Sydney
1990   Casting with David Reekie, Pilchuck Glass School, USA
1991   Casting with James Watson, Pilchuck Glass School, USA
Related Professional Experience
1990   Taught Fusing/Slumping workshop, Experimental Glass Workshop, New York
1991   Taught Fusing workshop, Bildwerk School, Fraeunau, Germany
1993   Guest Lecturer, Sydney College of the Arts
1987–94 Work and teach in own studio, Sydney
Solo Exhibitions
1987   Access Art Gallery, Sydney
1988   Hamilton Glass Gallery, Sydney
1989   Vincent Art Gallery (in conjunction with Macquarie Art Gallery), Adelaide
1991   Craft Showcase, David Jones Gallery, Sydney
1993   Exhibiton of glass and mixed media jewel boxes, Craftspace, Sydney

Group Exhibitions
1987   Beaver Galleries, Canberra
1988   Metro Arts Glass Show, Brisbane
       ANZ Glass Prize, Glass Artists' Gallery, Sydney
       'International Kiln-formed Glass', Craft Council of the ACT, Canberra
1989   'Australian Review', Primavera Gallery, Virginia
       'Of The Earth', Third Invitational Exhibition, Sydney
       Eighth Gold Coast National Ceramic Award, Qld
       'Australian Glass 1989', Distelfink Gallery, Melbourne
       'National Craft Acquisition Award', Craft Council of Northern Territory
       NSW Travelling Art Scholarship, The Works Gallery, NSW
1990–94 Craft Councils of NSW, QLD, NT, ACT, Glass Artists' Gallery;
       Blaxland Gallery; Pochoir, Phillip & Co; Studio Showcase, Sydney
       Meat Market; Distilfink Gallery, Victoria
       Beaver Galleries, Canberra
       Jam factory, Adelaide
       Australia Gallery; Archetype Gallery; Miller Gallery, New York
       Hermann Gallery, Germany
1990   'Essence of the 90s: Art & Design of Perfume Bottles', Bloomingdale's
       Dept Store, New York
       'Studio Artists Show', Experimental Glass Workshop, New York
       'New Romantics', Archetype Gallery, New York
1991   'Artists Show', Archetype Gallery, New York
1993   Ausglass Members Exhibition, Canberra
       Diamond Valley Art Award, Melbourne
       Wagga Wagga Limited Edition Series Exhibition, NSW
       ACI Glass Award, Meat Market, Melbourne
       Evolving Archetypes, Archetype Gallery, New York
       'The Glass Bowl', Distelfink Gallery, Melbourne
       'Contemporary Design in Jewish Ceremony', Jewish Museum of
       Australia, Melbourne
       '11th National Craft Acquisition Award', Museum of the Northern
       Territory, Darwin
       Sixth National Ceramics Conference, Brisbane
       'Making for Space', Architectural Glass Show, Ausglass Conference,
       Sydney
1994   Miller Gallery Figurative Exhibition, New York

Awards
1987   Craft Board Development Grant ($4000)
1990   Scholarship, Pilchuck Glass School, USA

Commissions
1992   'Secret Treasure of Russia', Art Gallery of NSW, Sydney

Collections
Queensland Regional Art Gallery, Brisbane
Museum of the Northern Territory, Darwin
Private collections in Australia, USA, Japan, Canada, Britain, France, Germany

Publications
Craft Arts, Craft Australia, Craft Australia Year Book 1986, Craft SW, Ausglass Magazine, Sydney Morning Herald, Manly Daily, Mosman Chronicle, Art Text, Canberra Times, Stiletto Magazine, Ragtrader

CEDAR PREST
1940   Born in Melbourne, Australia
Elected to the British Society of Master Glass Painters in 1968, and is a Foundation and Life Member of the Crafts Council of SA. Has served as Chairperson of the Crafts Board of the Australia Council 1980–83 and was awarded the Order of Australia Medal in 1987 for services to stained glass.

Commissions
1983/90/94 Macquarie University Library, Sydney
1987   St Peters College Memorial Hall, Adelaide
1988   Carmelite Chapel, St John, Box Hill, Melbourne
1988/89/94 Guildford Grammar School Chapel, Perth
1989   Ted Egan Residence, Alice Springs
1989–91 Church of the Resurrection, Kidman Park, Adelaide
1990   Kensington & Norwood Council Town Hall, Adelaide
1990–92 Daw Park Repatriation Hospital Chapel, Adelaide
1991   Cancer Ward Childrens Hospital, Camperdown, Sydney
       St Lukes, Mosman Park, Perth

1991–92 St Peters Cathedral, Adelaide: Clerestory windows
1992   Sydney International Airport Foyer

Community Projects
1979–80 Parks Community Centre, Corner Trafford and Cowan Streets,
       Mansfield Park, Adelaide, funded by Crafts Board, Australian Council
       and South Australian Department for the Arts
       80 volunteers made 5 windows totalling 4535 square metres: Cafeteria
       37 square metres — theme 'Streamers'; Library 32 square metres — SA
       landscapes with Mallee gums; Children's library 16 square metres —
       children's stories and sport; Sports lounge 22 square metres —
       Aboriginal land rights dreaming; Swimming pool entry 6.5 square
       metres — Wave
1983–84 Araluen Arts Centre, Larapinta Drive, Alice Springs, NT, funded by
       Crafts Board of Australia Council
       38 volunteers made 4 window sets, totalling 26.4 square metres: *Stage 1* – 8 boardroom windows 6.48 square metres — the ochre pits; 16
       foyer windows, 7.2 square metre frieze — Aboriginal student
       drawings; 4 bistro windows 9.2 square metres — Alice from Wet to
       Dry. *Stage 2* – 8 Green Room windows 5.52 square metres — Mt Gillen
       Chaffey Theatre, Eighteenth Street, Renmark, SA, for Riverland
       Cultural Trust, funded by Crafts Board, Australia Council and Theatre
       Building Fund
       31 volunteers made 40 panels totalling 27.14 square metres: 2 sets for
       mezzanine foyers of theatre — The River
1985   Yirara College, Stuart Highway, Alice Springs, NT, for Yirara College,
       funded through Northern Territory Artists in Schools Programme
       Participants were classes of Year 7 and 8 students: Paved stone
       courtyard, fountain and environment
1986   Uringa Hostel, behind Tumby Bay Hospital for Tumby Bay Branch,
       South Australian Arts Council, funded by Arts Council of South
       Australia and Crafts Board, Australia Council
       31 volunteers made 10 sets of unit entrance windows, totalling 8.95
       square metres — local scenes at various times of day and seasons
       Middleback Theatre, Nicolson Avenue, Whyalla, South Australia for
       Eyre Peninsula Cultural Trust, funded by South Australian Department
       for Arts Work in Public Places programme
       This project ran in tandem with Tumby Bay, 3 days each, 25 volunteers
       made 5 windows in foyer, totalling 10.77 square metres: 4 front foyer
       windows 7.72 square metres — from the open cut to the export; 1 back
       foyer window 3.05 square metres — crystalline structures below
       ancient landscape and western Myall tree
1987   Kalamunda Library, Railway Road, Kalamunda, Perth, WA, for
       Kalamunda Shire Council, funded by the Crafts Board of Australia
       Council, Western Australian Department of Arts, local fundraising
       committee
       60 volunteers made south wall of library 48 square metres: 48 panels
       on theme of the forest and local landscape and history
1987–88 Araluen Arts Centre, Larapinta Drive, Alice Springs, NT, funded by
       Australian Bicentenary Arts Programme
       15–20 volunteers from local Aranda camp made central foyer window
       of 17.3 square metres: 12 panels interpreting a Dreaming painting by
       elder Wenten Rabuntja that shows stories which traverse the Araluen
       site

STEPHEN PROCTER
1946   Born in West Sussex, England

Education
Studied engineering and agriculture

Related Professional Experience
1970   Established own engraving studio, Ashburton, Devon
1976   Major Bursary Award from Crafts Council
1977   Visiting Artist, working in Glass Studio Franzensbad, Baden, Austria
1978–79 Visiting Artist-in-Residence for 1½ years, Illinois State University, USA
1979–81 Glass Artist-in-Residence in conjunction with Northern Arts and
       Sunderland Polytechnic
1980–84 Visiting Lecturer, The Royal College of Art
1981–91 Senior Lecturer, West Surrey College of Art and Design
       Established own studio near Farnham

1991–92   Visiting Associate Professor for one year, with responsibility for the Glass Programme, Illinois State University, USA

1992   Appointed Head of Glass Workshop, Canberra School of Art

Selected Solo Exhibitions

1973   Exhibition of paintings, Chagford Gallery, Devon, England

1978   'Contemplations on a Cornish Landscape', Watercolours, Fine Arts Centre, Clinton, Illinois

1979   'Through Glass Forms', Contemporary Art Glass Gallery, New York

1980   Paintings and drawings, Windjammer Gallery, Salcombe, Devon

1981–82   'Passages Through Light', touring exhibition: Sunderland Arts Centre; Dudley Museum; Pilkington Glass Museum, St Helens; Cleveland College of Art; Plymouth City Museum and Art Gallery; British Craft Centre, London, UK; Glas-Galerie, Lucerne, Switzerland

1982   'Thoughts About Light', LYC Museum and Art Gallery, Cumbria, England

1983   'Art 83', International Art Fair (Glas-Galerie, Lucerne), Basel, Switzerland

1986–87   'Thoughts About Light', touring exhibition: Kunstmuseum Düsseldorf, Germany; Glas-Galerie Luzern, Switzerland; Augustiner Museum, Freiburg, Germany; Lobmeyr, Innsbruck, Austria

1988   'Stephen Procter', Holsten Galleries, Florida
'For The Gathering of Light', touring exhibition: McAllen International Museum, Texas; The Brunnier Museum & Gallery, Iowa; Matrix Gallery, Austin, Texas

1992   'Seeds Of Light', Galerie Rob Van Den Doel, Hague, Netherlands

Group Exhibitions

1975   British Crafts Federation, London

1976   'Official Gifts', Design Council, London

1977   'Reflections in Glass', two man show, Lobmeyr, Vienna
'Reflections in Glass', two man show, Galerie SM, Frankfurt, Germany
'Coburger Glaspreis 1977', Coburg, Germany
Hamburg Museum, Hamburg, Franzensbad Group Exhibition

1979   'Ten Concepts in Glass', Habitat Gallery, Detroit
'British Artists in Glass', Prescote Gallery, Banbury, England

1980   'Stephen Procter — Glass Forms', Illinois State University, USA
Summer Exhibition of Royal Institute of Painters in Watercolours, London
Contemporary British Crafts, Sotheby's, Belgravia, London

1981   Welsh Arts Council, Festival Showcase
'Around The Corner', British Artists in Glass, Mappin Art Gallery, Sheffield, England

1982   'Glas Today in Art and Craft', International Symposium, Glasmuseum Frauenau, Germany
Fellows of the Guild of Glass Engravers, Newbury
International Glass Symposium, Novy Bor, Czechoslovakia

1983   Glass Symposium Exhibition, Museum of Applied Art, Prague
'British Glass Artists', The Glass Art Society, Toronto, Canada
'Contemporary Engraved Glass', J. & L. Lobmeyr, Vienna

1984   'Studio Glass since 1945', Brighton Museum, UK
'Art 84', International Art Fair (Dan Klein, London), Basel, Switzerland
'Glass in Architecture', Glas-Galerie, Lucerne, Switzerland
'Seven Artists One Material', Glas-Galerie, Lucerne, Switzerland
'An Artists Selection', Laing Gallery, Newcastle, UK
Mostra International Arredamento, Monza, Italy

1985   'A Collection in the Making', Crafts Council, London
'Coburger Glaspreis 1985' (Honorary Award), Veste Coburg, Germany
'Sculpture in Glass', Finnish Glass Museum, Finland
'Studio Glass', British Craft Centre, London
'West Surrey College of Art & Design: Staff & Students', Glas-Galerie, Lucerne, Switzerland; La Galeria, Frankfurt, Germany
'The Art of Glass and Today's Creators', Clara Scremini Gallery, Paris

1986   Guest Exhibitor, Annual Exhibition, The Glasshouse, London

1987   'Glas Now', Sao Paulo Museum, Brazil
'Vitrine 1987' (Staff and Students, WSCAD), Berne, Switzerland
'Thirty Years of New Glass 1957–87', Corning Museum of Glass, New York
'Clear Through To The Wood', Fitzwilliam Museum, Cambridge

'Studio Glass', Contemporary Applied Arts, London
'A School of Glass' (Staff and Students, WSCAD), Maya Behn Gallery, Zurich
'Glass 87 in Japan', Japan Glass Artcraft Association, Tokyo

1988   'Contemporary British Glass', Kuala Lumpur
'1988 Palm Beach Glass Invitational', Holsten Galleries, Florida
'World Glass Now '88', Hokkaido Museum of Modern Art, Sapporo, Japan
International New Art Forms Exposition, Galerie Bergmann, Chicago

1988–89   'Contemporary British Crafts', National Museums of Modern Art, Kyoto and Tokyo

1989   'Expressions en Verre II', Museum of Decorative Arts, Lausanne, Switzerland
'WSCAD: Staff & Students', Galerie L, Hamburg, Germany
'Masterworks in Glass', Beckett Gallery, Ontario, Canada
International New Art Forms Exposition, Galerie Bergmann, Chicago
'Winter Lights', New Ashgate Gallery, Farnham, England
'Glaskunst Zeitgenössischer Europäischer Künstler', Bomann Museum, Celle, Germany

1990   'Glas —van Drinkbeker tot Kunstobject', Museum voor Kunstambachten Sterckshof, Antwerpen, Belgium
British Design Exhibition, Tokyo
'New Glass in Europe, 50 Artists — 50 Concepts', Kunstmuseum Düsseldorf, Germany

1991   Fondation pour la Céramique et le Verre Contemporains, Inaugural Exhibition, Yverdon-les-Bains, Switzerland
'A Celebration of Ten Years', Maya Behn Galerie, Zurich
'Favourite Things', Crafts Council Gallery, London
'The Festival of Contemporary Glass 1991', Opus#1 Gallery, London
'Illinois Glass', a University of Illinois and Illinois State University perspective, Marx Gallery, Chicago
CINAFE (Galerie Bergmann), Navy Pier, Chicago
'All Together Now', Illinois State University Faculty Biennial, USA

1992   'Ode à la Coupe', Musee des Arts Decoratifs de la Ville de Lausanne, Switzerland

1993   'The Glass Show' a retrospective exhibition of Contemporary British Glass by the Crafts Council, London
Exhibition to celebrate the opening of 'Kito Glass', studio and gallery, Bremen, Germany
CINAFE (Galerie Bergmann), Navy Pier, Chicago
'Cloudbusting', staff exhibition, Canberra School of Art, Canberra

Collections

Corning Museum of Glass, New York
Victoria and Albert Museum, London
Lobmeyr Collection, Vienna
Kunstsammlungen der Veste Coburg, Germany
Royal Albert Memorial Museum, Exeter, England
Shipley Art Gallery and Museum, Gateshead, England
Augustiner Museum, Freiburg, Germany
Novy Bor Symposium Collection, Czechoslovakia
Collection of Illinois State University, Illinois
Kunstmuseum Düsseldorf, Germany
Schweizerische Kreditanstalt Bank, Lucerne
Crafts Council, London
Royal Museum of Scotland, Edinburgh
Museum of Decorative Art, Lausanne
Roberto Niederer Collection, Lucerne
National Museum of Modern Art, Kyoto, Japan
The Brunnier Gallery and Museum, Iowa
The Borowsky Collection of Contemporary Glass, Philadelphia
The Immenhausen Glas Museum, Immenhausen, Germany
Ebeltoft Glasmuseum, Denmark

Publications

1976   *Crafts Magazine*, May/June

1977   *Austria Today*, Vol. 2, Summer
Craft Horizons, December

1977/78   *Contemporary Glass Microfiche*, Corning, New York

1979   Crafts Council, Slidepack, July

1981   Charles Bray, 'Passages Through Light', *Craft Quarterly*
       Neues Glas, 4/81
1983   *New Glass Review 4*
       Vytvarn Kultura, 3
       Czechoslovak Life, 3
1985   *Czech Glass Review*, 6
       Crafts Magazine, Jan/Feb
       New Glass Review 6
1986   *Neues Glas*, 2/86
       Crafts Magazine, Sept/Oct
       Stephen Procter, 'Thoughts About Light'
1988   *World Glass Now*, catalogue
       Contemporary British Crafts, catalogue, Japan
1989   *Expressions en Verre II: Collection du Musee des Art Decoratifs, Lausanne*
       Dan Klein, *Glass: A Contemporary Art*
       Susanne Frantz, *Contemporary Glass*, Abrams
       Helmut Ricke, *Reflex der Jahrhunderte*, Kunstmuseum Düsseldorf
1990   *Glas — van drinkbeker tot kunstobject*, catalogue, Antwerpen
       Helmut Ricke, *New Glas in Europe*, Verlagsanstalt Handwerk

Selected Published Articles
1987   Paper on the 'Vessel' for Gulbenkian Foundation
1988   'Colin Reid', *Glass Art Japan*
1990   Glass schools: 'West Surrey College of Art and Design', *Glasswork*, December

KIRSTIE REA
1955   Born in Australia
Education
1986   Bachelor of Arts (Visual), Glass Major, Graphic Investigation Minor, Canberra School of Art
Related Professional Experience
1979–80   Attended various Stained Glass courses
1981–85   Attended workshops covering Design, Lampworking, Neon Photo Image on Glass and Painting on Glass
1982   Travelled overseas visiting glass exhibitions, galleries, collections in the UK and France
1983   Part-time teacher in Stained Glass
1987   Established studio in Canberra
1988   Part-time Lecturer, Glass Workshop, Canberra School of Art
1988   Participant, Kilnformed Techniques, International Master Workshop in Glass, Canberra
1989–91   Part-time Lecturer, Glass Workshop, CITA, Canberra
1990   Workshop Lecturer, ANU Arts Centre
1991   Conducted Jewellery/Glass Kilnwork Course, Crafts Council of the ACT
1991   Attended Occupational Heath and Safety Seminar, Dr Alan Pomeroy, Crafts Council of the ACT
1991   Attended AICCM Stained Glass Conservation Seminar, S.H. Ervin Gallery, Sydney
1991   Attended Fifth Ausglass Conference, University of NSW, Sydney
1991–92   Vice-President and committee member, Ausglass International
1992–94   Part-time Lecturer, Glass Workshop, CITA, Canberra
1993   Participant, Printmaking from glass plates, International Summer School workshop, Canberra School of Art
       Ausglass Conference and Workshops, Canberra

Exhibitions
1985   Third National Glass Biennial, touring exhibition, WWCAG, Wagga Wagga, NSW
       Ausglass Members Exhibition, Sydney College of the Arts
1986   'Glass Gems '86', Venture Gallery, Michigan
       'Survey Two', Devise Gallery, Melbourne
       'Australian Crafts 1986', Meat Market, Melbourne
1987   'Pilchuck Staff Show, session 5, Pilchuck Glass School, USA
       'Australian Crafts 1987', Meat Market, Melbourne
       'Glass in Public Spaces', Westpac Gallery, Arts Centre, Melbourne
       'Glass', Canberra School of Art Graduates, Victorian State Craft Collection Gallery, Melbourne
1988   'Fourth National Studio Glass Exhibition', WWCAG, Wagga Wagga, NSW

       ANZ Prize Show, Glass Artists' Gallery, Sydney
       'Kilnformed Glass: An International Exhibition', Crafts Council Gallery, Canberra
       'Australian Crafts 1988', Meat Market, Melbourne
       'Glass From Canberra', Despard Street Gallery, Hobart
1989   'Australian Kilnformed Glass', Kurland/Summers Gallery, Los Angeles, Habitat Galleries, Detroit
       'International *Pâte de Verre* Exhibition', Galerie Bergmann, Germany
       Staff Show, CITA, Canberra
1990   'Australian Kilnformed Glass', Heller Gallery, New York
1991   'Canberra Souvenir Show', Canberra Contemporary Art Space, ACT
       CAPO Annual Art Auction, ACT
       'Appreciating the Medium', Glass Artists' Gallery, Sydney
       'Challenging the Medium', Blaxland Gallery, Sydney
       Ausglass Members Show, St Andrews College, Sydney
       'Australian Kilnformed Glass', Habitat Gallery, Miami
1992   'Treed', Canberra Contemporary Art Space, ACT
       'Design Visions', Art Gallery of WA, Perth
       'Blundstone Invitation Exhibition', Tasmanian Contemporary Art Space, Hobart
1993   'Off the Beaten Track', solo exhibition, Edith Cowan University, WA
       'Eleven Women Sculptors', Beaver Galleries, ACT
       'Women Under Glass', The Door Exhibition Space, Fremantle, WA
       'Directions Glass Jewellery', Canberra School of Art Gallery Foyer
       'Origins & Originality', Ausglass Members Exhibition, Drill Hall Gallery, Canberra
1994   Collectors Circle Exhibition (for a touring group of American collectors affiliated with The American Craft Museum of New York), Beaver Galleries, ACT

Grants
1988/89   ACT Arts Development Fund Grant for workshop development
Collections
AGWA, Perth
Victorian State Craft Collection, Melbourne
Latrobe Valley Art Centre Collection, Vic
Private collections in the USA, Japan and Australia
Slide Collections
'New Glass Review 8', Corning, New York
Crafts Council of Australia Slide Library
Crafts Council of the ACT Slide LIbrary
Publications
1985   *Craft Australia*, 1
1986   *Craft Australia*, 1
       Craft Australia Year Book
       Neues Glas, 1/86
1987   *Craft Australia*, 1
1988   *Craft Australia*, 2, 3
1992   *Glasswork*, No. 13
1993   *Neues Glas*, 1/93

SERGIO REDEGALLI
1962   Born in Milano, Italy
Tertiary Education
1984   Bachelor of Arts (Visual Arts), Sydney College of the Arts
1988   Graduate Diploma Visual Arts, Sydney College of the Arts
Related Professional Experience
1985–88   Tutor, Sydney College of the Arts
1987–88   Private workshops, Sydney; Brisbane
1984–88   Various commissions
1987   Established 'Cydonia, The Glass Studio'
1988–91   Glass Kiln Work, Life and Leisure workshops, Macquarie University Union
1991   Casting workshops, Sydney College of the Arts
Boards
1984–87   Sydney Youth Festival
Exhibitions
1984   Graduate Exhibition, Sydney College of the Arts
       Small Work Exhibition, Glass Artists' Gallery, Sydney

Christmas Show, Glass Artists' Gallery, Sydney
1985 Two-man show, Glass Artists' Gallery, Sydney
Ausglass, Sydney
Third National Glass Biennial, WWCAG, Wagga Wagga, NSW
Meat Market, Melbourne
1986 Penrith Regional Art Gallery, NSW
1987 'Glass In Public Spaces', Westpac Gallery, Arts Centre, Melbourne
1988 World Expo 88, Brisbane
Stock Show, Glass Artists' Gallery, Sydney
Graduate Exhibition, ex Sydney College of the Arts, Pier 2–3, Sydney
1989 Park Royal Hotel, Parramatta, NSW
1990 Fisher's Ghost statue/marquette, Campbelltown City Council, NSW

Publications
1985 *Australia*, No. 1, Autumn; No. 2, Winter
1986 *Australia*, No. 2, Winter; No. 3, Spring
1986 Year Book
1988 *Outlook*, No. 147, February, Pilkington
1988 *World Expo 1988*, 30 April, Brisbane
'Australia Celebrates 11', *Australian Womens Weekly*
A Touch Of Glass, Pathways Board of Botanic Gardens of Adelaide, July
'Up Pompe 11', Richard Walsh, *Mode Australia*, September
1989 *Interior Designers and Decorators Handbook of Australia*, Vol. 6, No. 2,
Interior Architecture and Design, No. 20
The Advertiser, 13 October, p. 3
Interior Designers Handbook, Vol. 8, No. 1

Commissions
1984 National Tourism Awards
'Pop Art' Show, Art Gallery of NSW, Sydney
1985–88 Private commissions
1986–87 Specific interior/architectural commissions
World Expo 88, Brisbane, commissioned by John Truscott for the
World Expo Authority, purchased by Pilkington Australia
1988 Specific interior commissions
George Hayim (Duchess of Cremorne): Magic egg light
Pilkington Australia: Glass lectern for Ingleburn float plant opening,
currently resides at Pilkington Service Centre, Melbourne
1989 Private residence, Vaucluse
Trikon Corporation: Crystal logo
Limited Edition glass sculptures, Small Business Awards
L. J. Hooker International: Sculpture 100th Birthday
Glass Trophies, Limited Edition, Australian Entrepreneur Awards
Crystal 'G'Day' Chair in association with D4 Design, second annual
'G'Day' Gala Benefit Auction, November
Skygarden, Pitt Street, Sydney: Custom lighting (including all art glass
lights)
Glass floor, main entry; Glass, steel and brass wall
Custom Glass Walls, private home, of 3m x 3m of kiln patterned
glass/fused glass, Balmoral, Sydney
Main entry light form (raindrops of glass 2.8 metres long), drops of
glass and neon, private home, Burraneer, NSW
1989– Glass Awards, VIDA (Video Industries Distributors Association), (on
going)
Glass Lectern 2, Pilkington Australia, 1990
1991 Exchange Plaza, Perth (Cydonia): Art glass panels
Westpac lift refurbishment, Sydney: Art glass panels
Sculptural Award for Billy Joel, commissioned by Sony

Collections
Works held in a number of private collections
Parliament House Collection, Canberra
Bicentennial Conservatory, The Botanic Garden of Adelaide
Private collection, USA
George Hayim (Duchess of Cremorne) Collection

MEZA RIJSDIJK
1955 Born in the Netherlands
Education
1982–86 Attended a number of short workshops, covering a variety of glass
techniques

1983–86 Bachelor of Arts (Visual Art), Glass Major, Canberra School of Art,
graduated with distinction; studied under Klaus Moje, Neil Roberts and
guest lecturers
1985 Pilchuck Glass School, USA, assisted by the Crafts Board of the
Australia Council
Related Professional Experience
1982 Stained Glass worker, Lightplayers Glass Studio, ACT
1983 Attended Third National Ausglass Conference
1985 'Education: A Student's Perspective', presentation, Fourth National
Ausglass Conference
Teacher of Stained Glass, Crafts Council of the ACT; Cooma CCE, NSW
1985–87 ACT Ausglass Representative
1987 Teaching position, Glass Workshop, Canberra School of Art
1988 Participant, International Masterworkshop at the Canberra School of Art
Established a workshop in Sydney, with the assistance of the Visual
Arts/Crafts Board, Australia Council
Glass Casting Teacher, World Education Fellowship Creative Arts
Summer School
1989 Artist-in-Residence, conducted a workshop in Advanced Lost-wax
Casting, Glass Workshop, Adelaide CAE
Workshop in experimental kiln work, Sixth National Ausglass
Conference
1989–90 Member, Executive Committee, Ausglass
1991 Attended opening, Australian Kiln Formed Glass Exhibition, Boca
Raton, Florida (funded by the Australia Council)
Glass Artists Society (GAS) Conference, Corning, New York
1993 Artist-in-Residence, University of New England, Lismore, NSW
Presentation at the Eighth National Ausglass Conference
Solo Exhibitions
1992 Trio, 'Highly Strung', Blaxland Gallery, Sydney
1987 'Works in Glass', Crafts Council of the ACT, Canberra
Group Exhibitions
1983 Members Exhibition, Crafts Council of the ACT
1984 'Small Goods', Glass Artists' Gallery, Sydney
1985 Third National Glass Biennial, WWCAG, Wagga Wagga, NSW
1986 'Glass Gems 1986', La Gallerie Trois, Geneva, Switzerland, with Seguso
Art Glass Venture Gallery, Michigan
1987 'Australian Crafts 1987', Meat Market, Melbourne
'Melbourne Glass', Victorian State Craft Collection Gallery, Melbourne
1988 Fourth National Studio Glass Exhibition, WWCAG, Wagga Wagga, NSW
'Kiln Formed Glass: An International Exhibition', Crafts Council of the
ACT
ANZ Glass Prize, Glass Artists' Gallery, Sydney
'Glass from Canberra', Joyce Gallery, Tas
1989–91 'Australian Kilnformed Glass', touring the USA: Habitat Galleries,
Chicago; Kurland/Summers Gallery, Los Angeles; Heller Gallery, New
York
1989 'An International Exhibition of Fused Glass', Monica Trujen, Glass
Galerie, Bremen, Germany
'President's Choice', Meat Market, Melbourne
ANZ Glass Prize, Glass Artists' Gallery, Sydney
1990 'Scale Detail', Habitat Gallery, MI, USA
'Glass Sculpture', The Blaxland Gallery, Melbourne
'Australian Crafts 1990', Meat Market, Melbourne
'Wearable Glass 1990', Glass Artists' Gallery, Sydney
1991 'Challenging the Medium', The Blaxland Gallery, Sydney
'Appreciating the Medium', Glass Artists' Gallery, Sydney
'Australian Kilnformed Glass', Habitat Gallery, Florida
'Glas Verschmelzungen', GlasMuseum Rheinbach, Germany
1992 'Glass Jewellery', Deutsches Goldschmiedehaus, Hanau, Germany
(touring to eight galleries in Germany during 1992 and 1993)
'Design Visions', The Australian International Crafts Triennial, AGWA,
Perth
1993 'The Second Landing', NGV, Melbourne
ACI Glass Award, Meat Market, Melbourne
'Coast to Coast', an exhibition of 24 Artists from the Blaxland Gallery,
Myer, Perth
'Fire and Ice', Golden Canvas Gallery, Sydney

Awards

1983   Second Prize, Hawker College Art Prize
1985   Crafts Board of the Australia Council Grant for overseas study at Pilchuck Glass School, USA
1987   Grant for Workshop Development, Visual Arts/Crafts Board of the Australia Council
1989   ANZ Glass Prize, section 'Wall Panels'
1991   Ausglass Award, 'Appreciating the Medium', Glass Artists' Gallery, Sydney:
       work suited for reproduction and/or limited edition — joint award with Brian Hirst

Selected Commissions

1987   New Parliament House, Canberra: Two windows for stairwells, one in the Senate wing, one in the House of Representatives wing
1988   The Craig Brewery Bar & Grill, Darling Harbour: Glass mural in collaboration with Cherry Phillips
1990   Ethnic Business Awards, National Australia Bank
       Hakoa Club, Bondi: Glass sculpture placed in fountain in entrance hall
1991   Ethnic Business Awards, National Australia Bank
       Libesa Trading Co., Singapore: Large cast glass candle-holders
       Light fittings for refurbishment of Qantas Building, Sydney
       Jolly Knight Motel Seafood Restaurant, Casula: Feature light shades
       Danny Venlet (designer), for refurbishment of the Burdekin Hotel, Surry Hills: Light shades
1992   Private Residence, Bondi: Cast glass bedhead rim
       Park Lane Hotel, Sydney: 2 cast glass sculptures
       Southbank, Brisbane (Expo Site): Exterior light fittings
       ICAA Microsoft: Trophies
1993   Private Residence, Vaucluse: Wall sculpture *Nexus*
       Private Residence, Birchgrove: Wall construction
       ABC Fine Music Awards
       Papua New Guinea Commemorative Games Award
       St Bridgets Catholic Church: Cast glass eagle
       Birchmore Productions: Miniature glass film set

Collections

Corning Museum of Glass, New York
Parliament House Collection, Canberra
St George Building Society
Victorian State Craft Collection, Melbourne
AGWA, Perth
WWCAG, Wagga Wagga, NSW
Private collections in Australia and overseas

Publications

1985   'New Glass Review 6', *Neues Glas*, p. 125
1986   *Craft Australia Year Book*
1987   Lorraine Kloppman, 'Pate de Verre', *Craft Arts*, October/December, p. 57
1988   *Expressing Australia*, Art in Parliament House, p. 22–3
       Nola Anderson, 'Process and Idea', International Master Workshops in Glass, *Craft Australia*, No. 2, Winter, p. 93/*Craft Australia*, No. 3, Spring, pp. 63–4
       Marilynne Bell, 'Studio Glass Profile', *Craft Arts*, February/April, p. 69
1989   'Contemporary Glass Goes Everywhere', review, *Neues Glas*, 1/89
       Victorian State Craft Collection Catalogue
       Pottery in Australia, Vol. 28, No. 4, December
1992   *Glasswork*, No.13, November, Japan, pp. 11–12
1993   'Design Visions', *Neues Glas*, 1/93, front cover, pp. 11–21
       Ausglass Conference Report 1993, pp. 20–21

ANN ROBINSON

1944   Born in Auckland, New Zealand

Education

1980   Degree, Auckland University School of Fine Arts

Related Professional Experience

1990/92   Canberra School of Art, ACT
1990/92/93   Carrington Polytechnic, Auckland, NZ
1992   Pilchuck Glass School, USA ('Lost Wax Casting of Hollow Forms')

Selected Solo Exhibitions

1984   Artisan Centre, solo exhibition, Auckland, NZ
1990   New Zealand Crafts Council Wellington, solo exhibition, NZ
1992   Master Works Gallery, solo exhibition, Parnell, NZ
1993   Solo exhibition, Elliott Brown Gallery, Seattle

Selected Group Exhibitions

1981   'Glass '81', Auckland Society of Arts, NZ
1982   'Fragile Art', Northern Regional Crafts Council, touring New Zealand
1983   'Glass '83', touring New Zealand
1986   'Phillips Glass Exhibition', Auckland Museum, NZ
       'Sunbeam Glassworks', Dowse Art Museum, Lower Hutt, Wellington, NZ
1987   'Winstone Biennale', Auckland Museum, NZ
1988   'Kilnformed Glass: An International Exhibition', Craft Council Gallery of ACT, Canberra
       'World Glass Now '88', Hokkaido Museum of Modern Art, Sapporo, Japan
       'Stones in Glass Houses', Villas Gallery, Wellington, NZ
       New Zealand Expo Exhibition of Craft, Brisbane
1989–91   'Australian Kilnformed Glass', touring the USA: Habitat Galleries, Chicago; Kurland/Summers Gallery, Los Angeles; Heller Gallery, New York
1991   'The Executive Suite', Crafts Council Gallery, Wellington, NZ
       'New Zealand Glass Review', Compendium Gallery, Auckland, NZ
1992   'International Pilchuck Exhibition', William Traver Gallery, Seattle
       'Cribbs, Marioni and Robinson' (Kate Elliott Contemporary Glass), CINAFE, Navy Pier, Chicago
       'Contemporary Kilnformed Glass', Contemporary Crafts Centre, Portland, Oregon
       'Glass Now '92', Tokyo
       'International Directions in Glass', AGWA, Perth
       'Treasures from the Underworld', Seville, Spain
1993   'Parriott, Perkins and Robinson' (Kate Elliott Contemporary Glass), CINAFE, Navy Pier, Chicago
       'Pilchuck Glass Exhibition', Seattle
       'Habitat International', Farmington Hills, MI
1994   Glass from the Pacific Rim, State University, San Francisco, California
       Art Departments Gallery, San Francisco, California

Awards, Scholarships and Commissions

1983/84   Equipment grant, Queen Elizabeth II Arts Council
1984/86   Phillips Glass Award
1986   Travel grant to USA, Queen Elizabeth II Arts Council
1987   Winstone Biennale Award
1991   Equipment grant, Queen Elizabeth II Arts Council
       'Treasures from the Underworld', commission for New Zealand Expo Exhibition, Seville, Spain

Selected Public and Private Collections

Auckland Museum, Auckland, NZ
Dowse Gallery, Lower Hutt, NZ
Irvin J. Borowsky, Philadelphia, Pennsylvania
Karen Johnson Boyd, Racine, Wisconsin
National Museum of New Zealand, Wellington
Queensland Art Gallery, Brisbane

Publications

1988   *World Glass Now '88*, Hokkaido Museum, Japan
1989   Dan Klein, *Glass: A Contemporary Art* , p. 208
       Australia Kilnformed Glass, Australia Council for the Arts and Kurland/Summers Gallery, pp. 16–17
1992   Helen Shamroth, 'Glass Art in New Zealand', *Neues Glas*, 1/92, pp. 40–6
       Contemporary Kilnformed Glass, Contemporary Crafts Association, Portland, Oregon, pp. 64–5
1993   *New Glass Review*, Corning, New York, p. 92
       Donna Sapolin, 'Glass Conscienceness', *Departures* magazine, April/May, pp. 76–81, *78*

PADDY (PATRICIA) ROBINSON

1944   Born in Northern Ireland

Education
1961–64   College Diploma (Stained Glass), Belfast College of Art
1965   Art Teacher's Diploma (N.I.), Belfast College of Art
Related Professional Experience
1966–68   Stained Glass Painter, Ars Sacra Studios (Stephen Moor)
1968–73   Stained Glass Artist, Eroica Studios (David Saunders)
1973–   Started Glin Studio
1989–   Formed Finglinna Studios with Neil Finn
Teaching Experience
1965–66   Art Teacher, NSW Department of Education
1979–88   Lecturer, Nepean College of Advanced Education
1970–   Private teaching, Eroica Studios and then in Glin Studio
Exhibitions
1964/65   Royal Dublin Society, Ireland
1979/83   Blake Prize, Sydney
1980   Window on Galoa
1982   Meat Market, Melbourne
1987   Group show of Glass Engraving, Sydney Opera House
1989   French Bicentennial Exhibition, Centre Internationale du Vitrail, France
          Glass Engraving, group exhibtion, Beaver Galleries, Canberra
1993   Balmain Showcase, Sydney
Major Commissions
Glin Studio and Finglinna Studios:
St Patricks Catholic Church, Sutherland, Sydney: Approx 100 square metre *dalles de verre* ceiling and other ceilings and windows.
St Josephs Church, Camperdown, Sydney: Approx 15 square metre leadlight.
Anglican Cathedral, Grafton, NSW: Five painted windows approx 1/2 square metres each.
Church of the Good Shepherd Catholic Church, Plumpton, NSW: Approx 30 square metre leadlights, one ceiling light.
Sacred Heart Hospice, Darlinghurst, Sydney: Approx 6 square metre bent, laminated and carved window.
Waverley Friary Chapel, Waverley, Sydney: Approx 20 square metre leadlight, acid-etched and engraved.
Sacred Heart Church, Pymble, Sydney: Approx 40 square metre leadlight in ceiling.
Sacred Heart Church, Mona Vale: Approx 2 square metre window and life-size laminated glass statue of Sacred Heart, tabernacle (glass) and sanctuary lamp.
Liverpool RSL Club: Approx 20 square metre sandblasted and laminated screen, with three-dimensional figure on bent-glass display stand.
Our Lady of the Way Catholic Church, Emu Plains, NSW: Decorative glazing of church, approx 14 square metre three-dimensional dichroic glass and antique glass ceiling light, glass tabernacle and sanctuary lamp.
Our Lady of Victories Catholic Church, Horsley Park, Sydney: Approx 30 square metre traditional painted glass in small and large Gothic-shaped windows.
Paradiso Wedding Reception Centre, Fairfield, Sydney: Approx 6 square metre sandblasted, engraved and laminated screen, fanlights and leadlights.
Bellevue Function Centre, Bankstown, Sydney: Approx 9 square metre sandblasted, etched, engraved and laminated glass screen.
Loreto Home for the Aged, Bronte, Sydney: Approx 20 square metre copperfoil window.
Bankstown Sports Club: Approx 3–6 metre high glass sculpture, water and sandblasted and engraved.
Our Lady of Mt Carmel Catholic Church, Mt Pritchard, NSW: Approx 100 square metre of *dalles de verre* incorporating kiln-laminated enamelled float glass.
Mt Pritchard Community Club, NSW: Approx 6 square metre multi-layered blasted, engraved and laminated glass screen.
Major Collections
College of Obstetrics & Gynaecology, Melbourne
University of Western Sydney, Kingswood, NSW
University of Adelaide, SA
Private collections in Australia, USA and the UK
Publications
1966   *Bulletin*
1978   *Pol*
1981   *Belle*
1988   *Vogue*
          Craft Australia
1990   *Craft Arts*

KEITH ROWE
Born in 1952
Education
1977–70   Studied Photography, Australian Centre of Photography
1979–81   Studied Photography and Glass, Sydney College of the Arts
1981   Bachelor of Arts (Visual Art), Glass and Photography, Sydney College of the Arts
Workshops and Tuition
1980   Sheoak workshop in Hot Glass, Jerry King, Con Rhee, Julio Santos
1980   2 week exchange program, tutored by Dennis O'Conner and Julio Santos, CIT, Melbourne
1981   Ausglass conference, Hot Glass demonstrations, Melbourne
1983   Conference and workshops, Marvin Lipofsky (USA), Makato Ito (Japan) and Fred Daden (UK), assisted Makato Ito during demonstrations, New Zealand Society of Artists in Glass (NZSAG)
1984   Assisted Martin Lipofsky (USA), demonstrating in Glebe Hot Glass Studio, Sydney
1985   Ausglass Conference and workshop on Furnace Technology with Durk Valkema and Anna Carlgren
1986   NZSAG Conference and workshop, William Morris (USA)
1987   Ausglass Conference and workshop, Fred Daden (UK)
1988   NZSAG Conference and workshop, Dick Marquis (USA)
1989   Ausglass Conference and workshop, Gary Nash (NZ), assisted in workshop tuition
1990   NZSAG workshop, Rob Levin (USA)
1993   Ausglass Conference and workshop in Lost-wax Casting and Mould Building, David Reekie (UK) and Katsuya Ogita (Japan)
Related Professional Experience
1979–80   Operated and maintained Mobile Glass Furnace, Sydney College of the Arts
1982   Traineeship grant, Crafts Board of New South Wales, to work with Nick Mount of Budgeree Glass
1982–86   Co-director, Glass Artists' Gallery, Sydney
1983–90   Established Glebe Hot Glass Studio, operating as an access studio, hiring furnace time to competent glass workers and giving tuition in regular beginners workshops
1983–88   Tutor in Hot Glass, Sydney College of the Arts
1989/90/91 Guest Tutor, Underdale SACE
1990   Established Keith Rowe Glass at Blackheath, Blue Mountains, NSW
Solo Exhibitions
1982   Outsider Gallery
          Sketchbook Gallery
1983   Christopher Alexander Gallery, Wentworth Falls, NSW
1984   Pigments and Palettes Gallery, Orange
          Glass Artists' Gallery, Sydney
1985   Cuppacumbalong Gallery, Canberra
1987   Bonython Gallery, Woollahra, Sydney
1987/88   Hamilton Glass Gallery, Lane Cove, Sydney
1990/91   Bramae Gallery, Springwood, NSW
1991   Holdsworth Gallery, Woollahra
          Avenue & Art Gallery, Mosman
1993   Holdsworth Gallery, Woollahra
Group Exhibitions
1983/84   Virtu Gallery, Brisbane
          Stokers Siding Gallery
1985/86   Ausglass Conference Exhibition
1985–91   Hamilton Glass Gallery, Lane Cove
1982–90   Glass Artists' Gallery, Sydney
1986   Woodcraft Gallery
1987   Bonython Meadmore Gallery, Woollahra, Sydney
1988   Meat Market, Melbourne
          Ozart Gallery, Newcastle, NSW
1988/91   Classic Stained Glass Studio
1990   Avenue and Art Gallery, Orange, NSW
1991/92   Crafters Gallery, Tamborine Mountain, Qld
1991   Lewers Bequest; Penrith Regional Gallery, NSW
1991   Blaxland Gallery, Sydney
1993   Crafters Gallery, Tamborine Mountain, Qld

1993   'Egg Show', Meat Market, Melbourne
Major Commissions
1988   OTC Building, Sydney: Executive offices and foyer
1989   Hyatt Regency, Coolum, Qld: VIP suites and foyer
1990   Ritz Carlton Hotel, Sydney
1990/91   'Keep Australia Beautiful' Co. Ltd: Trophy
Major Collections
Powerhouse Museum, Sydney
Rockhampton Regional Art Gallery, Canberra
Parliament House, Sydney

LUNA RYAN
1957   Born in the Netherlands
Education
1987–90   Bachelor of Arts (Visual), CITA, Canberra
Exhibitions
1990   'Stand-By', Final Year Student Exhibition, Canberra School of Art
1992   Exhibition of International Glass Art, Glass Art Centre, Schalkwijk, The
          Netherlands
1993   'Ten Years of Acquisitions: A Selection from the ANU Collection', Drill
          Hall Gallery, Canberra
1994   'Collector's Show', Glass Artists' Gallery, Sydney
Awards
1990   ANU Award
1990   EASS
Collections
ANU, Canberra
Publications
1991   'New Glass Review 12', *Neues Glas*, 2/91

PAUL SANDERS
Born in 1963
Education
1990   Bachelor of Arts, Ceramics/Glass Design, Charles Sturt University,
          Riverina, NSW
1991   Post Graduate studies in Glass Design, produced paper on Glass
          Colouration Technique, graduated with High Distinction, Monash
          University Chisholm Campus, Melbourne
Solo Exhibitions
1990   H.R. Gallop Gallery, Wagga Wagga, NSW
          Blackwood Street Gallery/Meat Market, Melbourne
Group Exhibitions
1988   Fourth National Studio Glass Exhibition, WWCAG, Wagga Wagga,
          NSW
1989   'Crossing the Rubicon', H.R. Gallop Gallery, Wagga Wagga, NSW
1990   Veritas Galleria, El Dorado, Vic
1991   '4 New Artists', Glass Artists' Gallery, Sydney
          Fifth National Studio Glass Exhibition, WWCAG, Wagga Wagga, NSW
          'Fresh', Glass Artists' Gallery, Sydney
1992   'Vessel Variations', Glass Artists' Gallery, Sydney
1993   'Small Works', Glass Artists' Gallery, Sydney
          CINAFE, Navy Pier, Chicago
          'Glass Plus', Glass Artists' Gallery, Sydney
1994   'Collectors Exhibition', Glass Artists' Gallery, Sydney
Commissions
1993   Nu-Skin Award
1994   Australian Meat & Livestock Corporation Awards
Collections
Ebeltoft Glasmuseum, Denmark
Wagga Wagga National Glass Collection, NSW
Adelaide Institute of Higher Education, SA
Monash University Art Collection, Melbourne
Nikko Hotel Art Collection
Dennis Clifford Glass Collection, Australia
Private collections in the UK, France, USA and Australia

JULIO SANTOS
1933   Born in Portugal

Solo Exhibitions
1980   Australian Gallery, Melbourne
1981/83   Craft Centre, South Yarra, Melbourne
1982/84/88/90 Von Bertouch Galleries, Newcastle NSW
1983/91   Australian Craftworks, Sydney
1984   Beaver Galleries, Canberra
1985/86/93 Distelfink Gallery, Melbourne
1986   Alvin Gallery, Hong Kong
1987   Japan, Ube; Maitland City Art Gallery, NSW
1989/91   Maitland City Gallery, NSW
1991   Newcastle Region Art Gallery
Plus numerous group exhibitions
Commissions
His Excellency Sir Zelman Cowan: Plate, personal gift to Prince Charles
Premier of NSW: Plate, gift to member of Government of China
Australian Institute of Management, Sydney: Large chandelier
Plate presented to the Prime Minister of Australia
Several pieces of glass presented to various heads of State and international
visitors to Australia
Major Collections
Government House, Brisbane: 4 chandeliers and plate (Latticino)
Queensland Art Gallery, Brisbane: Glass plates
Queen Victoria Museum and Art Gallery, Launceston, Tas: Bowl
NGV, Melbourne: Vase
Hamilton Gallery Collection: Cylinder
Northern Territory Museum of Arts and Science, Darwin
ANG, Canberra

STEPHEN SKILLITZI
Education
1966   Ceramics Certificate, National Art School, Sydney
1970   Masters Degree in Fine Art, University of Massachusetts, USA
Related Professional Experience
1967–   Ceramics studio employee, London
1968–   First student of Dale Chihuly (now the world's most famous glass artist)
1968–82   Established a glass studio in USA and many in Australia for both
          students and own use
1969–75   Published articles, made a short film and lectured on the 'USA Hot
          Glass Studio Movement'; received a Craft Board grant for Glass;
          established a 'studio furnace' for glassblowing, public demonstrations
          and training glass assistants; exhibited blown glass; initiated blowing
          furnaces within art schools; experimented with kiln-glass and
          electroforming on glass; included in an international studio glass
          exhibition; employed as a glass artist-in-residence for glass industries
1987–   Full-time work on commissions, and exhibitions mostly in the USA
Teaching Experience
1969–70   Part-time, Ceramics, Glassblowing, Design, USA
1970–73   Part-time, Ceramics, Glassblowing, Sydney
1976–87   Full-time, Ceramics, Glass, Design, Bachelor of Design Degree at
          SACAE, Adelaide
1970–   Numerous lectures and workshops, including six national conferences,
          and overseas tours in 1981/89/90/91
Solo Exhibitions
Over 30 solo exhibitions since 1966 including:
1967   Aladdin Gallery, Sydney
1970   Graduate Show, University of Massachusetts, USA
1972   Realities Gallery, Melbourne
1979   Gallery 180, Melbourne
1981   Holdsworth Gallery, Sydney
1981   Bonython Gallery, Adelaide
1986   Studio 20, Adelaide
1988   Bethany Gallery, Tanunda, SA
1991   Judy Youens Gallery, Houston, Texas
1992   Miller Gallery, New York
Group Exhibitions
1975   International Glass Touring Exhibition, Europe
1981   Contemporary Glass, Japan
1987   'Glass in Public Spaces', Cultural Centre, Melbourne

1988   Sculpture Triennial, Mildura, Vic
1989   Pilchuck Glass School, USA
1990   Invitational, The Glass Gallery, Washington DC
1990/91 18th/19th Annual Internationals, Habitat Galleries, Detroit
1994/95 'Contemporary Glass', Japan

Awards
1966/71/76 Clay Art Prizes
1968–70 Scholarships, USA
1971/74/75 Craft Board Grants
1992   Silver Award, Kristallnacht Project, USA

Selected Commissions
1987   Mildura Shire Council, Victoria, Australia: Space divider — 'Columns of Life No. 1'
1988   Hyatt Hotel Adelaide, SA: Glass screen with neon — 'Waves'
1992   Alice Springs, NT: Trophies for Brolga Awards
1993   Adelaide Central Mission: Foyer sculpture

Performance Art
10 occasions from 1968–88 in USA and Australia

Selected Public Collections
ANG, Canberra
NGV, Melbourne
Most state and regional galleries in Australia
Ebeltoft Glasmuseum, Denmark
Private collections in Australia and overseas, 3 USA art museums

Publications
Solo articles:
1969–   *Pottery in Australia*: 6
1981   *Craft Australia*
1981–   *Ausglass*: 12
1982   *Ceramica*, Spain
1985/87/90/93 *SA Crafts*
1988/93 *Craft Arts*
1992   *Glass*, USA
Shared articles:
1985   *Glass Review*, No. 5, USA
1987   *Neues Glas*
Plus articles in journals about Australian glass art, including four magazine/book cover photographs

PAMELA STADUS
Born in 1953
Education
General:
1970   Higher Education Certificate
1976   Higher Diploma Teaching, Secondary Art & Craft, Painting Major, Design Sub-major, University of Melbourne
1980   Graduate Diploma, Visual Communication, University of Melbourne
1986   Computer Graphics, Hawthorn Institute of Education, Melbourne
1988   Etching, Victorian College of the Arts
        Lithography, Monash University, Caulfield
1993   Masters in Craft, Monash University
Glass:
1984   Leadlight, self taught
1984–85 Warm Glass Techniques, David Wright
1986   Surface techniques: Etching and Sandblasting, Tony Hanning & Graham Stone
        Kiln forming with Allan Crynes
1987–88 Kiln Casting, Warren Langely and self-experimentation
1989   Lampworking, Ginny Ruffner
1990   Sandcasting, Henner Schroder and Jose Chardiet
        Pilchuck Glass School, USA
1991   Illusory Space in Glass, Dana Zamenikova
1993   Fellowship in Casting, Creative Glass Centre of America, Wheaton Village, New Jersey

Scholarships
1990   Nominated for Corning Scholarship, USA
        Study at Pilchuck Glass School, USA
1993   Fellowship in Glass Casting, Creative Glass Centre of America, USA

Post graduate course award to complete Master in Craft, Monash University, 1 year duration

Related Professional Experience
1990   Artist-in-Residence, Caulfield Grammar, Melbourne
1990   Nominated for ACI Glass Award, Meat Market, Melbourne

Teaching Experience
1976–77 Art and Graphic Communication, Sunshine West High School, Vic
1978–82 Co-ordinator, Senior Art and Graphic Communication, Magazine, Art Department, Newlands High School, Vic
1984   Art and Graphic Communication, Prahran High School, Vic
1985–86 Art, Computer Graphics & Graphic Communication, Templestowe High School, Vic
1987–91 Art, Graphic Communication, Printmaking, Stage Set Design & Construction, Caulfield Grammar School, Vic
1988   Sessional Teacher, Glass Casting, Victorian College of the Arts
1988–93 Sessional Tutor, Kiln-Formed and Painted Glass, Council of Adult Education, Vic
1990   Sessional Teacher, Warm Glass, Monash University, Caulfield, Vic
1991   Sessional Teacher, Warm Glass, Deakin University, Warrnambool, Vic
1992   Sessional Teacher, Sandcasting, University of Sydney

Exhibitions
1984   Caulfield Art Gallery, Vic
        Fringe Festival
1986   'Australian Craft', Meat Market, Melbourne
        Glass Artists' Gallery, Sydney
1987   Blackwood St Gallery,
        'Australian Craft', Meat Market, Melbourne
1988   'Australian Craft', Meat Market, Melbourne
1989   'Australian Craft', Meat Market, Melbourne
        Blackwood St Gallery,
1990   Solo exhibition, Caulfield Art Gallery, Vic
1991   Jewish Ceremonial Design Travelling
1992   Solo exhibition, Glass Artists' Gallery, Sydney
1993   Glass Artists' Gallery, Sydney
        Miller Gallery, New York
1994   Artefact, South Yarra

Awards
1991   Honourable Mention, Mornington Peninsula Art Award, Vic
1993   Highly Commended, Diamond Valley Art Award, Melbourne

Commissions
1992   3 People's Choice Award, Channel 7/*Woman's Day*
        Builder Owner's Marketing Association Award
        Collins St, Melbourne: Architectural lighting
1993   Housing Industry Award

Collections
1987   City of Hamilton Regional Art Gallery, Vic
1991   Diamond Valley Shire Council, Melbourne
1993   Creative Glass Centre of America, New Jersey
        WWCAG, Wagga Wagga, NSW
        Monash University Art Collection, Vic

GRAHAM STONE
Born in 1950
Exhibitions
1981–83 'Australian Crafts', Meat Market, Melbourne
1981   'Contemporary German/Australian Glass', Meat Market, Melbourne
1982   'Australian Glass', Distelfink Gallery, Melbourne
1983   Second National Glass Biennial, WWCAG, Wagga Wagga, NSW
        Ausglass II, Jam Factory, Adelaide
1984   'Graham Stone', MGM, Melbourne
1985   'Graham Stone', Glass Artists' Gallery, Sydney
1986   'Glass Survey', Distelfink Gallery, Melbourne
1987   'Glass Expo', Prism Galleries, Perth
1989   'President's Choice', Meat Market, Melbourne
        'Decade', Meat Market, Melbourne
1990–91 'The Graham Show', Qdos Gallery, Lorne, Vic
1991   National Glass Triennial, WWCAG, Wagga Wagga, NSW
1992   'The Bowl Show', Meat Market, Melbourne

1993 'Origins & Originality', Canberra Institute of the Arts
ACI Glass Award, Meat Market, Melbourne

Awards
1981 Design Acquisition, Meat Market, Melbourne
1983 Australia Council Professional Development Grant
1986 Artist-in-Residence, Geelong Grammar, Highton

Collections
State Craft Collection of Victoria, Melbourne
NGV, Melbourne
Antony Pilkington, Chairman of Pilkington Group, UK
Collection of the Premier, NSW
City of Campbelltown Collection, NSW
Pilkington Australia Collection
Wiiken Collection, Chicago

Commissions
1983 Pearse Residence, Toorak, Vic
1986 Geelong Grammar, Highton, Vic
1988 Nunawading Arts Centre (collaboratory community project), Melbourne
1989 Pilkington Australia
1990 Mildara Wines Ltd, SA
1991 Earth Exchange Mining Museum, Sydney
1992 Monash University Gippsland, Vic

Publications
1981 *Contemporary German Glass in Australia/Contemporary Australian Glass*, catalogue, p. 58
1982 *Craft Expo '82*, Crafts Council of Australia, illus, statement
Neues Glas, 1/82 p. 20
1983 *Adelaide Advertiser*, 25 January, illus., p. 11
Neues Glas, 1/83, illus., pp. 4, 5
The Age, 19 July, p. 20
1984 *Craft Australia Year Book*, Crafts Council of Australia, p. 75
1985 Graham Stone, review, *Craft Victoria*, No. 154, April, pp. 9, 10
1988 *State Craft Collection*, catalogue, introduction by Geoffrey Edwards, illus.
Jenny Zimmer, *Craft Australia*, No. 4, Summer, p. 83
1989 *Outlook*, No. 159, March, illus., p. 2
1990 *Australian Furnishing Trade Journal*, February, illus., p. 45
Ease Newsletter, June, front cover, illus., pp. 1, 2
1991 *Geelong Advertiser*, February
Crafts New South Wales, Spring, front cover, illus., p.35
1991–92 Graham Stone, reviews, *Ausglass Magazine*, Spring/Summer, pp. 2, 3, 11–13
1992 Review by Marie Geissler, *Craft Arts International*, No. 24, illus., p. 100
Review By Geoffrey Edwards, *Artlink*, Vol. 12 No. 2, Winter, illus., pp. 40, 41
1992–93 *Ausglass Magazine*, Summer, History (As Author), p.13–16
1993 Graham Stone, review, *Craft Victoria*
Graham Stone, review, *Ausglass Magazine*, Autumn, pp. 6–9

ITZELL TAZZYMAN
1971 Born in Santiago, Chile

Education
1993 Bachelor of Arts (Visual Art), First Class Hons, Glass Major, Printmaking Minor, Honours project in Artist Books, Canberra School of Art

Related Professional Experience
1992 Co-ordinator, Ausglass Student Exhibition, Ausglass Conference
1993 Technical Assistant, Glass Printmaking (Elizabeth Tapper, USA Richard Whitely, Australia), Ausglass Conference
Wrote a technical and conceptual manual on glass print making: 'Paper Images for the Glass Artist'
1994 Tutor, Lost-wax Casting workshop, Glass Workshop, Canberra School of Art
Assistant to Kirstie Rea, Artist Commission for Public Works

Group Exhibitions
1993 'Interval', Graduate show, Drill Hall Gallery, Canberra
'Surfacing', Graduate show, Glass Workshop, ACT
'Women Under Glass', The Door Exhibition Space, Fremantle, WA

'S/HE Feminist Trajectories', Travelling show NSW, ACT
Ausglass Members show, Drill Hall Gallery, Canberra
Ausglass National Student Show, Contemporary Art Space, Canberra
1994 'Surfacing', Glass Artists' Gallery, Sydney
'ActOut', First Draft Gallery, Sydney

Commissions
1992 *Canberra Times*: 'Artist of the Year' award trophy

PAVEL TOMECKO
1948 Born in Slovakia (formerly Czechoslovakia)
1982 Immigrated and settled in Adelaide, SA

Education
1963–67 'Secondary School of Art Glass Making', Zelezny Brod, Slovakia
1967–73 'Glass in Architecture' studio, headed by Professor Vaclav Cigler covering all glass making techniques, theory and teaching of art, Academy of Fine Arts, Bratislava, Slovakia
1973 Degree in Art Sculpture: Teaching Certificate and title Academic Sculptor

Related Professional Experience
1973–82 Lived and worked as a freelance glass artist in Bratislava, Slovakia
Participated in many national and international glass and sculpture exhibitions, gaining international recognition
Undertook commissions throughout Czechoslovakia in co-operation with architects and other glass artists
Personally designed and crafted sculptures from solid optical and coloured glass for European and American patrons
In 1981 was selected in the Corning Museum's 'New Glass Review 2'
1983–85 Employed by the Jam Factory, Adelaide to set up glass cutting and polishing workshop, to assist in the design of new production line and to train apprentices
Became partner in 'Novart Glass' and designed and produced optical glass sculptures, many commissioned for trophies and awards
Developed technique to unite optical glass sculptures with precious Australian opal
1985 Established own business 'Uniart Glass'
Continued to create original glass sculptures, many with opal, for selected galleries nationally and internationally: a series of sculptures selected as VIP gifts for the Prime Minister and cabinet
After winning Australian-wide competition, commissioned to design and produce a series of sailing trophies for all pre-races and the 1987 America's Cup
Other commissions include: Australian Design Council Award; The Prince Philip Prize; Australian Business Monthly Top 500 Awards; WA Architecture Design Awards; SA Manufacturer of the Year Award; Telecom Small Business Awards and a number of others
1991 Formed partnership with Daniela Tomecko (nee Marthova)
Invited by 'Ausglass' to lead the glass sculpturing workshop in Sydney, January 1991
Spent two weeks lecturing at Glass Workshop, Canberra Institute for Arts
Currently Working on commissioned trophies and awards. Continuing to design and create original works (for galleries, exhibitions and private collections) in partnership with Daniela Tomecko and singularly, with many designs incorporating Australian opal

Exhibitions
1970–82 Throughout Czechoslovakia
1971 Athens; Cairo; Istanbul, Turkey
1975 Vienna; Moscow; Erfurt, East Germany; Budapest; Lima, Peru; Novi Sad, Yugoslavia; Mexico City
1979 Havana, Cuba; New York
1979–80 Chicago
1980 Valencia, Spain; Los Angeles; Moscow; Riga, USSR; Vilnius, USSR; Berlin; Budapest
1981 Sofia, Bulgaria; Vienna; Munich
1982 Budapest; Havana, Cuba; Lausanne, Switzerland
1983 Ausglass Conference, Adelaide; Den Hague, Netherlands
1984 Adelaide; Nieuwegein, Netherlands
1985 Royal Art Association, Adelaide; Jam Factory, Adelaide

1986   Melbourne; Adelaide
1988   Jam Factory, Adelaide
1989–90 Melbourne
1991   Toronto, Canada; Budapest; Den Hague, Netherlands
1992   Bratislava, Slovakia; Munich
1993   Adelaide; Toronto, Canada

Collections

Slovak National Gallery, Czechoslovakia
City Museum of Bratislava, Czechoslovakia
Craft Art Museum, Prague, Czechoslovakia
Quality Crystal, Toronto, Canada
Superlux, New York
Artistic Fund, Poland
Gallery Lobmeyr, Vienna
Gallery Rob van den Doel, Netherlands
Hon. R.J. Hawke (former Prime Minister of Australia)
HRH Prince Philip, Duke of Edinburgh
Private collections in USA, Germany, San Marino, Hong Kong, the UK, Australia, Netherlands, Japan and many other countries

VICKI TORR

1949–1992 Adelaide, South Australia

Education

1983   Bachelor of Design, University of South Australia, Adelaide
1984   Joined workshop of Ian Mowbray, Jam Factory, Adelaide
1987   Established workshop in Unley, SA

Related Professional Experience

1987   Temporary Glass Tutor, University of South Australia, Underdale
         Campus
1990   Temporary Glass Tutor, University of South Australia, Underdale
         Campus

Selected Exhibitions

1983   Experimental Art Foundation, Adelaide
         'New Edition', Jam Factory, Adelaide
1984   'On and Off the Wall', Contemporary Art Centre, Adelaide
         'Glass from Australia and NZ', Darmstadt, Germany and touring
1985   'Two Glass Artists', Glass Artists' Gallery, Sydney
         Third National Glass Biennial, WWCAG, Wagga Wagga, NSW and
         touring
1986   'Australian Crafts 1986', Meat Market, Melbourne
         'Survey Two', Devise Gallery, Melbourne
         'Group Glass 1986', Hamilton Design Gallery, Sydney
         'Hot Shot Glass Show', Australian Craft Works, Sydney
1987   'Australian Crafts 1987', Meat Market, Melbourne
         'Beaver Award Exhibition', Beaver Galleries, Canberra, ACT
         Form and Function 2, 'The Bowl Show', Meat Market, Melbourne
         'Touch of Glass', Gallery Indigenous, Melbourne
1988   'Australian Crafts 1988', Meat Market, Melbourne
         International Exhibition of Glass Craft 1988, Kanazawa, Japan
         'Kilnformed Glass', Crafts Council of the ACT Gallery, Canberra
         'Classics', Craft Centre Gallery, Sydney
         'In Tasmania, in Australia', Design Centre, Launceston, Tas
         'Glass', Distelfink Gallery, Melbourne
         Fourth National Glass Exhibition, WWCAG, Wagga Wagga, NSW, and
         touring
         'Women 1988 Awards Exhibition', Devise Arts, Melbourne
1989   'Australian Glass 1989', Meat Market, Melbourne
         Second New Zealand Crafts Biennale, Auckland Museum, Auckland,
         NZ 'Adelaide in Himeji' art exhibition, Himeji, Japan
         Jam Factory Gallery, Adelaide
1989–91 'Australian Kilnformed Glass', Kurland/Summers Gallery, Los Angeles;
         Habitat Galleries, Detroit; Heller Gallery, New York; Habitat Galleries,
         Miami
1990   'Australian Glass', The Glass Gallery, Bethesda, Maryland, USA
         'Kilnformed Glass', Beaver Galleries, Canberra
         'Personal Visions', Royal SA Society of Arts, Adelaide
         International Exhibition of Glass 1990, Kanazawa, Japan
1991   'Challenging The Medium', Blaxland Gallery, Sydney

'World Glass Now', Hokkaido Museum of Modern Art, Sapporo, Japan
         National Glass Exhibition, WWCAG, Wagga Wagga, NSW
         'Coupe Colossus', Jam Factory Gallery, Adelaide
1992   Vichealth National Craft Award
         NGV, Melbourne
         AGWA, Perth

Selections and Awards

1987   'Glass Art': Kiln Formed, Beaver Galleries Award
1988   Workshop Development Grant, Australia Council

Commissions

1984   ANL Headquarters, SA: Conical glass lightshade (701 mm diameter)
1986   Northfield High School, SA: Glass mosaic wall (4.3 m x 3.8 m)
1989   Piper Alderman, SA: Fused glass panels (24 x 500 mm x 500 mm)
1991   Concept and designs for eastern wall of proposed Adelaide Magistrates
         Court, SA
         Regent Arcade, Adelaide, SA: Fused glass panels (9.5 m x 1.2 m)

Public Collections

Hokkaido Museum of Modern Art, Sapporo, Japan
Powerhouse Museum, Sydney
Queensland Art Gallery, Brisbane
Parliament House Collection, Canberra
Diamond Valley Art Collection, Melbourne
University of South Australia, Adelaide
City of Hamilton Art Gallery, Hamilton, Vic
Latrobe Valley Arts Centre, Morwell, Vic
Victorian State Craft Collection, Melbourne
Queen Victoria Museum and Art Gallery, Launceston, Tas
Art Gallery of South Australia, Adelaide
WWCAG, Wagga Wagga, NSW

Publications

1983   *Artlink*, Vol. 3, No. 5
1984   *Craft Australia*, Autumn
         Design World, No. 6
         Neues Glas, 4/84
1985   *Craft Australia*, Winter and Summer
         SA Crafts Year Book
1986   *Vogue Living*, February
         SA Crafts Year Book
         Craft Australia Year Book
1987   *Ausglass Magazine*, June
         Ausglass Magazine, September
1988   'New Glass Review 9', *Neues Glas*, 2/88
         Vogue Australia, No. 11, November
1989   *Craft Arts International*, No. 15, March/June

PETER TYSOE

1935   Born in the UK

Education

1952–57 Oxford School of Art
1957–58 Goldsmiths School of Art, London University

Related Professional Experience

1958–59 Lecturer in Art and Design, Oxford and London
1959–62 Officer in Royal Army Educational Corps, UK
1962–65 Lecturer in Art and Design, Devon, UK
1965–66 Exhibitions Officer, Crafts Council of Great Britain, UK
1966–84 Self-employed artist, ran own professional studios in Dartington and
         Totnes, Devon, UK
1985   Appointed Head of Glass, Jam Factory Craft and Design Centre,
         Adelaide

Commissions

Work in welded steel, cast aluminium and bronze and cast and blown glass has
been commissioned by architects and designers for hotels, banks and other public
and private buildings in the UK, the Middle East and Nigeria
1993   Design concept for 5 m x 3 m cast glass screen, Magistrates Court,
         Adelaide

Public Collections

City Art Gallery, Plymouth, UK
City Art Gallery, Liverpool, UK

City Art Gallery, Portsmouth, UK
Parliament House Collection, Canberra
Hamilton Art Gallery, Vic
Kunstsammlungen der Veste, Coburg, Germany
Musee des Arts Decoratifs Lausanne, Switzerland
Art Gallery of South Australia, Adelaide

VELTA VILMANIS
1949   Born in Adelaide, Australia
Education
1974   Bachelor of Architecture, University of Adelaide
1975   Registered architect
1989   Bachelor of Arts (Visual), Glass Major, Canberra Institute of the Arts
Travel/Study
1979–80   Travelled Europe visiting glass studios and workshops
1980   Stained Glass Workshop — Patrick Reyntiens' Studio, England
          London Glassblowing Workshop
1985   Glassblowing Workshop, Gerry King, Adelaide
          Stained Glass Workshop, Jochen Poensgen, Canberra
1986   Glassblowing Workshop, Dennis O'Connor, Wagga Wagga
1987   Pilchuck Glass School, Diana Hobson, Libensky/Brychtova, USA
Related Professional Experience
1974   Architect
1987   Teaching Assistant, Ausglass workshop
1987–88   Ausglass Representative for ACT
1988   Exhibition Co-ordinator, 'Kilnformed Glass, An International
          Exhibition', Crafts Council of the ACT
1989   Established own studio
Exhibitions
1987   'The Vessel Show', Glass Artists' Gallery, Sydney
1988   Fourth National Studio Glass Exhibition, WWCAG, Wagga Wagga,
          NSW, touring Sydney, Melbourne, Brisbane, Adelaide
          ANZ Glass Prize, Glass Artists' Gallery, Sydney
          Graduate Exhibition, Canberra School of Art Gallery
1989   'Australian Glass 1989', Meat Market Crafts Centre, Melbourne;
          Distelfink Gallery, Melbourne
          'Glass', Taylor/McClure/Vilmanis/Williams, Despard Street Gallery,
          Hobart
          'Designed and Made', Craft Council of NSW, Sydney
          'Light and Living', Glass Artists' Gallery, Sydney
          Diamond Valley Art Award, Melbourne
          ANZ Glass Prize, Glass Artists' Gallery, Sydney
1990   'Architectural Glass', Judi Elliott/Velta Vilmanis, Beaver Galleries,
          Canberra
          'Australian Glass 1990', Meat Market Crafts Centre, Melbourne
          'Pate de Varre', Glass Artists' Gallery, Sydney
          Tenth National Craft Acquisition Award, Darwin
          'Light and Living', Glass Artists' Gallery, Sydney
          International Exhibition of Glass, Kanazawa, Japan
1991   'Challenging the Medium', Blaxland Gallery, Sydney
          'Appreciating the Medium', Glass Artists' Gallery, Sydney
          'Glass Now '91', Japan
          'Sightlines', Crafts Council of the ACT Gallery, Canberra
          'Cast of Shadows', Jam Factory Gallery, Adelaide
          National Glass Show, Sixth National Ceramics Conference, Brisbane
          'The Glass Bowl', Distelfink Gallery, Melbourne
          Diamond Valley Art Award, Melbourne
1992   Solo exhibition, Qdos, Lorne
          'Glass Now '92', Japan
          'Vessel Variations, Glass Artists' Gallery, Sydney
          'On-Tray', Jam Factory Gallery, Adelaide
          'Light Sources', Glass Artist' Gallery, Sydney
          'Jahresmesse Kunsthandwerk 1992', Hamburg, Germany
          'Studio Glass Design', WWCAG, Wagga Wagga, NSW
1993   'Sculpture in Glass', Beaver Galleries, Canberra
          'Glass Lights', Beaver Galleries, Canberra
          'Origins & Originalities', Drill Hall Gallery, Canberra
          'Glass Now'93', Japan

Solo exhibition, Distelfink Gallery, Melbourne
'The Vessel', Meat Market, Melboure
ACI Glass Award, Meat Market, Melboure
Solo exhibition, Glass Artists' Gallery, Sydney
'Women Under Glass', The Door Exhibition Space, Fremantle, WA
Awards/Acquisitions
1979   Australia Council Crafts Board Grant, Pilchuck Glass School, USA
1988   ANU Acquisition Award
          Canberra School of Art, Art Bank Acquisition
Commissions
Dome light for private residence, Forrest, Canberra
Sculpture for Capital Arts Patrons Organisation Auction
McDonnell Douglas Hargrave Trophy
Mallesons Stephen Jaques, Canberra: Office lights
Coombs & Barei, Adelaide: Wall mural
St Michael's Parish Church, Kaleen, ACT: Tabernacle light
David Jones Award for Fashion Excellence
Prime Ministerial Women and Sport Awards 1992
Prime Ministerial Women and Sport Awards 1993
Collections
ANU, Canberra
Canberra Institute of the Arts
Ebeltoft Glasmuseum, Denmark
OTC Collection, Sydney
Queensland Art Gallery, Brisbane
WWCAG, Wagga Wagga, NSW
Private collections in Australia, Japan and Europe
Slide Collections
Crafts Council of Australia, Selected Slide Library
Publications
1988   *Fourth National Studio Glass Exhibition*, catalogue, Wagga Wagga City Art
          Gallery
1990   *The International Exhibition of Glass* , catalogue, Kanazawa
1991   *Glass Now '91*, catalogue, Yamaha Corporation
1992   'Lighting the Way', *Craft Arts International*, No. 21, March/June
          Glass Now '92, catalogue, Yamaha Corporation
          'Just Made, Light Sauce', *Object*, Summer, Crafts Council of NSW

RICHARD WHITELEY
1963   Born in East Dean, England
          Australian resident 1963–
Education
1983   Art and Design, Dandenong TAFE, Vic
1987   Bachelor of Arts (Visual), Distinction, CITA, Canberra
1993   Master of Fine Arts (MFA Sculpture), University of Illinois at Urbana-
          Campaign, Illinois
Related Professional Experience
1982   Completed three-year apprenticeship in commercial leaded and stained
          glass at Spectrum Studio, Berwick
1987   Pilchuck Glass School, Washington
1988   Studio Assistant, Weinberg Glass, Providence, Rhode Island
          Commissioned by National Capital Development Commission to
          design and manufacture kiln-formed glass window for Chisholm
          Primary School, Chisholm, ACT
          Assistant in Glass to Steven Weinberg, International Master Workshops
          and Symposia, Canberra
1991   Visiting Artist, CITA, Canberra
1992   Fellowship/Residence from Harvey Littleton, Littleton Studios, North
          Carolina
1992   Visiting Artist, Hartwick College, Hartwick, New York
          Guest Speaker, City Associates of the Art Institute of Chicago, Marx
          Gallery, Chicago, Illinois
1993   Glass Art Society Conference, Toledo, Ohio
          Speaker, Ausglass Conference, Canberra
          President, Graduate Art Student Association, University of Illinois
Teaching Experience
1989   Teaching Assistant, Glass studies, Illinois State University, Normal,
          Illinois

1990	Teaching Assistant to Klaus Moje, Pilchuck Glass School, USA
1990–93	Teaching Assistant in advanced, intermediate and beginning undergraduates in glass studies; Personal Assistant to Professor William Carlson, University of Illinois
1992–93	Instructor and Co-ordinator, Continuing Education Glass class, University of Illinois state-wide programming
1993–94	Visiting Assistant Professor, School of Art and Design, Glass Studio, University of Illinois
	Workshop Instructor, Printmaking from Glass, Ausglass conference and workshops, Canberra
1994–	Lecturer, Glass, Sydney College of the Arts, University of Sydney

Selected Exhibitions

1988	'Glass Australia '88', Meat Market, Melbourne
	'International Exhibition of Kiln-Formed Glass', Crafts Council of The ACT, Canberra
	'New Work, New Artists', Glass Artists' Gallery, Sydney
1989	'Contemporary Glass 1989', Contemporary Crafts Gallery, Portland, Oregon
1989–90	'Australian Glass', Habitat Gallery, Detroit, Michigan; Kurland/Summers Gallery, Los Angeles, California; Heller Gallery, New York
1990–91	'Glass Art from Australia', Galerie Gottschalk-Betz, Frankfurt, Germany; Galerie L, Hamburg, Germany
1991	'Illinois Glass', Marx Gallery, Chicago
1993	69th Faculty Exhibition, Krannert Art Museum, University of Illinois, Champaign, Illinois
	Solo exhibition, Gallery 105, Champaign, Illinois
	Master of Fine Arts Exhibition, Krannert Art Museum, University of Illinois, Champaign, Illinois
1994	'Shattered Perspectives', Elliott Smith Contemporary Art, St Louis, USA
1994	'Capitol Invitational', The Glass Gallery, Bethesda, Maryland, USA

Grants/Awards

1987	Awarded overseas study grant by the Australia Council
1988	Awarded Queen Elizabeth II Silver Jubilee Grant for Young Australians
1990	Awarded tuition waiver and assistantship by the University of Illinois
1990	Grant from the Australia Council for assistance toward American tour of Australian kiln-formed glass
1991	Grant from the Australia Council for assistance toward European tour of Australian glass
1992	Named to the campus-wide roll of 'Outstanding Instructors', University of Illinois
1994	Capitol Glass Award, Bethesda, Maryland, USA

Collections

Queensland Contemporary Art Gallery, Brisbane
Victorian State Craft Collection, Melbourne
Private collections

Selected Publications

1990	Nola Anderson, 'The Story of Studio Glass', *Neues Glas*, 3/90, cover, pp. 210–16
	Judy Le Lievre, 'Art Glass from Australia', *Craft Arts International*, No. 20, October, pp. 63–69
1992	Grace Cochrane, *The Crafts Movement in Australia*, pp. 390–92
1993	David McNeil, 'An Ausglass Alchemy', Object, Aultum, p. 34
	Munro, Alison, 'Origins & Originality', *Craft Arts International*, No. 26, December, p. *103*

KERRY WILLIAMS

1949	Born in Wellington, New Zealand

Education

1971	Bachelor of Arts, University of Newcastle, NSW
	Diploma in Education, University of Newcastle, NSW
1980	Bachelor of Commerce, University of Newcastle, NSW
1985	Associate Diploma in Creative Arts and Crafts, Newcastle College of Advanced Education, NSW
1986	Graduate Diploma in Art, Canberra School of Art
1989	Master of Arts (Visual Arts), Sydney College of the Arts

Related Professional Experience

1971/82	Teacher, NSW Department of Education

1988	Lecturer, Sydney College of the Arts
1989	Lecturer, Sydney College of Arts
	Lecturer, University of Western Sydney
1990	Lecturer, Sydney College of the Arts, University of Sydney
1991/2	Lecturer/Co-ordinator, Ceramics, Co-ordinator of Post Graduate Studies, Curtin University of Technology
1993	Lecturer/Co-ordinator, Clay and Glass, Curtin University of Technology, Perth

Curatorial Experience

1990	'Metaphor & Metal', Sixth Festival of Women Performers and Artists, Bondi Pavilion Gallery, Sydney
1991	'Cappuccino & Clay', Fremantle Festival, Old Fremantle Gallery, Fremantle

Solo Exhibitions

1989	'Fleshing The Facade', The Performance Space, Sydney
1990	'Kaleidoscope', The Performance Space, Sydney
1993	'From Fleshing the Facade', Fremantle Arts Centre

Group Exhibitions

1985	'Clay Associates', Seaview Gallery, Newcastle
1987	Graduate Diploma Students' Exhibition, Canberra School of Art Gallery
1988	Box Hill City Exhibition, Vic
1989	The Performance Space, Sydney
	'National P-G Exhibition', University of New South Wales, Sydney
	'Terracotta', Queensland Potters' Gallery, Brisbane
	National Craft Award, Northern Territory Museum of Art and Sciences, Darwin
	Warringah Art Exhibition, Sydney
1991	'Current Direction', Metro Arts, Brisbane
	'Metaphor & Metal', Bondi Pavilion Gallery, Sydney
	'Austceram 90', Exhibition, Perth
	National Ceramic Award, Canberra
	'Casting A Wide Ceramic Net', Lake Macquarie City Art Gallery and Regional, Galleries of Taree, Muswellbrook, Campbelltown and Tamworth, NSW
1992	ARX 3, Perth Institute of Contemporary Art, Perth
	Mandorla Art Award, Moore's Building, Fremantle

Grants

1981	NSW Government School Based Initiatives Grant
1989	Australia Council Artists' Development Project Grant
1992	Curtin Research Grant, Curtin University of Technology, Perth
1993	Creative Development Grant, Ministry for the Arts, Western Australian Government
	Curtin New Researchers Grant, Curtin University of Technology, Perth

Publications

1985	*Newcastle Herald*, November
1987	Post Graduate Students' Exhibition, catalogue, Canberra
1988	*Power Play in Untitled*, catalogue, Performance Space, Sydney
	Equality vs Autonomy, in transcript of Conference Lectures, Proceedings from the Fifth National Ceramics Conference, University of New South Wales
	Pottery in Australia, December
	Pottery in Australia, February
	Untitled, catalogue, Sydney
1989	'Fleshing The Facade: The Manual', Master of Visual Arts Research Paper and Documentation, Sydney Arts Research Paper and Documentation, Sydney College of the Arts
	Interview, 2NUR/FM, University of Newcastle
1990	'Mad or Fuming?', *Austceram 90*, Proceedings of the International Ceramic Artist/Potters Conference, AGWA, Perth
	Alice in World of STEELMAN in Casting a Wide Ceramic Net, catalogue, Lake Macquarie City Art Gallery
	Metaphor & Metal, catalogue, Bondi Pavilion Gallery, Sydney
1992	'Cappuccino & Clay', *Pottery in Australia*, Vol. 31, No. 4
	'Say C.C.', *Pottery in Australia*, Vol. 31, No. 4
	'Ceramic Arts/Industry Interface: Possibilities for the Future', *Austceram 92*, Proceedings of the International Ceramic Conference, Melbourne
1993	Ted Snell, 'Winter's Tale', *Art & Australia*, Vol. 31, No. 2
	Fremantle Herald, May

NICHOLAS WIRDNAM

1956   Born in Portsmouth, England

Related Professional Experience

1975–83 Founding team member, Isle of Wight Glass Studio, England
1980/81 Teaching surface decoration techniques, Kerry Glass Studio, Ireland
1982   One man glass studio, Jersey, Channel Islands
1983–92 Lecturer, Glass Department, Monash University, Caulfield, Melbourne
1991   Monash University Professional Development Grant for extensive travel through United States: participation in studio glass workshops; two month studio residency with glass artists Benjamin Moore and Dante Marioni; conducted workshop demonstrations in US tertiary institutes
1990/92/92 Development of personal work, access glass workshop, Meat Market, Melbourne

Exhibitions

1984   'Directions', Australian Glass and Ceramics, Sydney Opera House
1985   'Glass from Australia and New Zealand', Darmstadt, Germany
1986   'Continuity and Change', Jiangsu Province, China
1987   'Australian Glass Designers', David Jones, Melbourne
1988   'Meat Market Easter Show', Meat Market, Melbourne
         'Gas and Fuel Glass Exhibition', Meat Market, Melbourne
1989   'Metro Arts: Second Annual Craft Survey', Brisbane Community Arts Centre
         'Made In House: Glass and Ceramics', Meat Market, Melbourne
1990   'Elegant Glass', solo exhibition, Ciclopii Gallery, Armadale, Melbourne
1991   'Appreciating the Medium', Australian Artists in Glass Exhibition, Glass Artists' Gallery, Sydney
         'Interpreting Tradition', solo exhibition, Glass Artists' Gallery, Sydney
         'Melbourne Makers', Glass Artists' Gallery, Sydney
         'Perfume Bottle Show', Distelfink Gallery, Hawthorn, Melbourne
         'Glass Spectrum', White Hill Gallery, Red Hill, Vic
         'Mornington Peninsula Craft Event', Balnarring, Vic
         Diamond Valley Art Award, Melbourne
1992   Q-dos Gallery, Lorne, Vic
         Eltham Art Exhibition, City of Eltham, Vic
         'Goblet Show', Nakama Gallery, Tokyo
         'Victorian Tableware Exhibition', Meat Market, Melbourne
1993   ACI Glass Award, Meat Market, Melbourne

Collections

Victorian State Craft Collection, Melbourne
Queensland Art Gallery, Brisbane
Diamond Valley Art Collection, Melbourne

DON WREFORD

1942   Born in England

Education

Studied Fine Art Painting and Sculpture, Hornsby College of Art, London
Completed Graduate Diploma with Julio Santos, Caulfield Institute of Technology, Melbourne

Related Professional Experience

1970–73 Self-taught glass artist, making stained glass windows and lampshades
1977   Came to Australia, worked in Sydney, continuing work in stained glass
1978   Worked briefly with Peter Docherty, who had practised hot glass blowing in his Gosford Studio
1979   Spent a year at the Jam Factory, Adelaide with Stanislav Mellis, furthering skills in glass blowing
         Artist-in-Residence, Phillip Institute of Technology, Bundoora
1988–89 Ran own Hot Glass Studio at Etherlings Gallery, Malmsbury, Vic
1990   Set up Hot Glass Studio in Gisborne
Recently moved to Daylesford, where building a new studio and plan to explore further techniques in hot glass blowing

Awards

1986   Development Grant, Craft Board of the Australia Council, for casting glass
1987   Town Gas and Fuel Award, Mt MKT

Acquisitions

1984   Wagga Wagga National Glass Collection

1986   Queensland National Gallery, Brisbane
1987   NGV, Melbourne
1988   Art Gallery of the Northern Territory, Darwin

DAVID WRIGHT

Born in 1948

Education

1966–72 Bachelor of Architecture, University of Melbourne

Related Professional Experience

David Wright has been working with glass for 26 years and has operated his own studio since 1972. His work ranges from exhibition pieces to domestic, ecclesiastic, commercial and public commissions.

Recent commissions include work for the New Parliament House in Canberra and one of Australia's largest glass commissions for St James, King Street, Sydney

Solo Exhibitions

1976   Deutsher Galleries, Melbourne
1982   Distelfink Gallery, Melbourne
1984   Distelfink Gallery, Melbourne

Group and Survey Exhibitions

1975   Survey exhibition, NGV, Melbourne
1976   Royal Australian Institute of Architects, Melbourne
1978   Travelling exhibition, Australia and New Zealand
1979   Mornington Peninsula Arts Centre, Vic
1979/83 Jam Factory, Adelaide
1980   Distelfink Gallery, Melbourne
1981   International travelling exhibition, National Museums of Modern Art, Kyoto and Tokyo
1981/83 WWCAG, Wagga Wagga, NSW
1982   University of Tasmania
1983   Govett Brewster Gallery, NZ
1984   International exhibition, The Glass Art Gallery, Toronto, Canada
1984–85 'Glass from Australia and New Zealand', Hessiches Landmuseum; Darmstadt, Germany
1987   'Glass in Public Places', Westpac Gallery, Arts Centre, Melbourne
1993   National survey, Meat Market, Melbourne
1994   'World Glass Now '94', Hokkaido Museum of Modern Art, Sapporo, Japan

Selected Commissions

1976   Royal Melbourne Zoological Gardens, Melbourne: State Reception Centre
1979/81/85/89 St Eanswythe Anglican Church, Altona, Vic
1980   State Government Offices, Ballarat, Vic
1983   St Columb's Anglican Church, Hawthorn,Vic
1983/85/89 St John's Anglican Church, Croydon, Vic
1984   Royal Freemason's Homes for the Aged, Prahran Vic: Chapel
         Dromana Estate Vineyards, Vic
         Wattle Park Birthing Centre, Wattle Park, Vic
1984/90 Christchurch Anglican, South Yarra, Vic
1984/86/88/90/91 St Oswald's Anglican Church, Glen Iris, Vic
1986   St Paul's Anglican Church, Thomastown, Vic
1987   Catholic Ladies College, Religious Education Centre, Eltham, Vic
         Johnson and Johnson, Head Office, North Sydney
1987/88 Parliament House, Canberra
1987/88/89/90 St James Parish Church, King Street, Sydney: 90 square metres
1988   Melbourne Girls Grammar School, South Yarra, Vic: Chapel
1989   St Stephen's Anglican Church, Kambah, ACT
1989   Australia Post: Queen Street Shootings Memorial Window, GPO Melbourne
1991   Austin Hospital, Melbourne: Cardiac Unit Offices
1992   City of Doncaster and Templestowe, Vic: Aquatic Leisure Centre
1993   Melbourne City Council: Bourke Street Mall, Mosaic
1994   St Frances Xavier Cabrini Hospital, Malvern, Vic: New Chapel

Community Projects

1987   Nunawading City Council, Vic: Arts Centre
1990/91 Grimwade, MCEGS, Vic: Sports Centre

Memberships

Director, Board of Management, Meat Market, Melbourne

1979/90 1980/81 President, Ausglass
1983/87   Member, Crafts Board, Australia Council
1986   Member, International Council, Pilchuck Glass School, USA

Public Collections
Victorian Contemporary Craft Collection, Melbourne
Meat Market, Melbourne
ANG, Canberra
Powerhouse Museum, Sydney
WWCAG, Wagga Wagga, NSW
Pilkington ACI Collection
Numerous private collections in Australia and overseas

Publications
1976   Lee, Seddon and Stephens, *Stained Glass*, Mitchell Beazley, London
1979   Jan Minchen, *Architecture Australia*, November
1982   *Glass in the Modern World*, Tankosha, Tokyo
1983   Lundstrom and Shwoerer, *Glass Fusing*, Vitreous Publications, USA
1984   Jenny Zimmer, *Stained Glass in Australia*
        Commissioned Craftworks, *Architecture Australia*
1987   Dawn Mendham, *The Refining Fire,* Albatross

Film Productions
1985   *Five Craftsmen*, Victorian Ministry for the Arts
1991   *Fire in the House of Light*, dir. Catherine Brown, Film and Television School

ROBERT JAMES WYNNE
1959   Born in Yarram, Victoria, Australia

Education
1977–79 Diploma of Visual Arts, Monash University, Churchill, Vic
1981   Graduate Diploma of Visual Arts
1982–83 Master of Arts (Art), California State University, Chico, California

Related Professional Experience
1979–81 Part-time employment, Budgeree Glass Studios, Budgeree, Vic
1980   Self-employed artist with part-time work in the construction industry
1982   Jody Fine Glass Studio, Berkeley, California (July)
1982–83 Teaching Assistantship (Glass Design), California State University, Chico, California
1989, 90 Lecturer in Glass (Part-time), Sydney College of the Arts, University of Sydney
1984–92 Self-employed glass artist
1991   Established Denizen Glass Studio, Manly, Sydney

Solo Exhibitions
1984   Distelfink Gallery, Melbourne
1985   MGM Glass Gallery, Melbourne
1988   Hamilton Design Glass Gallery, Sydney
1992   Golden Canvas Gallery, Sydney, Australia

Selected Group Exhibitions
1980   Emerging Craftspersons Exhibition, Meat Market, Melbourne
1981   Mornington Gallery, Vic
1982   California State Fair, Sacramento, California (Honorable Mention)
1982   '1078 Invitational', 1078 Gallery, Chico, California
1983   Three-person exhibition, 1078 Gallery Chico, California
1984   Glass Artists' Gallery, Sydney
1986   Hamilton Design Glass Gallery, Sydney
1986   Distelfink Gallery, Melbourne
1987   Glass Artists' Gallery, Sydney
1988   Adelaide Bicentennial Exhibition, Quality Five Crafts, Adelaide
1988   Crafts Council Gallery, Sydney
1988   'Glass Australia 88', Gas and Fuel Glass Award, Meat Market, Melbourne
1988   David Jones Glass Gallery, Sydney
1988   Jam Factory Gallery, Adelaide
1988   Fourth National Studio Glass Exhibition, WWCAG, Wagga Wagga, NSW
1989   Crafts Council of the Northern Territory, Darwin
1989   ANZ Glass Prize, Glass Artists' Gallery, Sydney
1990   'Australian Crafts 1990', Meat Market, Melbourne
1990   'Touch of Glass', Gallery Indigenous, Melbourne

1991   'Challenging the Medium', selected exhibition, Blaxland Gallery, Sydney
1992   Three-person exhibition, Q Dos Gallery, Lorne, Vic
1992   Work selected for Australia Shop at World Expo, Seville, Spain
1993   Ausglass Members Show, Drill Hall Gallery, ANU, Canberra
1993   ACI Glass Award, Meat Market, Melbourne
1993   CINAFE, Navy Pier, Chicago

Grants
1981/82 Crafts Board of the Australia Council

Awards
1982/83 Honourable Mention, California State Fair, Sacramento, California
1988   First Prize, cash award, Sydney Royal Agricultural Show, Sydney
1988   Highly Commended, 'Glass Australia '88', Meat Market, Melbourne

Collections
Victorian State Craft Collection, Melbourne
Latrobe Valley Regional Arts Centre, Morwell, Vic
Queensland Art Gallery, Brisbane
WWCAG, Wagga Wagga, NSW
Rockhampton Art Gallery, Rockhampton, Qld
Parliament House, Canberra

Publications
1983   Masters Thesis (in Art), California State University, Chico, California
1984   *Craft Australia Year Book*, Crafts Council of NSW, Sydney
1985   MGM Gallery Exhibition, *Ausglass Magazine*
1988   *Classics*, catalogue, Crafts Council of NSW, Sydney
1988   *Glass Australia '88*, catalogue, Meat Market, Melbourne

KLAUS ZIMMER
1928   Born in Berlin, Germany

Education
1947–52 Diploma of Graphic Design, Master School of Arts and Crafts, Berlin
1961–66 Diploma of Fine Art (Painting), Royal Melbourne Institute of Technology
1967   TTTC, Technical Teachers College, Melbourne
1966–70 Diploma of Printmaking, Royal Melbourne Institute of Technology
1986–87 Post Graduate Diploma (Ceramic Design), CIT, Melbourne
1989   Master of Arts by Publication, CIT, Melbourne

Workshops
1979   Design and Glass Painting, Crafts Council of the Northern Territory
1983   Workshop for Architectural Glass Design (Assistant to Professor Joh Schreiter, Germany), Inglewood, NZ
1984   Glass Design, Glass Painting and Kiln Work, Whitecliffe Art School, Auckland, NZ
1987   Glass Painting and Design, Darling Downs Association for Advanced Education, Toowoomba, Qld
1992   Stained Glass in Miniature, 23rd McGregor Summer School, University College of Southern Queensland

Related Professional Experience
1956–72 Numerous one-man exhibitions of prints and paintings in private and public galleries in the South Pacific, Germany and Australia
1976   First one-man exhibition of autonomous glass panels at the Caulfield Art Centre, Melbourne
         Since then shown work in over 60 exhibitions in Australia and Europe
         Studied glass with Bill Gleeson at RMIT during the 1960s
         Worked in stained glass studios in Cologne, West German, 1974; worked with Patrick Reyntiens and Ludwig Schaffrath at Burleighfield House, 1975
1976–77 Made a photographic survey of contemporary European stained glass
1979   Studied at the Staatliche Glasfachschule in Hadamar and worked at the studios for glass painting and mosaic of Dr H. Oidtmann, Linnich, Germany
1980   Organised and hosted, at CIT, the first international workshop in architectural glass design in Australia, directed by internationally acclaimed designer Ludwig Schaffrath
1983   Assisted Professor Johannes Schreiter during a workshop for architectural glass design in Inglewood, NZ
1983   Founded Australia Studios for the design and manufacture of architectural stained glass

1984   Organised, with art historian Jenny Zimmer, the first complete
        exhibition of Australian and New Zealand glass to travel to historical
        glass centres in Europe: Darmstadt, Germany; Chartres, France; and
        Romont, Switzerland
        Until March 1986 was foundation Senior Lecturer in Charge of Glass
        Studies at CIT; now promotes his firm, Australia Studios, and works on
        public and private commissions and on various exhibition work

Award
1983   Diamond Valley Art Award, Melbourne
Professional Bodies
1971   Fellow, Royal Society of Arts
1990   Fellow, British Society of Master Glass Painters

Select Bibliography

This text has principally relied on interviews and oral history as recorded from glass practitioners and others by the author. Other sources include exhibition catalogue essays and articles in journals which appear in chapter endnotes. The following select bibliography lists books on both historic and contemporary glass and craft, consulted in this book, as well as suggestions for further reading.

Arwas, Victor, *Glass: Art Nouveau to Art Deco*, Academy Editions, London, 1987

Ash, Douglas, *Dictionary of British Antique Glass,* Pelham Books, London, 1975

Bacri, Clotilde, *Daum: Masters of French Decorative Glass*, Thames and Hudson, London, 1993

Bayer, Patricia and Waller, Mark, *The Art of Rene Lalique*, Collins, Australia, 1988

Beard, Geoffrey, *International Modern Glass*, Barrie and Jenkins, London, 1976

Beverley, Sherry, *Australia's Historic Stained Glass*, Murray Child, Sydney, 1991

Cochrane, Grace, *The Crafts Movement in Australia*, New South Wales University Press, 1992

Cousins, Mark, *Twentieth Century Glass*, Quintet Publishing, London, 1989

Cummings, Keith, *The Technique of Glass Forming*, A.H. Reed, Syney, 1980

Flavell, Ray and Smale, Claude, *Studio Glassmaking*, Van Nostrand Reinhold, New York, 1974

Frantz, Susanne, *Contemporary Glass: A World Survey from the Corning Museum of Glass*, Harry Abrams, New York, 1989

Grover, Ray and Lee, *Contemporary Art Glass*, Crown Publishers, New York, 1975

Ioannou, Noris, *The Culture Brokers: towards a redefinition of Australian contemporary craft*, State Publishing, 1989

Ioannou, Noris, *Craft in Society*, Fremantle Arts Centre Press, 1992

Klein, Dan, *Glass: A Contemporary Art*, Collins, London, 1989

Klein, Dan and Llyod, Ward, *The History of Glass*, Orbis, London, 1984

Littleton, Harvey, *Glass Blowing — A Search for Form*, Van Nostrand Reinhold, New York, 1971

Margetts, Martina, *International Crafts*, Thames and Hudson, London, 1991

Marshall, Joe, *A Glass Source Book*, Collins and Brown, London, 1990

Mentasti, Rosa Barovier, *Venetian Glass 1890–1990*, Arsennale Editrice, 1993

Newman, Harold, *An Illustrated Dictionary of Glass*, Thames and Hudson, London, 1977

Ricke, Helmut, *New Glass in Germany*, Kunst and Handwerk/Verlagsanstalt Handwerk, Dusseldorf, 1983

Tait, Hugh (ed.), *Five Thousand Years of Glass*, published for Trustees of British Museum, British Museum Press, London, 1991

Vose, Ruth Hurst, *Glass*, The Connoisseur, London, 1975

Zimmer, Jenny, *Stained Glass In Australia*, Oxford University Press, 1984

Index

Numbers in **bold** refer to illustrations

Aboriginal: art and glass, 105, 121, 122, 144, 151, 159; culture, 93
abstract-expressionism, 49
Academy of Fine Arts, Bratislava,161, 162
acquisition policy, 77
Adelaide, 21, 24, 26, 33, 34, 46, 63, 66, 87, 90, 93, 134, 136, 157
aesthetic, 11, 13, 30, 31, 33, 34, 35, 38, 49, 61, 63, 65, 72, 74, 87, 104, 108, 112, 119, 134, 161, 171, 173, 176, 177, 179, 180, 185, 188
Aitken Kuhnen, Helen, 66, 67, 74, 84, **85**, 87, 112, 184
Alice Springs, 144
Allen, Ruth, 37, 126, 134
Almberg, Eva, 25, 27
alternative hot and cold-glass practices 38
America, 27, 34, 35, 44, 45, 49, 56, 75, 76, 77, 81,111, 126, 147; see also United States
American Glass Art Society, 51
American glass: artists, 19, 21, 38; making, 66; pioneers, 52, 175
American Hot Glass Movement, 15, 20, 21, 25, 115, 140
ancient: culture 82; processes, 121
Anderson, Nola,13, 41, 43, 48, 84, 172, 180
Anderson, Michael, 26
Andersson, Willy, 27
Annand, Douglas, 20, 22
'antipodean perspective', 56
applique, 66
apprenticeship, 35
appropriation, 177
archaic, 68, 102
architectonic, 96, 103, 111, 154
Architectural, 46, 52, 53, 54, 66, 68, 98, 105
architectural: form, 72; glass, 96, 140–144, 151–153; installations, 26, 28, 76, 93,106, 151; glass movement, 142; images, 106; location, 166; stained glass, 140–151, 155
Argy-Rousseau, Gabriel, 99
Arrowsmith, Edward, 111
Art Gallery of New South Wales, 116
Art Gallery of Western Australia, 73
art glass, 54, 173
Art Glass From Australia, exhibition, 71, 93
art nouveau, 102, 128
Art Works Glass, exhibition, 48, 63
art-versus-craft, 51, 177; debate, 103; dilemma, 188; rhetoric, 172
Aspinall, Jan, 66
assemblage, 67, 72; see also multi-media
Atkins, Anne, 72
attitude, 20, 21, 45, 49, 51, 53, 56, 62, 68, 81, 88, 112, 134, 140, 142, 171, 172, 175, 176, 177, 180, 187–188
Auckland, 125
Ausglass, 3, 28, 34, 37, 41–59, 61, 63, 65, 73, 77, 78, 149, 158, 164, 172
Ausglass journal, 41,173
Australia Council, 21
Australia-New Design Visions, exhibition, 73, 74, 87

Australian Association of Glass Artists; see Ausglass
Australian: bush, 108, 148, 149, 158; designs, 142, 158; environment, 72, 121; flora, 122, 158, 159; glass movement, 44; glass overseas, 36; history,159; imagery, 121,144; geographic isolation, 35; landscape,108; opal, 161; Outback, 95, 148, 162
Australian International Crafts Triennial, exhibition, 73, 87–76
Australian Kilnformed Glass, exhibition, 84
autonomous glass panels, 62, 67, 72, 76, 141, 142, 148
avant-garde, 20, 34, 54

baroque, 68
Bauhaus, 34, 35
beadmaking, 57
Beaston, Terry, 72
Behn, Berin, 72
Belfast College of Art, 155
Belfrage, Clare, 33, **42**, 122, 126
Bell, Robert, 43, 76, 77
Bellicci, Andre, 25
Ben Tre, Howard, 75
bench-working, see lamp-working
biennial; see conferences and triennial
Bingley, Christopher, 72, 142
Bloch, Martin, 158
blowing, 11, 15; 37, 38, 45, 66, 77, 81–82, 84, 87–88, 90, 92, 93, 95, 103, 115–137; 139, 148, 162, 166, 179, 180, 187; blowing workshop, 111–112; early to contemporary,114–138; pioneer period,19–22; at Jam Factory, 25–33;
blown work, 20, 30, 31, 37, 56, 62, 63, 65, 67, 67, 68, 69, 72, 76, 84, 87, 93, 95, 98, 101, 103, 105, 115–137, 144, 147, 148, 151, 152, 158, 184, 185
Blum, Janice, 66, 67, 68, 71, 87, 112, 134, **173**, 187
Bodger, Lorraine, 72
Bohm-Parr, Judith, 57, 68, 74, 87, 88, **90**, 99–101, 112, 187
Bolli, Francoise, 111
Boysen, Bill, 21, 25
Brennan, Anne, 51
bricolage, 67, 184, 187
bricoleur, 184
Brisbane, 66
Britain, 22, 28, 37, 56, 185: see also UK
British Craft Council, London, 93
British Museum, 109
bronze mould, 45; -casting, 67, 92, 98, 102
Brown, Mikaela, 125, **129**, 184
Brugel, Karl, 87
Brychtova, Jaroslava, 20
Buddle, Roger, 88, **94**, 102, 112
Bullseye, 74, 102
Bush, Liza, 66

Cahill, Maureen, 20, 22, 26–27, 38, 39, 43, 62, 68, 72, 73, 76, 84, 92, 96, 112, 151–153, **152**, 166, 176

Cairns, 101
California, 30, 31, 121; Funk, 63
cameo glass, 68, 158,
Campbell, Robyn, 88, **104**, 111, 112
Canada, 73, 104
Canberra, 38, 74, 83, 87, 92, 108, 147, 151
Canberra School of Art Glass Workshop, 22, 26, 28, 31, 33–38, 41, 52, 72, 74, 81, 87, 96, 108, 109, 111, 124, 125, 131, 145
Candy, Judith, 24, 87, **97**, 102, 112
Carducci, 173
Carlson, William, 56
Carlson, Robert, 75
carving, 158; negatively,157
cased, blown-glass, 158
casting, 56, 67, 74, 77, 81, 103, 112, 181; see also lost wax
catalogue, 61, 69
Caufield Institute of Technology, Melbourne, 24, 27, 30
Central School of Art, London, 142
centre-periphery, 54, 57
ceramic, 26, 49, 109, 125, 153
ceramic: design, 129; idiom, 171
ceramics, 20, 22, 31, 63, 88, 102, 111, 145, 165, 170–172, 185, 188; movement, 171; practice, 171
chaos theory, 131, 187
Chalain, Daniel de, 72
Challenging the Medium, exhibition, 52
Charles Sturt University, Wagga, 25, 103, 111
Chaseling, Scott, 28, 37, 126, 134, **135**
Chelsea glass, 76
Chicago, 136
Chihuly, Dale, 20, 30, 36, 56, 75, 87, 122, 126, 131, 134
Chisholm Institute of Technology, Melbourne, 22, 72, 112
Cigler, Professor Vaclav, 161
cire perdue, 91, 93, 95; see also lost wax
clay, 12, 22, 82, 111, 169, 171, 176; history, 185; maquettes 134
clay and glass: cross-over, 56; studies, 171
Clegg, David, 72
Clements, Richard, 33, 39, 57, **157**, 164
Cochrane, Grace, 43, 51, 54, 77
Cocks, Deborah, 26, **40**, 57, 111, 147, 166, **174**
cold-working, 15; -kilnforming, 56; -laminating, 15; workshop, 24; -working, 15, 74, 77, 116, 153
collaboration, 46, 59, 119, 134–137, 162; see also teamwork
collages, 134, 142
collecting, 54
collector's: network, 54; market, 69
College of Art, Brisbane, 26
coming-of-age, 52
community, 33, 36, 37, 38, 59, 77, 84, 169
computer, 166; designs, 109, 148–149, 153–154, 184
conceptual: approaches, 26, 37, 66, 67, 74, 82; drama, 75; concerns, 46; privileging, 112; versus material seductiveness, 176; tools, 91

conferences, 16, 28, 34, 41–59, 63, 65, 73, 77, 116, 149, 158, 164, 169, 172,
constructivist, 76
Cooke, Glenn, 43, 68
Corning Glass Review, 109
Corning Museum of Glass, USA, 20, 51, 93, 102
Cotter, Maud, 56
Courtney, Giselle, 26, **156**, 164
Cowcher, Joseph, 66
Cowie, Jane, 26, 68, 122, **124**, 125–126
craft, 34, 36, 41, 49, 52, 70, 76, 145, 187; aesthetic 75; debate, 49; education, 34–35; industry, 45; issues in, 49; media, 63, 172, 174,179; movement, 153, 172, 175, 187; perspective, 175; practice and theory, 48, 51, 56, 183; practitioners, 166; revival, 49; values, 119, 169, 177; qualities, 61, 177, 188; crafting process, 92,169,188
crafts, 59, 63, 69, 77
Crafts Council of Australia, 45
craftsmanship, 48, 52, 75, 92, 154, 158, 184
Crawford, Michael, 65, 66
Creative Glass Centre of America, 165
creativity, 11, 15, 24, 34, 46, 53, 65, 84, 119, 122, 137, 141, 166, 169, 183, 184
crisis, 48, 53, 56, 171, 174
Crisp, Peter, 87, 164
critic, 62, 63, 119, 171, 173
critical, 68; approach, 48; context for glass, 174; faculties, 184; literature, 172; re-evaluation, 56; writing, 51, 57
criticism, 50–52, 57, 66, 73, 172–174
critics, 44, 57, 174
Cros, Henri, 99
Crosby, Graham, 28
cross-disciplinary, 57, 147
Croucher, John, 57
Crown Corning Glass, 27, 158
Crynes, Allan, 36, 84, 87, 88, 101–102, **107**, 112
crystal glass, 109, 158
crystalline, 174, 184
cultural: associations 99, 113, 179, 188; baggage, 181; function of 'art glass', 54; heritage, 53, 116; influence, 59; issues, 50; layering, 105, 106; make-up, 41; nuances, 188; perspective, 51; practices, 48; representation, 81; theory, 172, 180; traditions, 75, 187; traits, 73; transfer, 14; meanings, 56, 169, 179;
curators of glass, 31, 43, 44, 51, 61, 77, 78, 171, 174, 176, 177
curator-practitioner nexus, 14
'curatorial stigma', 68
Curtin University of Technology, Perth, 26, 33, 165
Cutting Edge, exhibition, 69
cycles, 113, 169, 187
Czechoslovakia, 27, 161
Czechoslovakian, 171, 175, 185; glass, 75, 161; artists, 20

D'Aquino, Michael, 31
Daden, Fred, 46
Dartington Glass, 93
Daum brothers, 101
Davis, Iestyn, 126
De Sumo, Patrick, 67, 87
deconstruction, 69, 108
Decorchemont, Francois, 84, 93, 99

Delaney, Pauline, 28, 72, **117**, 128–131
Denmark, 53, 77
Derix, Hein, 145
design, 33, 34, 37, 45, 48, 62, 65, 69, 78, 93, 96, 104–106, 109, 111, 124, 125, 126, 129, 131, 133, 134, 136, 141, 142, 147, 149, 151, 153, 158, 161, 164, 166, 176, 184, 185; study of, 22, 53, 56, 102, 141, 142; *see also*, glass
Design Council Award, 161
designer, 20, 21, 22, 28, 33, 34, 67, 75, 92, 93, 95, 97, 99, 133, 134, 41, 144, 147, 149, 181
designer-maker, 21, 24, 33, 98
Despret, Georges, 99
Detroit, 84
Docherty, Peter, 131
Dodson, James, 28
Dorsteenhutte Glass Works, Germany, 136
Douglas, Mark, 33
Dybka, Anne, 36, 52, 73, 155, 157, 158–159, **160**, 166

Ebeltoft Glass Museum, Denmark, 53, 77
eclectic, 72, 126, 145, 153
eclecticism, 67, 177
Edith Cowan University, Perth, 26, 165
Edols, Ben, 33, 36, 68, 122, **123**, 124–125, 134, 187
education, 34, 37, 41, 46, 52; *see also*; glass: courses
educators, 3, 4, 13, 14, 31, 104, 111, 112, 131, 151
Edwards, Geoffrey, 43, 44, 46, 51, 53, 66, 76, 77
Eguchi, Kazuko, **62**, 112, 147–148, 166, 184
Egypt, 82, 99, 109
Egyptian, 102; core-vessel, 151; technique, 102
electroforming, 46, 88, 91, 164, 184
Elliott, Judi, 66, 68, 74, 77, 84, 87, 88, 106–108, 112, 134, **180**
Elliott, Kathy, **123**, 125
Elsegood, John, **24**, 25, 66, 87, 103–104
Emmerichs, Gerhard, 36, **54**, 66, 72, 76, 139, 142, 144–145, 166
Emmett, Peter, 48, 63, 65
enamelling, 37, 111, 126, 147, 148, 165
England, 27, 28, 84, 95, 100, 106, 129, 142, 158
engraved, 67, 75, 87, 121, 147, 158, 184
engraving, 15, 37, 57, 131, 139, 145, 151, 155, 158
environmental concerns, 91, 139, 155, 184
Esson, Michael, 73
etching, 15, 66, 95, 109, 116, 142, 154, 159, 165
Euro-American practices, 54
Europe, 21, 30, 34, 35, 44, 53, 71, 72, 73, 75, 76, 77, 93, 99, 140, 141, 148, 164, 187
European traditions, 28
exhibitions: 61–78; international, 71–77; pivotal, 72; programme of, 41; survey type, 41, 43, 63, 65–71; thematic, 63, 65; experience, 3, 16, 19, 20, 22, 28, 30, 33, 36, 44, 51, 52, 53, 56, 72, 78, 98, 121, 126, 131, 133, 147, 148, 166, 171, 182, 184, 188
experiential, 181
expressive niches, 19

Fabrica Angolana, Portugal, 136
Farley, Jennifer, 26
Feeney, Lance, 52
feminist, *see* glass
figurative: depiction, 166; exploration, 147, 155; imagery, 91, 111; moulded glass, 88; work, 56, 67, 96, 111, 147

filligrano, 136
fine art, 50, 51, 84, 116, 131, 177; approaches, 104
Finland, 93
Finnish, 185
First National Exhibition of Australian Glass, 28
first public glass-blowing, 19
flame-working; *see* lamp-working
flat glass, 19, 37, 38, 46, 62, 63, 66, 72,142
Flek, Joseph, 27
float glass, 96, 153–158, 164
Ford, Gwendoline, 84
formal approaches, 72; language, 185
formalist language, 175
France, 98
Frantz, Susanne, 51, 52, 54
free-blown techniques, 148
Fremantle Art Centre, 111
French, 84; glass masters, 102; tradition of *pâte de verre*,101
Fujita, Kyohei, 75
functional, 19, 48, 54, 65, 66, 67, 69, 103, 119, 125, 136, 151, 177, 184, 185, 188
furnace, 31, 81, 82, 87, 88, 115, 162; mobile, 21; -working, 15, 137
fusing, 66, 74, 75, 84, 98, 112, 142, 151
Fynnaart, Abraham, 66

Galle, Emile, 99
German, 56, 126, 185; glass, 34, 140; School of leaded and stained glass, 30, 140–142, 151
Germany, 34, 36, 71, 84, 136, 141, 142, 145, 148
Gippsland, 30, 31, 128; Institute of Advanced Education, 30
Glancy, Michael, 46, 164
Glass Artists Gallery, Sydney, 27, 52
'glass art', 19, 37, 44
glass: art-craft gap, 36; blowing, 19, 20–22, 27–33, 38, 45, 81–82, 95, 115–138, 179, 180, 187; -blowing pipes, 90; carving, 155; community, *see* Ausglass; courses, 22–27, 24, 26, 33, 38, 51, 82, 111, 129, 141; criticism, 50–52, 56, 57, 66,171–174; design, 56, 109; ethics, 52; ideology, 50; idiom, 65; in public spaces, 46; jewellery, 48, 84,164, 172; language of, 51, 56, 63, 109, 142, 169, 175, 179; manufacture, 21, 119; movement's values,172; narrative, 13–14, 48, 75; painting, 57, 66, 72, 144–147; paste, 99; 42; philosophy, 30, 44, 52; politics, 37; practice, 49, 53; programmes, 22–39, 56, 57; properties of,11, 56, 67, 119, 174, 176; schools, 33, 34, 145; styles, 65, 66, 68, 101, 102, 106, 119, 122, 125, 128, 131, 133, 136, 142, 145, 159, 161, 181; *see also* imagery; theory, 53, 56; training courses, 22–39; values, 43, 56, 57; women in/feminist issues, 46, 73–74, 109, 119, 134, 155,165; *see also* seduction; blowing
Glass From Australia And New Zealand, exhibition, 71–72
glass-clay cross-over, 14, 56,
'glass rush', 169–172
Glasshouse, London, 93
Gleeson, Bill, 141
Gordon, Alasdair, 57, 157
Goss, Peter, 27, 28, 121
Great Britain; *see* United Kingdom
Greig, John, 72
Gropius, Walter, 34

Grunseit, Marc, **67**, 73, 112, 139, 148–149, 166
Grybaitis, Mies, 88, 111, 112, **168**
guild, 34, 41, 57

Halkidis, Effie, 164
Hancock, Bridget, 92, **105**, 112
Hancock, Judy, 164
Hand, Anne, 31, 67
hand-skills, 116, 125, 181
Hanning, Tony, **10**, 33, 36, 44, 45, 52, 68, 157,
    158, 166, 172, 175, 184, 188
Hayhurst, Kate, 24
Hayworth, Paul, 21
Heaney, Colin, 121, **127**
'Heart of Glass', film, 57
Herman, Sam, 20, 21, 25, 27, 62
Hill, Cindy, 112
Hirst, Brian, **2**, 26, 31, 37, 45, 52, 66, 67, 71, 72,
    74, 77, 95, 116, 173, 184
historical, 11, 53, 81; analysis, 172; associations,
    56, 116, 151, 179,184; cast-glass, 102;
    historical contexts, 96, 153 ; links, 87, 117;
    models, 66, 121; perspective, 46–48;
    technique, 74, 99, 180
history, 11–39, 45, 46, 54, 169–171,185
Hobson, Diana, 84, 100
Hoffmann, Anthony, 26
Hokkaido Museum of Modern Art, Japan, 53, 76,
    176; Prize, 77, 116
Holland, 45, 71
Holler, Franz Xaver, 56
Hook, Michael, 28, 31, 32, 33
Hot Glass Access Workshop, Melbourne, 33, 126,
    129;
Hot Glass Gathering, 43; see also American Hot
    Glass
hot-glass: philosophy 31; workshop; 24, classes
    36
Huff-Johnston, Rosemary, 66
Hughes, Bronwyn, 41, 59, 87, 119, 136
human emotion, 72
humanism, 176
humanistic: potentialities of glass, 100, 188; states,
    88; qualities, 177
Hunter, Gisela, 72, 142
Hunter, Sally, 24, 142
Huth, Ursula, 75, 126
Hutton, John, 155

iconography, 96
icons, 67, 76, 119, 145
ideology, 81; of glass 50; 'of making', 180
illusion, 68, 91, 93, 95, 144, 151, 157, 158, 159,
    161, 165, 166, 184
imagery, 141, 142, 157, 164, 185; abstracted, 145;
    Australian, 121, 144; archaic, 102; colour-field,
    75; computor-generated, 147, 148;
    deconstructivist, 69; emotive, 45, 145; eroded,
    95, 105, 106, 116; etched, 116, 159; evocative,
    184; figurative, 82, 91, 111, 147; formal, 91,
    106; functional, 125; illusionary, 92, 98, 158,
    159, 184; ironical, 63; organic, 102; outmoded,
    181; representational, 112; sacred, 109; source
    of, 46; see also glass: styles
impressionistic, 144, 145
industrial, 21, 33, 119, 134, 161
inner vision, 56, 181, 184, 188
'inner being', 179

innovation, 144, 148, 159, 161, 177; technological,
    19, 46, 65, 95–96, 98, 121;
Inspiration, 22, 25, 53, 57, 7392, 97, 101, 106,
    121, 125, 133, 144, 166
Installation, 38, 56, 57, 66, 73, 88, 98, 126, 159
institutional promotion, 61; values, 43
printing, 109, 111, 141, intaglio, 56
integrity, 52, 57, 179–181
interdisciplinary, 50, 51, 172
International Crafts Triennial, exhibition, 53, 87
International Directions in Glass Art, exhibition,
    72–73, 74, 75, 87,147
international glass: artists, 44–46, 56; debut, 14;
    exhibitions: 43, 71–77, 84, 87, 147; influence,
    46, 57, 59; movement, 19–22, 30, 38, 53, 57,
    77; network, 14, 31, 39, 53, 59; recognition,
    35, 77, 83, 96, 121,161; scene, 12, 35, 37, 52,
    53, 77, 96;
International Masterworkshop in Kilnformed
    Glass, 37–38, 83, 108
international studio glass, 36, 53, 68, 72
International Summer School, 52, 56
internationalism, 46
Ireland, 155
iridescent glass, 102, 121, 128, 164
irony, 37, 63, 77, 175
Italian functional glass, 66; glass making, 122, 185;
    style, 125
Italian Glass Workshop, 125

Jam Factory Glass Workshop, 21, 27–33, 34, 35,
    38, 41, 61, 72, 87, 93, 116, 125, 126, 129, 131,
    134, 153, 161, 164
Japan, 36, 37, 73, 75, 126, 133, 147, 164
Japanese, 56, 76, 77; art, 134; style 148; work, 53
Jungian: model, 182; symbolism, 106
jurors, 14, 43, 61, 65, 66, 68, 78

Kalifa, Marc, 88, 98–99, **110**, 112
Kalnins, Annete, 157
Kaluza, Irena, 68
Kelly, Elizabeth, 66, 68, 125, **130**
Keslake, Meg, 24
kilns, 31, 44, 82, 88, 90, 106, 153
kiln innovation, 98
kiln-cast, 67, 88, 91, 95, 184, 184, 185,
kilnformed, 15, 34, 35, 37, 62, 65, 67, 59, 75, 76;
    ancient 81–82; 113, 126, 148, 159; exhibitions
    of, 84–88; glass workshop, 33–38;
    Masterworkshop in, 83–84, 108; kilnforming,
    19, 26, 30, 31, 33, 34, 37, 38, 63, 67, 74, 77,
    84, 115, 121, 124, 139, 164, 179, 180, 181;
    advantages of, 81–83; character of, 81, 87
Kilnformed Glass — An International Exhibition,
    84
King, Gerry, 21, 24, 26, 37, 43, **50**, 66, 73, 74, 77,
    84, 87, 88, 104–106, 112
Klein, Dan, 76, 161, 177
Kleinert, Sylvia, 49–50
Klos, Joachim, 151
Knottenbelt, Rob, 20, 21, 26, 27, 28, 32, 33, 37,
    39, 43, 62, 63, 66, 71, 72, 76, 77, 84, **138**,
    153–155, 166, 176, 184
Koplos, Janet, 175
Koss, Gene, 165
Kosta Boda, Sweden, 22, 93
Kuspit, Donald, 57
Kyoto City University of Arts, Japan, 147

Labino, Dominic, 20, 175
Lalique, Rene, 92
laminated glass, 76, 98, 139
laminating, 66, 142, 153–157
lamp-work, 67, 87, 134, 162–164, 187
lamp-working, 15, 57, 66, 139, 162–164, 166
landscape, 95, 108, 124, 133, 144, 148, 184
Langley, Warren, 20, 21, 26, **35**, 36, 37, 39, 43, 52,
    54, 59, 62, 66, 67, 69, 71, 72, 73, 74, 76, 77,
    84, 87, 88, 95–96, 98, 112, 164, **170**, 177,
    184–185
language: of craft 66; see also glass
Larwood, Matthew, 24
latticino, 136
layered glass, 68, 102–103, 141, 148, 157, 158,
    159, 165
Le Lievre, Judy, 25–26, 43, 65, 69, 70, 77
Leach, Bernard, 49, 93
lead embroidery, 142
lead-crystal, 67, 87, 92, 158; -wares, 136
leaded glass: panels, 15, 30, 67, 72, 139–144;
    German School of, 141–142, 144; see also
    stained glass
Lee, Lawrence, 142
Leonora Glass, New South Wales, 22, 27, 136
Leperlier, Antoine, 84
Levi-Strauss, Claude,184
Levin, Robert, 124
Libensky, Stanislav, 20, 75, 161, 175
Lichtman, Linda, 57
light-affecting properties 179
limited editions, 69, 99, 125; see also, Studio Glass
Lipofsky, Marvin, 20
Lipschitz, Annie, 24
Lipsky, Oldrich, 27
literary, 13, 145, 155, 172
Littleton, Harvey, 20, 27, 77, 88, 98, 175
London, 20, 21, 46, 93, 131, 142, 151, 158, 164
Los Angeles, 84
lost wax casting, 67, 84, 88–99, 101, 102, 109,
    137, 165, 184
lustre, 66, 76, 116, 151, 164
Lynggaard, Finn, 53, 54, 77–78, 187

Mace, Flora, 75
Mann, Gillian, 67, 69, 84, 87, **89**, 109, 145, **162**,
    166, 184
mannerist, 184
Marcheschi, Cork, 57
Marioni, Dante, 31, 33, 45, 117, 122, 124, 125,
    126
Marioni, Paul, 44, 45, 117, 124
market, 27, 46, 54; -conscious, 62; -driven, 54, 88,
    175; international, 46, niche, 70; success, 172
marketing, 28, 48
Marquis, Dick, 21, 30, 33, 117, 121, 122, 124, 125
Marr, Edward, 155
Marthova, Daniela, 162
material culture, 13, 50, 63, 172, 188
McClure, Elizabeth, 36, 37, 53, 68, 77, 84, 108,
    125, **128**, 133, 185
McKeown, Patrice, 66, 67
McLeod, David, 125
McMillan, Alison, 66, **70**, 72, 112, 149, 151
McNeil, David, 41, 53
McPhee, John, 43, 68, 76
Meat Market Craft Centre, Melbourne, 24, 32, 45,
    126, 129

media-specific, 175; -based, 63; aesthetic, 49
medium: artistic, 62, 147; criticism of, 172–174;
    -based aesthetic, 49; control of, 108,
    exhibition, 43, 61; idea into, 43, 109, 187;
    language of, 56, 87; potential of, 63; highly-
    charged, 177; pushing the, 11; resistance of,
    174–177; versus idea, 65
Meitner, Richard, 44, 45, 116
Melbourne, 24, 26, 32, 44, 46, 66, 126, 129, 141,
    142, 147, 158
Melis, Stanislav, 26, 27, 62, 131, 161, 162
membership, (Ausglass), 43
Mesopotamia, 82, 109
metaphor, 63, 76, 81, 155, 161
metaphorical, 38, 56, 91, 98, 106, 142, 176;
    allusions 88, 164; associations, 185; illusions
    95; power of glass, 179; properties, 169;
    qualities, 57, 112; terminology, 181
Middle East, 93, 148
milestone, 38, 83
millefiori, 136
millifiore, 102
mimicry, 56
Minson, Peter, 21, 39, 87, 136, 162–154
Minson, James, 26
'misshapen bubble', 137
mixed media, 38, 66, 76, 87, 88, 126
model, 21, 171, 184; of creativity 183
models, 24, 75, 182; art-versus-craft, 51;
    collaboration, 46; historical, 66; Jungian, 182;
    traditional,181; patriarchal-dominated, 131;
    Venetian, 124
modernism, 49, 54
modernist, 68; discourse, 172
Moje, Klaus, 31, 33–37, **36**, 44, 52, 65, 66, 74, 76,
    77, 81, 83, 84, 87, 88, 93, 101, 111, 112, 126,
    176, 181
Monash University, 22, 26, 28, 30, 32, 33, 128,
    129, 131, 136, 141, 145, 147, 149, 165
Moor, Stephen, 155
Morrell, Richard, 32, 66, 67, **86**, 87, 88, 95, 112, 185
Morris, Billy, 52, 121
mosaic, 62, 66, 76, 84, 93, 102, 108, 112, 145, 151
motivations, 13, 14, 43, 54, 57, 181, 188
mould, 37, 74, 102, 103; forms, 92; -blown, 72,
    116, 129, 184
moulds, 45, 93, 102, 153
Mount, Nick, 20, 21, **23**, 26, 27, 30–33, 36, 39,
    62, 73, 76, 116–119, 122, 128, 158, **179**, 184;
    Pauline, 30, 31, 33
Mowbray, Ian, 84, 88, **100**, 102–103, 112
multi-faceted, 66; -media, 65, 67, 90; -skilled, 72
Murano, 119; see also Venice
Murray, Kevin, 78

narrative: glass,11–14, 41, 52, 77, 185; complexity,
    67; content, 75, 88, 98, 106, 111, 116, 125, 166
Nash, Garry, **118**, 121
National Art Glass Collection, 26, 69, 70, 117
national characteristics in glass, 53, 75, 76–77
National Conference, 44
National Fabrica de Vidros, Portugal, 136
National Gallery of Victoria, 44, 68
national studio glass, 25
National Studio Glass Exhibition, 28, 65, 66, 87
neo-baroque,126; -dadaist, 63, 90
neon, 66, 116
networking, 32–33, 35, 37, 43, 44, 54, 57, 84

Neues Glas, 53
New South Wales, 21, 22, 25, 103, 104, 136, 162
New York, 20, 25, 84, 104
New Zealand, 51, 57, 71, 73, 75, 77, 84, 92, 100,
    111, 121, 125, 133
Newcastle, 136, 165
Nishi, Etsuko, 75, 87

O'Callaghan, Judith, 66
O'Connor, Dennis, 21, 24, 39, **58**, 66, 71, 88, 103,
    111
Ogishi, Setsuko, 28, **132**, 134
Ogita, Katsuya, 57
one-off pieces, 69, 70, 54
opal, 144, 161
opalescent, 92, 113, 176
'opalino-shard', 121
optical glass, 139, 161
organic nature of glass, 62, 115, 137, 155, 174
origins and originality, 53–57, 76, 171, 172, 177,
    179, 182, 187, 188
Out of Canberra, exhibition, 84

Pacific region, 51, 57, 92
painterly, 66, 67, 106, 133, 148, 165, 175, 184
panels, 62, 67, 72, 76, 96, 108, 116, 131, 141, 153,
    159; see also autonomous
Pantano, Chris, **120**, 121–122
Paris, 96, 109
pâte de crystal, 99
pâte de verre, 15, 37, 57, 66, 67, 68, 74–75, 84,
    99–104, 108, 109, 111, 112, 145, 184
patination, 67, 69, 103
performance, 72, 136
personal: allegory, 184; idiom, 66, 103, 126, 187;
    language, 185; narrative, 75; style, 68;
    symbolism, 111
Persson, Tom, 27
Perth, 26, 33, 53, 73, 87, 111
Petrova, Sylvia, 171, 172
phases, in glass development, 19–20
philosophy, 22, 30–33, 34, 37, 44, 45, 46, 49, 52,
    101, 108, 122, 125, 131, 144, 153
Pilchuck Glass School, USA, 31, 32, 36–37, 56, 57,
    84, 92, 96, 101, 105, 109, 122, 126, 141, 147,
    164, 165
pioneer glass blowers, 13, 19–22, 39, 69, 96, 116,
    142, 151
pioneering, 19–22, 38, 111, 136
Pistor, Willi, 84
pivotal, 12, 14, 21, 33, 45, 57, 72
Playford, Phillippa, 26
poesis, 14, 180, 182, 187
political: commentary, 63, 66, 96, 104; processes,
    57
Pop Art, 20
popular culture, 125, 177
Portnoy, Sallie, **71**, 84, 109–111
Portugal, 136
post-fired: fired, 184, patination, 103
post-modernism; 49, 56, 172; philosophy of, 125;
    strategies, 171; language of, 142
pottery, 36, 158
Powerhouse Museum, 54
praxis, 14, 180, 182, 187
Prentice, Rosemary, 24
Prest, Cedar, 22, 45, 52, 62, 72, 73, 112, 139, 142,
    144, **154**, 166

primitive, 109, 159, 164, 182
process, of making, 181; alchemical, 41, 98
Procter, Stephen, 37, **60**, 131–133, 183, 185
production glass, 27–33, 37, 48, 54, 57, 65, 68, 69,
    92, 96, 136
promotional activity, 65
prototypes, 33
prototyping, 69, 98
psychoanalytic perspective, 185
psychodynamics of glass, 177–184
psychological, 11, 61, 88, 111, 148,

Queensland, 98, 121
Queensland Art Gallery, 68

Rake, Anthony, 66, 87
Rayson, Wayne, 72
Rea, Kirstie, 36, **63**, 66, 74, 84, 87, 88, 108, 112
Read, Herbert, 181
Redegalli, Sergio, 26, 66, **83**, 88, 96–98, 112, 157
Reekie, David, 56, 109
regionalism, 46, 49, 53, 56
Reid, Colin, 84
Renfield, Cecil, 157
representational: potential of glass, 81; imagery,
    106, 111, 112, 119; modes 166; realism, 166;
    strategy,179, 187
revival, 12, 49, 62, 101, 122, 140, 175, 176
Reyntiens, Patrick, 141, 142
Ricke, Helmut, 53, 171–172
Rijsdijk, Meza, 66, 69, 74, **75**, 84, 87, 88, 108,
    112, 176
Roberts, Neil, 57, 66
Roberts, Philippa, 72
Robinson, Ann, 73, 75, **80**, 84, 87, 88, 92, 98, 100,
    112, 177, 181, 185
Robinson, Paddy, **140**, 155–157, 166
Roman, 28, 81, 121, 137, 185
Roubicek, Rene,161
Rowe, Keith, **25**, 26, 31, 122–123, 124
Rowley, Sue, 54, 56, 57, 59, 172, 177
Royal, Richard, 32, 56, 126
Royal College of Art, London, 46
Royal Melbourne Institute of Technology, 141
Ryan, Luna, **82**, 88, 108–109, 112

Saito, Reiko, 26
sand-blasting, 66, 72, 75, 103, 108, 116, 119, 124,
    131, 148, 151, 153, 158
sand-casting, 84, 93, 139, 164–165, 184
Sanders, Paul, 67, 68, 69, 87, 88, 103, 112, **182**,
    184
Santos, Julio, 21, 22, 31, 39, 62, 66, 73, 131,
    134–137, **146**, 151
satire, 63, 67, 72, 76, 88, 125, 184
Saunders, David, 62
Scandinavia, 66, 93
Schaffrath, Ludwig, 141, 142, 151
scholarship, 36
School for Glass, Zwiesel, 56
School of Design, Adelaide, 22, 24, 26, 28, 44,
    102, 105, 112, 153
School of Visual and Performing Arts, Wagga, 111
Schreiter, Johannes, 141, 151
Schreyer, Lothar, 34
Scotland, 133
sculptural: 38, 52, 67, 71, 72, 76, 159; concerns,
    77, 81, 175; figures, 164; glass, 68, 88;

potential 113; processes, 126; treatment, 66, 73, 103, 134; trophies, 161; vessel forms, 68, 95, 134; work, 84, 96, 108, 137, 148, 155, 177, 184
sculpture, 44; computer-generated, 153
Seattle, 36; *see also* Pilchuck
seductive qualities of glass: 11, 41, 74, 112, 131, 169, 174–177
semiotic, 50, 172, 184
Signoretto, Pino, 126
'signature style', 181
silk-screening, 93
'Skangaroovian Funk', 63
skills: exchange, 21–22, 56; transfer, 44, 112
Skillitzi, Stephen, **18**, 13, 19, 20–21, 24, 25, 26, 27, 30, 37, 39, 44, 46, 54, 62, 63, 66, 67, 69, 72, 73, 77, 84, 87, 88–92, 96, 98, 102, 111, 112,115, 134–137, 137, **146**, 161
Slovakia, 161
slumping, 15, 37, 66, 75, 84, 92, 108, 112, 142, 144, 145, 151, 153
Smith, Rod, 24, 26
Smith, Neville, 24
Smyers, Steve, 30
social, 43, 78; commentary, 63, 72, 96, 106; history, 54; issues, 72, 111, 188; meaning, 51, 57
society, 185
South Australia, 93, 95
South Australian School of Art, 24, 63
Spacek, Dr Jaromir, 27
Stadus, Pamela, **6**, 164–165, 166, 184
stained glass, 45, 66, 72, 131, 139–145; *see also* leaded
Stinsmuehlen, Susan, 46
Stone, Graham, 66, 68, 112, **143**, 159, 166
Stonor, Bernie, 57
Street, Ron, 21, 111
Stourbridge: 26; School of Art, England, 95
Studio Glass Design: Limited Edition Series, exhibition, 69–70
studio glass revival, 19–22, 176
studios: Australia Studios, 142; Britannia Creek Glass, 153; Budgeree Glass, 31; Cydonia, 96, 97; Freedom Glass, 144; Glass, Earth and Fire, 88,136; Lights of Fantasy Studio, 148; MoTo Glass, 103; Ozone Glass Design, 96; Resolution Glassworks, 126
style; *see* glass
stylistic issues, 57; trends, 61
Swedish, 27
Switzerland, 111
Sydney, 27, 45, 49, 63, 66, 95, 136, 144, 155, 158
Sydney College of the Arts, 22, 26, 27, 38, 43, 82, 112, 125, 147, 151, 164
symbol, 122, 185
symbolic, 56, 66, 67, 81, 96, 142; achievements, 182; communication, 116; complexity, 76; contradictions, 174; form, 179, 185; imagery, 77; language, 141, 166; representations, 184; systems, 187; properties,176
symbolise, 148
symbolism, 69, Jungian, 106

Tagliapietra, Lino, 31, 121, 124, 125, 126
Takeda, Atsushi, 176
Tapper, Elizabeth, 56
Tassie, James, 99
Tazzyman, Itzell, 88, 111, 112, **186**

teaching philosophy, 35, 37
team approach, 32, 119–126, 129, 134, 136
techne, 141
technical: achievement, 62; virtuosity, 65, 68, 91
technique: '… is cheap', 175, 187; 'death by', 134
Tenth Australian Glass Triennial, 172
theory, 15, 34, 35, 41, 49, 51, 53, 56, 106, 125, 131, 172, 180, 187
Thompson, Catherine, 56
Thornton, Dylan, 72
Tiffany, Louis Comfort, 45, 128
Tilgen, Michelle, 26
Timoko, Marea, 111
Toledo, USA, 20, 98
Tomecko, Pavel, **145**, 161–162, 166
Torr, Vicki, 24, **91**, 68, 74, 84, 87, 102–103
tradition in glass, 75, 119, 187
traditional, 77, 161; craft practice, 119; flat glass painting, 144; forms, 81; glass blowing, 119; leaded and stained glass, 148; techniques, 54
trailblazing, 39, 116
trainee glass makers, 27–30, 31, 33, 62, 125, 126, 128, 129, 134, 153, 161
Trenchard-Smith, Janette, 112
trends, 37, 38, 48, 56, 59, 65, 78, 81, 175; future, 76, 169, 171–172
triennial glass surveys, 53 65, 68, 76–77
'truth to materials', 49, 185
turning point, 52, 72; *see also* pivotal
Tysoe, Peter, 28, 30, **32**, 36, 69, 71, 87, 88, 93–95, 112, 164, 176, **183**

United Kingdom, 36, 93, ,95, 122, 141
United States, 30, 31, 32, 51, 53, 54, 56, 57, 63, 69, 73, 84, 87, 88, 92, 95, 104, 119, 121, 122, 124, 128, 134, 137, 147, 165, 175
University of Illinois, 56, 57, 147
University of South Australia, 24, 44, 112

Vallien, Bertil, 93, 101, 165
Van Ginnecke, Vincent, 75
Venetian: aesthetic, 31; glass 30, 162; glass-making, 121, 122, 126; imagery,126; influence, 30; model, 119–126; tradition, 125, 137
vessel, 67, 68, 69, 81, 82, 84, 92, 93, 108, 126, 131–133, 166; concept of, 145; exploration of, 38, 181, 185–187; form, 66, 67, 88,101, 116, 125, 128, 133; language of, 175, 185; -based, 71, 77, 136
Victoria, 30, 32, 131, 149
Vilmanis, Velta, 69, **74**, 87, 88, 108, 112
Viscetin, Bettina, 24
visual arts, 53, 54, 63; perspective, 177
Visual Arts and Crafts Board (of Australia Council), 31
visual idiom, 155
vocabulary, 106, 133, 184; for glass expression, 20, 181; of the vessel, 185; *see also* glass: language

Warff, Goran, 22
Wagga City Art Gallery, 25, 28, 65–71, 87, 117
Wagga National Studio Glass Exhibition, 68
Walsh, John, 27
Warmus, William, 171, 172
Watson, James, 109
watershed, 12, 19; *see also* pivotal, *and* turning point

Weinberg, Stephen, 84
Western Australia, 21, 33, 111, 165
Western intellectual tradition, 49
wheel-cutting, 56,125; -engraved, 158, 159; *see also* engraving
Whitehall Enterprises, Melbourne,145
Whiteley, Richard, 26, 36, **47**, 57, 69, 71, 84, 87, 112, 145–147, 166
Williams, David, 45
Williams, Kerry, 33, 111, **163**, 165, 166
Williams, Maureen, 68
Wirdnam, Nick, **29**, 122
With Care, exhibition, 61
Wittman, Jim, 21
Wolfe, Ann, 109
workshops, 57; demonstrations, 44, 53, 56
World Glass Now, exhibition, 53, 57, 76, 77
Wreford, Don, 28, 87, **114**, 131, 187
Wright, David, 20, 26, 36, 62, 73, 77, 84, 112, 139–141, **149**, 159, 166, 183
Wright, Christopher, 66,
writers, 31, 48, 52, 53, 174
Wynne, Robert, 31, **64**, 128, **178**

Yamano, Hiroshi, 56, 75, 126

Zacko, Askold, 162
Zimmer, Jenny, 28, 43, 44, 46, 48, 54, 72, 119,
Zimmer, Klaus, 62, 66, 73, 76, 77, 112, 139, 141–142, 145, 147–148, 149, **150**, 166
Zynsky, Toots, 75